The Dimensions of Elder Abuse

Also by the authors:

Alzheimer's Disease and Other Causes of Confusion by Gerry Bennett

Essentials of Health Care of Old Age by Gerry Bennett and Shah Ebrahim

Elder Abuse: Concepts, Theories and Interventions by Gerry Bennett and Paul Kingston

Family Violence and the Caring Professions edited by Paul Kingston and Bridget Penhale

Elder Abuse in Perspective by Simon Biggs, Chris Phillipson and Paul Kingston

Reviewing Care Management edited by Judith Phillips and Bridget Penhale

The Dimensions of Elder Abuse

Perspectives for Practitioners

Gerry Bennett

Paul Kingston

Bridget Penhale

Consultant editor: Jo Campling

MACMILLAN

First published 1997 by
MACMILLAN PRESS LTD
Houndmills, Basingstoke, Hampshire RG21 6XS
and London
Companies and representatives
throughout the world

ISBN 0–333–62568–4 paperback

A catalogue record for this book is available
from the British Library.

This book is printed on paper suitable for recycling and made from fully managed and sustained forest sources.

10 9 8 7 6 5 4 3 2 1
06 05 04 03 02 01 00 99 98 97

Editing and origination by
Aardvark Editorial, Mendham, Suffolk

Printed in Hong Kong

To our late fathers whom we miss greatly:
Dennis Kingston, Allin Penhale and Jim Bennett

Contents

Acknowledgements

There are a number of people without whom this book would not have been possible. The initial concept for the book came from discussion with Jo Campling who has remained enthusiastic throughout the process; Catherine Gray, of Macmillan, has been supportive and enduringly patient, allowing time for necessary changes. Johannah McGowan typed earlier sections of the manuscript with unfailing good humour and willingness.

The support of our US colleagues Rosalie Wolf and Karl Pillemer always proves to be inspirational. Fellow trustees from the Council of Action on Elder Abuse continue to inform our thinking and move the debates forward. Thanks are also due to colleagues, many of whom are practitioners, past and present, who stimulate much needed discussion and creativity in this complex area and who are too numerous to name individually. Heads of Departments have been supportive to the endeavour.

Our families have experienced much disruption and unavailability throughout the process of this book and yet remain steadfast in their support and goodwill; without them this work would not have been completed. The support which we have given to and derived from each other has maintained our commitment to the issue and to this book. Any errors or omissions are, of course, our own and are acknowledged as such.

The authors and publishers wish to thank the following for kind permission to use copyright material:

Council on the Ageing (Australia) for Tables 7.1 and 7.2 from the *Australian Journal on Ageing*, **12**(4):5–9 (1993), © S.E. Kurrle; *The New England Journal of Medicine* for inclusion of work by Lachs, M. and Pillemer, K., **332**(7):437–43 (1995); Stanley Thornes (Publishers) Limited for Table 1.3, from Bennett and Kingston (1993).

Introduction

Elder abuse is the largely unknown violence phenomenon of the 1990s. Although recognised for centuries and reported in the professional press increasingly since the mid-1970s, it is the least acknowledged of the types of human violence. The spectrum of violence has been well publicised with reports of child abuse and spouse abuse, but the entry of another area of abuse has been met by the equivalent of battle fatigue. This seems to be true for both professional and lay person. This book seeks to examine the contemporary dimensions of elder abuse. It aims to provide the reader with the accumulated knowledge base concerning this obviously complex human experience.

Raising awareness of the reality of elder abuse and the dissemination of information and knowledge about it is fundamental to the education process for the public and professionals. Indeed, it forms part of the mission statement of the only UK charity specialising in the issue – Action on Elder Abuse. The range of issues covered in this book provides readers with the basic facts needed to give a solid framework concerning this topic. Each chapter adds dimensions to the framework, allowing the subject to be analysed from many different perspectives.

The typology of the differing forms of elder abuse and their societal position and potential cause have been described by Kingston and Penhale (1997) and form a common thread throughout the text. Their typology outlines that for each type of abuse there is a political (macro), community (mezzo) and individual (micro) dimension. This concept is expanded upon in Chapter 1.

Many people view the essence of any education process on elder abuse as securing the issue as a social problem, i.e. providing a major impact on public awareness. The pathway to this goal has distinct steps, as outlined by Blumer (1971). Recognition as a social problem secures legitimation of the issue not only by society as a whole but more importantly by 'stake-holders' in government and other important institutions.

This book is but one step on that pathway. It does, however, aim to be both educative and informative for a wide readership, from student to seasoned clinician. To address this critical audience, the text includes brief introductory and concluding remarks for each chapter, aiming to allow a cover-to-cover update on the topic or selective reading.

1

Elder abuse as a comparatively recent phenomenon was first described in the UK in the mid-1970s, yet the research and legislative creative force resided in the US for the next 15 years. There has, however, been a significant shift in the last 5 years in this country, as will be seen in Chapter 1, which aims to provide a contemporary overview of the phenomenon in the UK.

Understanding some of the issues involved in other forms of abuse can help to shed light on one particular age group – older people. The chapter on family violence, Chapter 2, provides this illumination, pointing out relative similarities and differences between elder abuse and other forms of familial violence. There is also a focus on the likely predisposing factors and theories of causation that have been developed.

Institutional abuse, the violent cancer in the world of caring, has come of age. This topic is covered in Chapter 3. Of all the dimensions of abuse, it is perhaps the one closest to public awareness due to the frequent scandals that are superficially publicised. The messages are clear, become more refined with the passage of time, yet continue to be virtually ignored. We know how to recognise and indeed prevent most institutional abuse – by quality: quality staff, quality resources, quality accommodation and quality management. We also know how to achieve quality – up to a point, one has to pay for it.

The role of the medical profession within the complex quilt of inter-ested parties is rapidly evolving. The ageing population makes reluc-tant geriatricians of many doctors. Current knowledge indicates limited awareness within the medical profession even in countries where education and general awareness are considered comparatively advanced. In the UK, contrary to the situation with child abuse, geria-tricians as a group are not rushing towards the problem and, with a few exceptions, are not in the forefront of education and research into the issue (Vernon and Bennett, 1995). The chapter concerning medical dimensions, Chapter 4, outlines what is known about clinical presenta-tions of abuse. History-taking and the examination process are funda-mental within the medical environment. They provide the building blocks on which a diagnosis is made. Doctors of the future will need to incorporate questions on domestic or institutional violence during the history-taking process to enable them to begin the demanding task of putting together the holistic jigsaw. Expertise in examination and forensic pathology for the general clinician will develop away from the current, somewhat crude, associations that tend to be made of 'bruises equal abuse'. The detailed examination process, coupled with expert forensic guidance, will help to inform the situation. Research is essential to understanding, and general as well as specific illustrations are given to illustrate this important dimension.

There has been little apparent interest within the media for elder abuse as an issue. There has been scant reporting of government or voluntary sector initiatives that may have an influence on elder abuse, for example the English Law Commission report on mental incapacity and decision-making. An elderly lady being mugged or a scandal within an institution is likely to result in a comparatively large amount of publicity for a day or so. This publicity is rarely informative about the topic, only about the sensational aspects and personal details of the individual.

However, by contrast, there has in the US been an explosion of information and services to inform the public in general and older people in particular. These have taken the form of high-profile television campaigns and the use of billboards and advertisements on buses and trains to promote telephone helpline numbers. Some campaigns have focused on one type of abuse, for example financial abuse, with specific literature and education programmes available. The stimulus for these varied approaches comes from many sources.

The US has a highly organised State structure including local departments of ageing. In California, this was the source of a video and booklet aimed at a general audience advertised by an actress, Betty White, from the popular television show *The Golden Girls*. At a practice level, in each State a government department called Adult Protective Services (APS), akin to a branch of the UK's Social Services, is specifically allocated the task of investigating all allegations of abuse, neglect or exploitation from whatever source. In New Jersey, for example, the APS have mounted a large public awareness campaign involving mass advertising of their own role and the toll-free APS number, as well as including a free information helpline number that is provided by the New Jersey Area Agency on Aging.

In many countries, it is central or local government that provides the resources to pump-prime the essential aspects of early initiatives. In the US, grants have been provided by the Government's Older Americans Act (1987 Amendment). One part of this extremely important government legislation deals specifically with elder abuse. The debate over what might be the most appropriate form of legislation in the UK is just beginning. Many people point to the US system to illustrate how their legislative system in this field has not worked to the older person's advantage. We would hesitate to decry the educational gains that have been obtained from a government bill specifically dealing with older people and addressing elder abuse within it. What the law has done in the US (at least initially) has been to provide limited funds for the empowerment of older people via the legislation, and a proportion of this money has been and continues to be spent on education and raising awareness about elder abuse.

Chapter 5 provides a focus on the legal dimensions of elder abuse. Legislation may prove to be a useful tool in the progression of the social debate over this issue and be one of the steps towards the resolution of the problem. The US picture gives contradictory messages: despite the existence of comprehensive legislation, there is a professional and social perception that the problem remains almost unabated. The current legal provisions and possible future changes in the UK are discussed in the chapter.

Intervention strategies are likely be the key to the management of many causes of elder abuse. This is an area in vital need of research, as it is from the current knowledge base that different intervention techniques are likely to be developed. Existing strategies documented in the world literature range from women's refuges specifically catering for abused older women, to advocates supporting older people in abusive situations. Chapter 6 aims to provide an overview concerning intervention: as it exists at present and as it might develop in future. All of the above interventions are examples of some of the vital questions in need of research evaluation; others are the role of alcohol addiction within abusive situations and the roles of various support agencies within strategies of intervention.

In recent years, the subject has begun to achieve social and clinical recognition around the world. The final chapter, Chapter 7, focuses on the way in which international awareness of the problem has been increasing. The chapter documents the diverse way the subject is being tackled across the continents, providing much-needed information about initiatives that are being developed around the world to combat abuse and neglect. Finally, the chapter includes a section on the research agenda and touches on some of the ethical dilemmas which are involved within research in this area. The conclusion aims to provide a synthesis, albeit brief, of the book as a whole.

In the interests of consistency, the term 'elder abuse' is used throughout the book to refer to elder abuse and neglect, although there are acknowledged differences between the phenomena. The term 'abuse' is used to refer to physical violence and also other forms of mistreatment that individuals may experience from others. 'Family violence' is used to mean all forms of violence that take place within familial settings and relationships; 'institutional abuse' refers to all forms of abuse occurring within institutional settings. 'Interpersonal violence' is used as a term to denote all forms of human violence, regardless of setting. 'Older people' is the principal and preferred term used when discussing individuals in later life; use of the terms elderly (people) and elders when they appear should not be viewed as implying homogeneity or any disrespect, as none is intended.

Elder abuse is a complex phenomenon in the infancy of its understanding. This book gives the current facts that are known and explores the major areas of interest in a challenging way. It is aimed at a range of professionals and students in training, and will be of wider interest to the general public. It gives the foundation of information necessary to begin to understand the dimensions of the problem and a framework on which to build and develop those dimensions further towards resolution of the problem. Information is knowledge, knowledge is power and power enables. Older people must be enabled to live their lives free from abuse, abusive situations or the threat of abuse. For those people wanting to know more, this book will provide that much-needed information and knowledge, whilst generating additional questions that will need to be tackled in the future.

1
Contemporary Overview

Introduction

During the 1980s and 90s the term 'abuse' became synonymous with a multitude of behaviours and stereotypes that individuals sometimes experience, both in the private world of the family and in the public domain of residential and nursing care. These diverse types of abuse can be found in varying degrees on a continuum from severe physical abuse and violence, including murder, assault and sexual violence, to almost imperceptibly subtle forms of stereotyping, marginalisation and social stigma. It is also clear that these behaviours and stereotypes are inflicted upon individuals throughout the life course: individuals of all ages are victims. The aim of this chapter is to provide an overview of the currently accepted dimensions of the phenomena of elder abuse and neglect as they have developed in the UK in order to provide an introductory framework for the reader.

Historical background

The terms 'child abuse' and 'domestic violence' became, in the early 1970s and 80s, acceptable nomenclature that denoted forms of abuse to specific individuals in certain age groups. However, it was not until the late 1980s that the phrase 'elder abuse' began to be used as a term to describe the mistreatment of older people. At this point, this latest form of abuse also gained legitimation as a political phenomenon alongside child abuse and domestic violence (DOH/SSI, 1993). Thus the phenomena of familial violence, including elder abuse and neglect, can be seen to traverse the life course:

> Violence or abuse is truly found from 'cradle to grave' (Kingston and Penhale, 1995a, p. 4).

Within the wider arena of abuse, the issues of concern are constantly changing; it seems that as soon as society believes that it has recognised a new form of abuse and responded, sometimes effectively although often inadequately, another type of mistreatment is recognised or discovered. For example, the normative boundaries of family behaviour were shattered in the 1960s when doctors claimed that parents were physically abusing their children (Kempe *et al.*, 1962). These so-called normative values within the family were further tested when adult survivors of sexual abuse began to disclose their childhood experiences (Finkelhor, 1984).

Just at the time when society was trying to come to terms with the discovery of child abuse, the 'women's movement' began to demand a response to issues raised by a substantial number of women about violence inflicted upon them by men (for an overview, see Johnson, N., 1995).

In the contemporary arena of familial abuse, new forms of mistreatment are increasingly becoming recognised. For example, sexual abuse of children was not a recognised social problem in the early 1960s and date rape was not considered as an issue of concern until the 1980s (Murphy, 1988; Koss and Cook, 1993).

The early 1990s have also seen the emergence of suggestions of satanic ritual abuse of children (House of Commons, 1992); additionally, sexual abuse of people with learning disabilities has been acknowledged as a legitimate area of concern (Brown and Craft, 1989; ARC/NAPSAC, 1993). Bullying, long known as a problem in certain schools and communities, has only gained recognition as a serious problem since 1987 (Tattum and Herbert, 1993). Retrospective analysis of social problems in the familial abuse arena therefore shows that the boundaries of what is considered, and accepted, as being abusive to different generations appear to be increasingly widening in scope.

Within the sphere of elder abuse, the different types of abuse that have been recognised include physical, psychological, financial and neglect (Bennett and Kingston, 1993). More recently, the issue of sexual abuse of older people has been reported (Holt, 1993; Ramsey-Klawsnik, 1993). Additionally, older people are also disclosing that they themselves were victims of sexual abuse in earlier years (Nichol, 1993).

The entire realm of familial abuse appears therefore to be in a state of continuous transformation, with a constant redefinition of the issues involved and frequent discoveries of other forms or types of abuse. In the US in recent years, for example, sibling abuse and abuse of parents by their children have been raised as areas of increasing concern. As more knowledge is gained in the field of familial abuse at different times, definitions may also fluctuate:

> Ideas of what constitutes abuse change over time and vary from place to place, reflecting differing national problems and professional and societal preoccupations (Hallett, 1995, p. 29).

Since 1989 the re-emergence of elder abuse and neglect as a new field of social concern has been predominately located within the more generic field of familial abuse and has led to a steep learning curve for health and welfare professionals. Elder abuse and neglect as a phenomenon has clearly not been as high on the agenda of health and welfare professionals as either child abuse or domestic violence. This is reflected in the education and training of professionals. Inadequate curriculum time covering family violence more generally, and elder abuse more specifically, is still the norm (Kingston *et al.*, 1995). Additionally, there is in the UK a paucity of research to assist professionals in understanding the issues involved in the abuse and neglect of older people.

However, it is becoming noticeable that since 1989 this state of affairs has been slowly redressed, and there are an increasing number of publications now available to assist health and social care professionals to deal with this complex area of the dynamics of abuse. These range from training packages (Phillipson and Biggs, 1992; Pritchard, 1992), reviews of the knowledge base (McCreadie, 1991, 1995; Penhale and Kingston, 1995a) and texts (Bennett and Kingston, 1993; Decalmer and Glendenning, 1993; Biggs *et al.*, 1995; Kingston and Penhale, 1995a), to journal articles aimed at specific professional groups (Penhale, 1993c; Kingston and Phillipson, 1994; Kingston and Penhale, 1995b).

At this juncture, it is also necessary to reinforce the fact that the abuse of older people within institutions continues to cause growing concern. Institutional abuse has a long history within the continuing care sector in the UK. This is largely because institutional abuse has never been adequately addressed within a clear and satisfactory social policy framework. Scandals in institutions continue to be reported in the media, but only the most alarming cases have been subject to the scrutiny of government inquiries (further analysis of this aspect is considered in Chapter 3). The fact that the apparent revival of interest in elder abuse and neglect has tended to focus on mistreatment in the domestic setting should not, however, lead to a situation in which institutional abuse and neglect are forgotten about or ignored. Indeed, there is evidence to suggest that cases of abuse and neglect may be increasing in the private nursing home sector (UKCC, 1994). The United Kingdom Central Council for Nursing, Midwifery and Health Visiting (UKCC) is the regulatory body for the nursing profession; the decisions of the Council's committee concerning professional misconduct are published on a regular basis. The document produced in 1994 catalogued an increase in the number of cases being considered by the Professional Conduct Committee relating to the nursing home sector rising from 8 per cent in 1990 to 26 per cent in 1994. A superficial explanation would suggest an increase in the numbers of cases of abuse, most of these relating to elder abuse (given that the highest amount of provision of nursing homes beds is for older people). However, other explanations may include a more empowered workforce willing to 'blow the whistle' or a residential or nursing home sector more prepared to police itself following the changes in assessment and admission processes accompanying the implementation of community care (DOH, 1989a, b, 1990).

Clearly, a balance needs to be struck between the two phenomena so that the issue of institutional abuse continues to appear on the political agenda. Although it should not lead to a minimalisation of abuse that occurs in the domestic setting, it is arguable that the position of institutional abuse as an issue of concern should be strengthened and moved more to centre stage. M. Nolan (personal communication, 1994) highlights this by suggesting that it is important not to overlook the mistreatment of older people who live in some form of institutional care, which in his view is probably a more prevalent and pervasive area of potential concern.

This view is further reinforced by Phillipson and Biggs who stated:

> Attempts to define and map the extent of elder abuse indicate that it should not be seen as a single, monolithic phenomenon, but that it takes a variety of forms in different settings and in different kinds of relationships (Phillipson and Biggs, 1995, p. 202).

One way of deconstructing the different forms of abuse that are found is to consider abuse by type, which includes the victim, perpetrator, relationship and setting (see Table 1.1). It then also becomes possible to align the type of abuse at different structural levels, for example (macro–political), (mezzo–institutional) and (micro–individual). The advantage of such a taxonomy is to locate the type of abuse within a framework that could both suggest the potential causes of such abuse and also offer insights into the structural level at which potential remedies may be developed.

Table 1.1 Typology of differing forms of elder abuse and neglect: their societal position and potential cause

	Macro Level 3	Mezzo Level 2	Micro Level 1
Types	Political	Community	Individual
Elder abuse related to informal care in the domestic setting	Ideological assumptions of community care resulting in limited choice for recipients of care (resource issues)	Reality of community care with limited choice and sometimes limited resources	Known risk factors for elder abuse and neglect exacerbated by factors at levels 2 and 3
Elder abuse as a form of domestic violence	Inadequate policy response to domestic violence vis-à-vis child abuse	Fragmented provision for adult victims vis-à-vis child abuse. No specific lead agency with responsibility	Known risk factors for domestic violence exacerbated by factors at levels 2 and 3
Elder abuse by professionals found in domestic settings	Ideological assumptions that the mixed economy of welfare can always provide a quality service and can be adequately monitored	Inability of social services to adequately regulate and monitor a mixed economy of welfare. Inadequate system for police checks of staff	Known risk factors allied to issues of vulnerability
Elder abuse by professionals found in institutional settings	Ideological assumptions that the residential sector can always provide a quality service and can be adequately monitored. No current legal support for whistleblowers	Inability of the registration and inspection services to regulate the residential sector. Disincentives to whistleblow within all forms of institutional care: statutory, independent and voluntary	Known risk factors for institutional abuse and staff burn-out exacerbated by factors at levels 2 and 3
Elder abuse in institutional settings	Inadequate social policy response with questionable safety and protection within residential settings	Inability of social services to regulate a mixed economy of welfare	Known risk factors exacerbated by factors at levels 2 and 3 and issues of vulnerability, consent and risk
Elderly people as victims of crime sometimes caused by vulnerability	Inadequate social policy response that ignores vulnerability in later life	Not considered within the remit of the health and welfare agencies even in cases of vulnerability. Thus far construed as a crime or law issue	Not thus far professionally considered as a distinct form of elder abuse; seen as an issue predominately for the police

This taxonomy locates elder abuse as potentially found within caring relationships in later life as a form of domestic violence (familial abuse). Just as importantly, this taxonomy recognises different forms of institutional abuse. The forms of abuse that have not so far been located within the definitions of elder abuse relate to the abuse of older people who are vulnerable, perhaps because of psychological or other impairments, who are targeted by criminals, to use the American term 'exploitation'. These perpetrators choose their victim simply because of the ease with which they can commit the crime. The chances that they will be caught are restricted, and if they are, there is a stereotypical view that the victim will not make an adequate witness. The issue of crime targeted upon vulnerable older people will be considered in more depth in the definitional section.

This list of forms of abuse is clearly not exhaustive, and as other forms of abuse are identified, they will no doubt expand the taxonomy.

An absence of concern

It is significant that although the first reports of elder abuse were reported in medical journals in the UK in the mid-1970s (Baker, 1975; Burston, 1977), the issues raised were not adequately dealt with or even properly discussed at that time. The moral panic associated with child abuse was then very much to the forefront of public consciousness (largely due to a number of public inquiries held concerning child deaths). Domestic violence and elder abuse therefore took second place in professionals' list of concerns. Serious attention from professionals and the media in the UK was not forthcoming until the late 1980s. A consideration of the field of social problem construction can help to explain this state of affairs.

The development of elder abuse as a social problem can be seen to have followed Blumer's taxonomy of social problem construction closely; the stages suggested by Blumer (1971) being:

- emergence
- legitimation
- mobilisation of action
- formulation of an official plan
- implementation of the plan.

The discourse surrounding social problem construction has suggested that certain sociopolitical circumstances need to be present in order to allow a society to acknowledge a phenomenon as existing and as worthy of attention. When the first accounts of elder abuse were reported in the mid-1970s, the ground was not fertile for discussion or interest. Blumer has perceptively documented that not all social issues that are potentially worthy of note become legitimated as social problems:

> given social conditions may be ignored at one time yet, without change in their make up, become matters of grave concern at another time (Blumer, 1971, p. 301).

This seems to have been the case with elder abuse in the UK, with a noticeable void in terms of attention and reaction to the topic between 1975 and 1989, despite claims by professionals concerning its existence (Eastman, 1982; Cloke, 1983). It is perhaps somewhat premature to attempt to analyse why, despite the evidence, elder abuse remained something of a non-issue as a social problem until 1989. However, certain structural factors appear to have been important.

For example, identification of, and the development of responses to, family violence more generally have had a 30-year time frame in which to develop in the US. In the UK, this time frame has only been 20 years, with the death of Maria Colwell in 1973 attracting 'enormous press and media interest' (Hallett, 1995). It is therefore not surprising that any early insights into elder abuse were overshadowed by the formative research into both child abuse and domestic violence. Children had advocates in the form of social workers and the National Society for the Prevention of Cruelty to Children (NSPCC) and are protected by legislation, whilst the women's movement and the feminist lobby have empowered women to complain and lobby against abuse inflicted on them by men. Whilst not rejecting older women from their remit, the women's movement has focused on younger women, often those with young children. Evidence for this can be seen in the laudable Zero Tolerance campaign that originated in Edinburgh (Kitzinger and Hunt, 1993) and has been replicated elsewhere, which includes only one image of an older woman with the slogan, 'From three to ninety-three, women are raped'.

Phillipson and Biggs (1995) have also suggested that elder abuse was rediscovered in part because of the increased confidence and power of what Estes has called the 'ageing enterprise':

> the programs, organisations, bureaucracies, interest groups, trade associations, providers, industries and professionals that serve the aged in one capacity or another (Estes, 1979, p. 2).

The analysis undertaken by Blumer would suggest that once these individuals, groups and organisations start to discover the 'problem', the 'problem' becomes:

> the object of discussion, of controversy, of differing depictions, and of diverse claims (Blumer, 1971, p. 303).

The accuracy of Blumer's insight is noticeable when the report of the British Geriatrics Society conference held in 1988 is analysed, a conference which stimulated a widespread and controversial debate. Within the report of the conference a figure of 500,000 cases of elder abuse in Britain was suggested (Tomlin, 1989). The statistics suggesting that 10 per cent of older people were victims of abuse were taken from Eastman and Sutton (1982).

Conversely, Virginia Bottomley (then Junior Minister of Health) stated on television on BBC2's *Newsnight*:

> I don't frankly think that abuse of elderly is a major issue, thank goodness, in our society (*Newsnight*, 4.6.1991).

These diverse claims continued until September 1993 when the organisation Action on Elder Abuse was launched by John Bowis, Junior Health Minister at the time. The launch of Action on Elder Abuse occurred shortly after the publication of the practice guidelines from the Social Services Inspectorate/Department of Health (SSI/DOH) which indicated that Local Authority Social Services Departments within England, Wales and Northern Ireland should be establishing their own guidelines and procedures (DOH/SSI, 1993). Within the guidelines, there was a clear expectation that such policies should be developed and implemented by a multiagency group and, wherever possible, owned and operationalised by all members of that group.

Referring once again to Blumer's taxonomy, the stage had been reached where:

> the career of the social problem represents a decision of a society as to how it will act with regard to the given problem (Blumer, 1971, p. 304).

In England and Wales, we appear currently to be at the stage where the 'official plan' is being formulated (Blumer, 1971, p. 304), particularly when considered in relation to the DOH/SSI (1993) guidelines and the English Law Commission's (1993) proposals and (1995) report on legislative change (see Chapter 5 for a further exposition of these).

Whether the final stage, that of implementation of the plan for action, will be achieved is yet to be seen and will be subject to further development in the arena of elder protection.

Emerson and Messinger (1977) describe relatively accurately how 'troubles' (a term they use as a generic description for emerging social concerns) develop. Within this framework, elder abuse as an emerging concern in the time frame between 1984 and 1993 clearly fits their analysis:

> In sum many troubles when first noted appear vague to those concerned. But as steps are taken to remedy or manage that trouble, the trouble itself becomes progressively clarified and specified. In this sense the natural history of a trouble is intimately tied to – and produces – the effort to do something about it (Emerson and Messinger, 1977, p. 123).

Allied to professional concerns about elder abuse, there has been an increase in specialisation in work with older people by health and social care professionals. It could be argued that this developing interest in ageing studies is a symptom of 'Foucauldian panopticism'[1] (Foucault, 1979), in other words a desire to maintain total surveillance over certain groups within society. The medicalisation of interest in ageing studies is described by Armstrong as:

> The geriatric gaze over the domestic, as well as the hospitalised lives of the elderly (Armstrong, 1983, p. 88).

Just why, in the territory of family violence, the medical gaze appears to focus on the two extremes of the life course is an interesting question in itself. There is no doubt that both child abuse and elder abuse have been medicalised, with domestic violence being seen as predominantly a social issue in need of more socially orientated interventions. One answer might be that there are medical specialities that can 'claims-make' and promote an interest in the issue: paediatricians for child abuse and geriatricians for elder abuse. As yet, the medical profession does not appear to have a specialism focus or, as Foucault would describe it, 'a clinical gaze' (Foucault, 1976) over the field of domestic violence, although this may alter in future.

The increasing specialisation in work with older people has therefore stimulated the need for a greater understanding of older people's health and social needs, especially with regard to the social world of older people. Augmenting these aspirations has been a growth in professional and academic courses specific to social gerontology. Such courses have promoted a greater understanding of the sociological dimensions of ageing and have seen an attempt to dissociate professionals' views of later life away from the traditional biomedical thesis of functional decline of older people, to a more positive view of ageing.

However, on a more negative note, demographic changes have prompted a view of the apocalyptic dangers of an ageing population producing a fiscal burden on the state and more particularly on the working taxpayer (Robertson, 1991). Almost all gerontological texts have a mandatory section or chapter explaining the change from a pyramidal age distribution to a more rectangular structure, with increasing numbers of older people in the total population. Many authors describe in graphic statistical detail the numerical changes with their potential fiscal burden! From the social gerontological viewpoint, this particular view of impending disaster should be:

> combatted with vigour, otherwise it will be a self-fulfilling prophecy (Bond and Coleman, 1990, p. 5).

The view that rarely arises in these texts is of the heterogeneous nature of the elderly population, in particular with regard to health status. Commentators have noted extremely healthy older people of 85 years and above and extremely unhealthy 40-year-olds, with age *per se* not being a valid predictor of functional status or of the consequential health and social requirements (Kingston and Hopwood, 1994, p. 167).

Indeed, the concept of heterogeneity of older people in general terms (not just in terms of health status) is of relevance in this respect as an attempt to counteract some of the more stigmatising and discriminatory effects of applying a blinkered homogeneous view of ageing and later life. Furthermore, the undoubted talents and expertise that older people could contribute to society is given little credence, as Bond and Coleman state:

> People of all ages should be valued not only for their past contribution to society but also for their present and potential contribution (Bond and Coleman, 1990, p. 5).

The apocalyptic fiscal scenario of increasing numbers of older people has led to a re-evaluation of the entire infrastructure of health and social care for older people, with a vociferous debate surrounding the need for continuing care and community care. It was therefore almost inevitable that the issue of elder abuse and neglect would arise as a potential side-effect of increased pressure on carers from inade-

quate resourcing of community care and the rapid decline and reduction in the numbers of continuing care beds available in health care
settings. In these latter stages of the 20th century, we are beginning to
see evidence of the effects that such changes have wrought and suggestions that the levels of such side-effects will continue to rise (Penhale
and Kingston, 1995b).

There is, however, also a difficulty in the acceptance of elder abuse as
an area worthy of attention within some social gerontological circles, due
to the implied problem focus contained in much of the discourse to date.
The absence of concern may be due to the tension of including elder
abuse within the remit of gerontology. Whilst this is to an extent understandable, given the desire to portray positive images of ageing, it clearly
seems to warrant attention and to be included in the wider sphere of
studies on ageing. In view of the powerful rhetoric and the often
shocking reality of elder abuse, omission of the subject from the curricula
of gerontologists and other professionals is clearly unacceptable.

The view of older people as frail, dependent and vulnerable, if not
incompetent, that appears in much of the writing about elder abuse may
not assist, however, in attempting to counter the negative assumptions
and views of our ageist society. Salend *et al.*, albeit from an American
perspective, have cautioned against the development of particular
procedures, in particular mandatory reporting laws, for older people on
the grounds that such 'special treatment' might accentuate existing
tendencies to infantilise older people (Salend *et al.*, 1984).

It has also been noted (Baumann, 1989) that the reason that elder
abuse was readily accorded social problem status in America may be
linked with the traditional focus of research interest concerning older
people in that country, with a strong focus on the problem areas
surrounding ageing. The widely held view of elderly people as potential victims may in part also result from this focus on dependency and
vulnerability in later life, and the same trends are beginning to be
noticed in the UK. This may be particularly apparent in terms of the
negative views of age that such concentration on abuse and neglect
tends to promulgate. These negative views are also reinforced by
debates now developing as to whether practice guidelines and procedures should focus specifically on older people or instead focus on all
vulnerable adults.

Finally, the fact that elder abuse had been accepted and legitimated
as a social problem in the US and Canada from the late 1970s onwards
meant that North American research and knowledge of the phenomenon was almost certain to filter over to the UK. When eventually the

research did reach the UK (and other European countries, as will be seen in Chapter 7), many practitioners had a sense of *déjà vu,* and a second wave of interest was stimulated. This second wave of interest has seen a prolific escalation in interest in the plight of abused older people, particularly amongst a small group of concerned professionals.

Dimensions of abuse

The form of abuse mentioned above mainly relates to mistreatment (abuse, violence or neglect) at a micro level, in effect at an individual level, between 'perpetrator' and 'victim'. However, within the compass of elder abuse it is also necessary to consider mistreatment at the macro (society) and mezzo (community) levels.

Table 1.2 Macro, mezzo and micro levels where abuse and neglect can be found

	The actors	Theories
Macro level	Society	Political economy (Walker, 1981; Estes *et al.*, 1982; Phillipson, 1982), structured dependency (Townsend, 1981)
Mezzo level	Community	The situational model, interactionist theory (McCall and Simmons, 1966; Blumer, 1969)
Micro level	Individuals	The situational model, symbolic interaction (McCall and Simmons, 1966), social exchange theory (Dowd, 1975)

Micro level abuse

When elder abuse is alluded to by policy-makers, professionals or academics, they are usually referring to forms of abuse between two individuals, usually a 'perpetrator' and 'victim': abuser and abused. Reciprocal abuse, however, is not unknown, where it is difficult to specify who is perpetrator or victim (McCreadie, 1991). In effect, the roles may change frequently, with both individuals being both abused and abuser. Furthermore, commentators have indicated that abuse and neglect may not be a one-sided affair, that situations may occur at least in part, as a response to provocation or longstanding relationship difficulties (Homer and Gilleard, 1990; McCreadie, 1991; Grafstrom *et al.*, 1992).

The individuals concerned may be blood relatives from within the same family, or the relationship may be one of carer and cared for beyond familial boundaries. What is not included within the broad conceptual domain of elder abuse, at least not in the UK at present, is the view that violent behaviour, fear and intimidation, social marginalisation or financial abuse by third parties should be considered as a form of elder abuse. In this respect, mugging or harassment of older people by strangers would not be included in the majority of definitions of elder abuse in the UK. Elder abuse and neglect as usually defined in the UK at present normally concern behaviours between individuals who are known to each other.

However, in the US, third party fraud, often referred to as fiduciary abuse, is clearly defined within the elder abuse arena (WISE Senior Services, 1993). It may well be that this debate will emerge in the near future in the UK. In responding to questions at the 1st International Symposium on Elder Abuse held in the UK in 1993, Wolf suggested that the way forward in the US was to open up the definitional process (Wolf, 1993).

It has already been suggested that older people who are targeted by perpetrators because they are vulnerable have not so far been included within definitions of elder abuse. There does not appear to be any logical reason for this; analogies from both the child abuse field and abuse inflicted upon people with learning disabilities suggest that 'stranger abuse' was not initially included as part of the definition of abuse and struggled to be accepted as a concept because of the obsession with abuse found within the family. A reappraisal is necessary to consider on what basis older people who are vulnerable and are exploited by strangers are excluded from definitions of elder abuse.

This would not be the case with children. Anderson *et al.* (1993) reported on the prevalence and nature of sexual abuse in childhood found in a community sample of women. In their study, 38.3 per cent were abused by a family member, 46.3 per cent by an acquaintance and 15 per cent by strangers. However, the children abused by strangers were still considered to be victims of child sexual abuse.

Within the field of learning disabilities Williams, C. (1995) argues that perpetrators include people with learning disabilities who abuse their peers, children, for example schoolchildren on a bus calling people with learning disabilities 'dimwits' and other derogatory terms, and employees who abuse a colleague in the workplace.

Williams, C. (1995, pp. 19–41) goes further and suggests that in his opinion the media, the police, the justice system and organisations, for example health and welfare organisations, could all be considered as perpetrators at certain times because of their treatment of people with learning disabilities.

Furthermore, vulnerable older people who reside in some form of residential care and are abused by their peers (who may be strangers) are clearly located within existing definitions of abuse. However, their counterparts with similar if not the same levels of vulnerability residing in the community who are mistreated or exploited by strangers are currently excluded from such definitions.

These wider definitions will be further explored at the mezzo levels of abuse in Chapter 3 concerning institutional abuse.

Macro level abuse

It has already been suggested that a broader definition of elder abuse and neglect is required to encompass behaviours inflicted upon older people at three distinct, although often overlapping, levels: macro, mezzo and micro. This section will explore phenomena that could be construed as abuse and neglect found at mezzo and macro levels. In order to place forms of abuse found at mezzo and micro levels within a conceptual sociological framework, a brief analysis of the historical and contemporary social position of older people in societies is needed.

This wider view is necessary for three reasons. Firstly, in order to frame the historical context of abuse and neglect, extrinsic sociological, cultural and economic factors affecting the family life of older people in previous centuries need a brief exploration. Secondly, it is also necessary to analyse the impact of these wider historical social, cultural and economic factors on both contemporary family life and the social circumstances of older people. Thirdly, an analysis of the effects of changing health and welfare policies for older people, and their ability to support older people in the community, augments our understanding of the totality of the social worlds and experiences of older people.

Historical perspectives

Reverence towards older people for their wisdom, experience and ability to inform and to act as links between differing generations within the community has been much overplayed in many societies. Evidence to the contrary suggests that later life has generally been a time of major difficulties for older people, with indications of numerous Western societies endorsing behaviours that may be considered significantly life threatening for older people. Anthropological data also indicate that, in certain non-industrial societies, death-accelerating behaviours are inflicted upon older people (Maxwell *et al.*, 1982; Glascock, 1990). Minois graphically described the ambivalence suffered by older people at various times in history in different cultures:

> Since the dawn of history, old people have regretted their youth and young people have feared the onset of old age. According to western thought, old age is an evil, an infirmity and a dreary time of preparation for death (Minois, 1989, p. 303).

In analysing this depressing state of affairs, Minois suggested five factors influencing the social status of the older people from an historical perspective. Firstly, physical frailty: it appears that the social conditions for older people were always worse in societies that were least policed, whilst in more structured societies the weakest individuals could be protected from the stronger elements. Secondly, the ability to act as a link between generations was seen as a positive attribute that enabled status in societies without the written word. Conversely, after the arrival of the written word, the ability of older people to inform and carry knowledge over generations was virtually obsolete. Thirdly, the body, with its decremental changes with age, was unacceptable to societies who worshipped the idol of beauty. Minois explained that:

> this was particularly obvious in Greece and during the Renaissance. Societies which entertained a more abstract and symbolic aesthetic ideal were, conversely, less revolted by wrinkled faces because they were aiming at a spiritual beauty above and beyond the visible; this was the case in the middle ages especially (Minois, 1989, p. 305).

The fourth factor relates to the type and size of the family. Those societies with an extended family structure cared not only for their elders but also for other members who were incapable of work. Societies that entered a period of deconstruction of the extended family in favour of the conjugal family tended to neglect their elders. Finally, wealth was a significant factor which to some extent assured a certain concern amongst family members for their elders. However, the phenomenon of inheritance could itself cause conflict within the family, younger members wishing to inherit rather earlier than an elder would otherwise choose. In effect, as Minois suggested:

It has always been better to be old and rich than old and poor (Minois, 1989, p. 306).

Many of these historical legacies appear to be re-emerging in the postmodern world of the late 20th century with a vengeance. For example, the issue of inheritance has caused much recent concern in the UK because of policies concerning payment for long-term care of older people. This is because the value of any property is taken into account within financial assessments concerning the contributions which individuals should make towards the cost of their care. This is irrespective of any future inheritance rights of relatives to the property. The historical framework, as outlined above, clearly needs to be understood alongside the contemporary world of older people in the 1990s.

Abuse and neglect: mezzo level

Whilst referring to abuse or neglect at the mezzo level (community), it is important to consider the link between structural and economic factors and sociological theories such as the situational model and interactionist theory. The situational model, whilst focusing on the dependency of the older person and the likely effect on the carers' potential for elder abuse and neglect, will also be affected by wider structural forces. Phillips (1986) noted that this model relies to a certain degree on frustration–aggression theory, which views violence as:

> a learned reaction that is displayed by an aggressor when goals are blocked or frustrated (Phillips, 1986, p. 199).

Clearly, there are goals that may be frustrated by the difficulties of caring for an older person; alternatively the goals may be frustrated by an inadequate community support system. Other factors may include the wider community acceptance or otherwise of older people, intergenerational conflict and behaviours such as community harassment. Such community-orientated abuses have not found themselves referred to as 'elder abuse' in the wider debate surrounding elder abuse and neglect until now. However, in the US the definition has clearly widened away from the somewhat restricted 'two-actor phenomena' to include, for example, third party theft, denoted as 'fiduciary abuse', by police authorities (WISE, 1993).

Macro level: the economics of ageing and health care

Within considerations of the macro, or societal, level of abuse, it is necessary to differentiate the economics of ageing and health from other forms of marginalisation found at macro level, purely because of the known health changes in later life. This stance could, of course, be construed as ageist. Nevertheless, by arguing that the situation for older people in terms of health and social care is different from that of younger adults, the ageist nature of health and welfare policy direction can be seen in sharp relief.

The thrust of the public debate in health and social care in the US can be noted from the titles of books and articles.

- *Setting Limits: Medical goals in an aging society* (Callahan, 1987);
- *A Good Old Age: The paradox of setting limits* (Homer and Holstein, 1990);
- *Too Old for Health Care: Controversies in medicine, law, economics and ethics* (Binstock and Post, 1991);
- *Diagnosis-related groups-based funding and medical care of the elderly: a form of elder abuse* (Wilkinson and Sainsbury, 1995).

So far, the indications in both the UK and US suggest that health rationing for older people exists and that a public debate has not emerged with a consensus view that rationing is acceptable. The noticeable absence of any debate around the issue of funding for long-term care, for example, has been expressed by the Director of Carers National Association:

> Have we really discussed with society at large the whole issue of how long term care is to be funded? Has there been any public debate about the issue of inheritance, the fact you can no longer expect to inherit the value of your parents' property because you are probably going to have to spend that money to pay for their care? These changes have happened by stealth in society, there has been no public debate about it and they have been predicated on the unpaid contribution of carers (Pitkeathley, 1994, p. 38).

This policy appears to be so contentious in 1996 that political 'U' turns regarding long-term health care funding are being considered. The question to consider in this context, however, is whether this form of rationing could be considered abusive or neglectful. When members of Action on Elder Abuse met representatives of pensioner organisations to seek their views on elder abuse and neglect, their response was unequivocal. Although almost all the representatives stated that they were aware of cases of physical, psychological and financial abuse towards elderly people, forms of abuse at the macro social level appeared to be of more concern to them.

Difficulties with access to health and social care, rationing of health care on age grounds rather than need, inadequate pensions, hypothermia because of difficulties with heating payments (exacerbated by VAT on fuel) and the general social marginalisation of elderly people within society were all considered by the forum to be forms of abuse and neglect. The forum did not consider whether these forms of abuse could be construed as macro, mezzo or micro; rather, they referred to them as 'political abuse'. Such grass-roots views should not be ignored. If they are not heeded, the danger is of a professional construction of the problem and the creation of an 'elder abuse enterprise'. This point is reiterated by Kingston and Penhale (1995a) who suggest that:

> When policies are formulated to intervene in cases of elder abuse and neglect it will be necessary to question whether they are being designed with the best interests of elders to the fore... The vested interests of service providers should have no part in the construction of elder abuse and neglect as a social problem (pp. 239–40).

The danger of expanding elder abuse and neglect beyond the rather constricted view of a two-actor phenomenon, means that almost any form of attitude, behaviour or policy might potentially be considered to be abusive or neglectful of older people. This does not include, however, any consideration of the views of older people themselves on what might constitute abuse and neglect (other than the example given above). However, critics in the US of mandatory reporting laws justify their position by arguing that:

> greater abuse exists in the form of the inability for older people to live a life free from poverty (Callahan, 1986, p. 2).

In an attempt to expand the definition beyond the two-actor phenomenon, Kingston and Penhale (1995a) modified the work of Gil (1981), which originally focused on child abuse:

> abuse of elders is human-originated acts of commission or omission and human created or tolerated conditions that inhibit or preclude unfolding and development of inherent potential of elders (Kingston and Penhale, 1995a, p. 6).

This expanded definition allows for the inclusion of behaviours found at the more structural political and social level, for example poverty, social marginalisation and other forms of stigmata, found under the broad term 'ageism'. Of equal importance is the notion of 'lay legitimation', i.e. the ability of older people to voice their opinions around the issues of elder abuse and neglect, to allow a climate of discourse originated by, manifested by and legitimated by the voices of older people, in the total absence of professionals of any description.

The debate concerning definitions is considered in more depth later in the chapter.

Terminology

From a contemporary perspective, the terminology utilised clearly symbolises certain aspects of the phenomenon. The terms used suggest, to professionals and lay persons alike, specific notions of what constitutes the phenomenon. In retrospect, it is illuminating to reconsider how the terminology evolved, and to review how misleading the early terminology was. It was misleading in terms of not only the gender of victims but also the forms of behaviours inflicted upon those individuals.

The chronology of terminology

- Granny battering (Baker, 1975);
- elder abuse (O'Malley *et al.*, 1979);
- elder mistreatment (Beachler, 1979);
- the battered elder syndrome (Block and Sinnott, 1979);
- elder maltreatment (Douglass *et al.*, 1980);
- granny bashing (Eastman and Sutton, 1982);
- old age abuse (Eastman, 1982);
- inadequate care of the elderly (Fulmer and O'Malley, 1987);
- granny abuse (Eastman, 1988);
- mis-care (Hocking, 1988);
- vulnerable adults (Staffordshire Social Services, 1994);
- adult protection (Keele University, 1996).

It appears that the phrase 'elder abuse' has stood the test of time, and it is the term that has been adopted most frequently to describe the phenomenon. With further research and a wider understanding of the issues, developing the terminology may well need to be challenged, modified or changed. Certainly, much more discussion is required with older people themselves in order to understand their interpretation of the phenomenon and, indeed, whether their perception of abuse and abusive situations accords with others in this field of enquiry. What is increasingly apparent, as Callahan stated, is that:

abuse like beauty is in the eye of the beholder (Callahan, 1988, p. 454).

Within the field of child abuse, there has been a shift in the use of terminology over the years from 'baby battering' to 'child abuse' to the current day usage of 'child protection'. It is possible therefore that there may be a move away from 'elder abuse' to 'elder protection' or even 'adult protection' in due course. There are, however, major difficulties in linking protection with older people, who are in the main considered as autonomous adults afforded the same freedoms and citizenship as any other adult. In addition, as with child abuse/child protection, the phenomenon of elder abuse appears to have been predominantly constructed by professionals and has not arisen, as happened with domestic violence, from the voice of the victims themselves (Kingston and Penhale, 1995a, p. 239).

There is therefore, as suggested earlier, the danger of the construction of a professional 'elder abuse enterprise' (Manthorpe, 1993b) fabricated by professionals to effectively 'solve' the problem. To pursue this a little further: it is possible that professionals will act to perpetuate notions of abuse and mistreatment, perhaps even where none exist, in order to protect their own self-interests. In order to counter this tendency, it is necessary to develop an empowering structure that listens to the voice of older people and acts with their interests as paramount.

One major void in the UK is an organisation as large and powerful as either the American Association of Retired Persons (AARP) (Douglass, 1991) or the Grey Panthers. These organisations have assisted in the empowerment of older people, particularly in the area of community involvement. They have also acted in a pressure group capacity to lobby and create pressure on the US federal government for adequate pension rights and global health care cover.

In the UK, neglect as a phenomenon is often added to definitions of mistreatment but is infrequently mentioned in the research studies which have been conducted so far. Self-neglect was referred to as far back as 1975 and as a phenomenon in its own right has been recognised for many years. This phenomenon has been described as the 'Diogenes syndrome' (Clark *et al.*, 1975).[2] The study by Clark and colleagues of 30 elderly people who were admitted to hospital with acute illness and extreme self-neglect was the seminal work in this area (Clark *et al.*, 1975).

More recently, however, a case study by Cole and Gillett (1992) has been reported. The prevalence of both neglect and self-neglect are unknown, but practitioners will be familiar with the conditions, particularly those situations in which they have tried to persuade an individual suffering from neglect to receive some form of service intervention and assistance without success.

Indeed, in the US it would appear that much, if not the majority, of the work of Adult Protective Services Teams concerns elders who self-neglect.[3]

Definitions of abuse

One of the most common themes that arises in any discussion on abuse throughout the life course is the difficulty in attempting to 'define' the phenomenon in question (Kingston and Penhale, 1995a, p. 2). This is also a complicating and exacerbating feature that is apparent within the sphere of elder abuse and neglect. Numerous academics, policy-makers and professionals have tried unsuccessfully to define elder abuse both in the US and UK, and the debate continues (Hudson, 1994; Action on Elder Abuse, 1995a; Kingston and Penhale, 1995a).

There is, however, an apparent consensus concerning the various dimensions of abuse, the five most common (Wolf and Pillemer, 1989) being:

- *physical abuse:* the infliction of physical harm or injury, physical coercion, sexual molestation and physical restraint;
- *psychological abuse:* the infliction of mental anguish;
- *material abuse:* the illegal or improper exploitation and/or use of funds or resources;
- *active neglect:* the refusal or failure to undertake a care-giving obligation (including a conscious and intentional attempt to inflict physical or emotional stress on the elder);

- *passive neglect:* the refusal or failure to fulfil a care-taking obligation (excluding a conscious and intentional attempt to inflict physical or emotional distress on the elder).

Within the UK, more generic global definitions have been sought. Certainly, in order to widen the debate beyond the restricting parameters of a two-actor phenomenon, a more progressive definition may be necessary.

These more generic definitions that include abuses inflicted at the three structural levels previously mentioned – micro, mezzo and macro – whilst conceptually sound, do not offer tangible parameters for practitioners to work with. Moreover, the definition found most frequently in policy guidance will probably be the definition found in *No Longer Afraid*, the first guidance issued by the DOH/SSI (1993):

> Abuse may be described as physical, sexual, psychological, or financial. It may be intentional or unintentional or the result of neglect. It causes harm to the older person, either temporarily or over a period of time (DOH/SSI, 1993, p. 3).

The organisation Action on Elder Abuse, as one of its first tasks, was commissioned by the Department of Health in England to develop a definition of elder abuse. Whilst not wishing to be too prescriptive, and acknowledging both the difficulties involved in defining the phenomenon and the fact that there might need to be change or at least modification in future, a definition was developed following a process of consultation with the membership of the organisation. The agreed upon version was:

> Elder abuse is a single or repeated act, or lack of appropriate action occurring within any relationship where there is an expectation of trust, which causes harm or distress to an older person (Action on Elder Abuse, 1995a).

What can be seen in the above definition are notions concerning the frequency of abuse (single or repeated act); that abuse (or neglect) might consist of a lack of a necessary action (omission as well as commission); that there is some relationship between the parties consisting of at least an expectation of trust; and that the action causes some harm or distress to the elder. Encompassed within the definition is the importance of the elder's perception of the relationship and also the action (or lack of action) and whether it causes the person distress or harm.

It is also evident, however, that even this definition is not without difficulty. For example, there may be problems within the delineation of relationships (some, any, all?) and expectation of trust (by whom, from whom, who determines?). It is apparent, too, that the definition may need to be altered in future.

A further difficulty seems to be caused by the different backgrounds of professionals involved in the family violence debate. Whilst considering the arena of child abuse, Ogg and Dickens used the term 'discourse analysis' to describe the tensions that arose during the implementation of the Children Act 1989 (Ogg and Dickens, 1995, pp. 81–4). The discourses they considered were 'law', 'welfare', 'the market economy' and 'managerialism'. Discourse analysis is described as of value in that it:

> focuses attention on the way that certain forms of harm (to children) are presented and understood in such a way that they become the subjects of public debate... whilst others... have not received the same treatment (Ogg and Dickens, 1995, p. 82).

Using a similar framework within the arena of elder abuse and neglect, albeit rather briefly, the tensions that arise because of the way in which various professional groups view and respond to elder abuse and neglect becomes apparent.

Since 1989 in England, the Law Commission has been considering changes in legislation to protect victims of abuse and others who may be vulnerable (Law Commission, 1993a, b, c, 1995). A debate has been developing between those factions who clearly believe that new legislation is not necessary, or who at least believe that caution is required (see, for example, Phillipson, 1992; Alzheimer's Disease Society, 1993; Phillipson and Biggs, 1995) and those who support legislative changes (Age Concern, 1990; Stevenson, 1995a; see also Chapter 5).

The obvious tensions that exist between the discourses of 'law' and 'welfare' seem to have been taken to their extreme in the US. Legislation enacted in each state has resulted in the development of different mandatory reporting laws and differing perceptions of how abuse and neglect should be dealt with. Taking into account the fact that there is no standard or agreed definition of what constitutes elder abuse, it becomes apparent that this has led to a rather fragmented response from a legislative perspective. If we are usefully to learn from the US experience in this field, it is necessary to acknowledge that criminalisation following the US model of mandatory reporting may not be the most appropriate route to take in the UK (Callahan, 1986; Crystal, 1986; Hugman, 1994). It should be possible, however, to enact legislation in the UK without following the adversarial route so familiar in the US; this aspect will be pursued further in Chapter 5 on the legal framework.

Ogg and Dickens also consider the discourses of 'market economy' and 'managerialism' with regard to child abuse (Ogg and Dickens, 1995, pp. 82–3). Again, a preliminary consideration of the effect that these perspectives might have on intervention strategies in the field of elder abuse may offer valuable insights. The introduction of the NHS and Community Care Act (DOH, 1990) has stimulated both a mixed economy of welfare and care management with an emphasis on the management of the care of individuals.

The discourse of 'market economy' has been apparent as a cornerstone of the community care arrangements introduced by a Conservative administration but endorsed across all political parties in the UK. The key concepts used are: 'greater consumer choice and flexibility', leading to 'increased independence for individuals'; 'increased usage of private/independent services' (and a decrease in the perceived monopoly of state provision of services); and 'improvements in the value for money of services provided'. The managerial strand is evident in the tighter managerial control over resources and budgetary constraints surrounding the introduction and maintenance of care management systems for Social Services/Social Work Departments in the UK. Specific documentation for managers concerning the implementation of care management systems and detailing the need to develop improved managerial and information systems was also provided by government (DOH/SSI, 1991a).

With regard to elder abuse and neglect, guidance from the English government via the SSI (DOH/SSI, 1993) has indicated that the assessment of situations or allegations of elder abuse should take place within the wider context of the assessment and care management processes. There is a need to acknowledge, however, that whilst the assessment should be needs led and holistic, it may also require a specific focus on abuse in order for it to be fully effective in such difficult and complex situations which practitioners often face. The care package developed for an individual as an outcome of the assessment may also need a specific focus on protection (see Chapter 6 for a further exposition of these aspects).

Tensions also exist within the framework suggested by Aber and Zigler (1981), who assert that definitions are necessary within different professional spheres, for example:

- legal definitions
- case-management definitions
- research definitions.

The situation in England at present is that the Law Commission has reported to parliament, and a full decision is awaited as to how far the recommendations will be accepted as it was decided by government in January 1996 that a further period of consultation is necessary. In the interim, definitions that already exist in law will require careful utilisation (see Chapter 5 for further detail on this).

It has already been argued that definitions that are likely to be used in practice, i.e. care management definitions, are probably the most volatile and may be subject to frequent modification. The majority of policies in use at present appear to be utilising the SSI definition (Action on Elder Abuse, 1995b).

One necessary debate is to rethink the position of vulnerable elderly people who are exploited by strangers, and to reconsider whether modifications of existing definitions to include such victims are necessary.

As in all areas of social concern, the debate about definitions will continue as more insights are gained, so that perceptions are modified and the semantics reconstructed. It can be seen that this has already occurred in the terminology used to describe mistreatment; the same modification process with regard to definitions is likely occur in future.

Prevalence of abuse

In order to legitimate the existence of a social problem quantitative evidence as to the size of the problem which exists is clearly necessary. The evidence concerning elder abuse was not available in the UK until 1992; the lack of evidence did not, however, stop various commentators suggesting diverse figures for the prevalence of abuse. As we have seen earlier, Blumer's hypothesis suggests that at the stage of 'mobilisation of action', the potential social problem is controversial and subject to diverse claims (Blumer, 1971). This was clearly the case in the UK, with various prevalence figures being alluded to without any empirical evidence to support such claims. There are certain parallels in the sense that, in the US, the issue of elder abuse had clearly been constructed as a social problem 10 years before the first prevalence study was completed (Pillemer and Finkelhor, 1988). This state of affairs has led at least one commentator to suggest that:

> Research in the preceding nine years before Pillemer and Finkelhors' (1988) prevalence study... had addressed every conceivable perspective of elder abuse without knowing what percentage of the population is abused, or are potentially at risk, of abuse (Kingston, 1990).

In the UK, the first prevalence study was completed in 1991 (Bennett and Kingston, 1993); therefore the UK is in a position to predict the volume of potential victims within 95 per cent confidence intervals.

Table 1.3 Prevalence figures in the UK with 95 per cent confidence intervals

	Type of abuse	95% confidence intervals for British population (x 1000)
Abuse reported by elderly people	Verbal	561–1123
	Physical	94–505
	Financial	94–505
Reported abuse to elderly people by adults aged 16+ years	Verbal	2411–3305
	Physical	134–402

Source: Bennett and Kingston (1993).

There are now several prevalence studies, and different international prevalence rates can be compared. What is clearly missing within the studies on incidence and prevalence are data concerning institutional abuse in the UK. The scale of the problem in the US is described in Chapter 3. It is a matter of urgency to replicate the work of Pillemer (1989) in the UK in this area, or at least to begin an attempt at empirical analysis of the dimensions of institutional abuse.

Table 1.4 Comparison of rates of abuse and neglect by country

Types of abuse	Rate (%)				
	US	UK	Canada	Australia	Finland
All types	3.2	–	–	–	6.7
Physical	2.0	2.0	0.5	2.1	
Verbal	1.1	5.0	1.4	2.5	
Neglect	0.4	–	0.4	1.4	
Financial	–	2.0	2.5	1.1	

Source: US, Pillemer and Finkelhor (1988); Canada, Podnieks (1989); UK, Ogg and Bennett (1992); Finland, Kivelä *et al.* (1992); Australia, Kurrle *et al.* (1992).

Risk factors

Attempts to understand the causes of elder abuse and neglect from research studies focusing on risk factors are scarce. Most of the empirical work originates from the US, and much of this work does not reach the gold standard of empiricism (Kingston and Reay, 1995). There are far too many survey studies, using unrepresentative population samples, disparate definitions and very few case control studies. The case control studies completed thus far in the US have not been replicated cross-culturally. Therefore it is not possible to state whether the risk factors found in US studies would be found in similar studies in the UK or elsewhere in the world. It is crucial that the US case control methodologies are replicated in the UK and elsewhere as soon as possible. Such replication is all the more urgent in the UK in the light of policy and procedure development occurring that quotes the US risk factors as if they were wholly applicable here. This usage of US data may therefore be misleading professionals in their quest to recognise and intervene with victims and perpetrators of elder abuse and neglect.

With the above caveats in mind, it is suggested that to base risk factors on the most credible scientific evidence available is preferable to basing them on unsubstantiated anecdotal evidence or poor-quality unrepresentative data, of which far too many are published. The evidence for risk factors considered in this chapter will be therefore drawn from the few case control studies available. The reasons for this are obvious: professionals from numerous backgrounds all have personal anecdotal evidence of working with both perpetrators and victims of abuse; these cases are not representative of the general population in later life; and most health and social care professionals work with individuals who are referred to them with specific health and welfare needs and problems. It is therefore crucial that professionals are presented with the most up-to-date research findings on which to base their practice.

If the debate surrounding elder abuse and neglect is to move forward, only the most robust scientific data should be evaluated and put forward as evidence of the phenomena. The presentation of out-of-date findings only causes confusion for professionals already trying to grapple with one of the most difficult areas of health and social intervention, that of interpersonal violence.

Unfortunately, examples of professionals stating their opinions either based on no evidence or on evidence based on dated, poor-quality research continue. In a recent publication, Eastman (1994, p. 24) suggests a series of characteristics of an abuser and an abused person:

- The abused person is severely physically or mentally impaired.
- The abused is very old (75+) and, not surprisingly, usually female.
- The abused tends to be victimised by relatives, lives with those relatives and experiences repeated incidents of abuse.
- Stress is still, in my opinion, a factor in abuse of elderly people, whether that stress be associated with alcohol, long-term medical problems (of the carer) or financial difficulties.

Few of the above factors have been found in the most recent case control studies, and in certain cases the opposite findings emerged. Eastman (1994) suggests that these characteristics have been consistently supported by American research quoting from O'Malley *et al.* (1979), Block and Sinnott (1979) and House of Representatives (1981). This research, however, is at least 14 years old and has been criticised by more recent commentators. Eastman does not reference the most recent evidence-based information from case control studies that have emerged since 1983.

Evidence presented here will be drawn from six case control studies (Phillips, 1983a; Pillemer, 1986; Bristowe and Collins, 1989; Homer and Gilleard, 1990; Grafstrom *et al.*, 1992; Anetzberger *et al.*, 1994) and will be correlated against the five risk factors that tend to be the most quoted:

- intra-individual dynamics (psychopathology of the abuser);
- intergenerational transmission of violence (cycle of violence theory);
- dependency and exchange relationships between abuser and abused;
- stress;
- social isolation.

Intra-individual dynamics (psychopathology of the abuser)

In four of the six case control studies, there is clear evidence of abusers having either mental health problems or alcohol misuse and abuse (Pillemer, 1986; Bristowe and Collins, 1989; Homer and Gilleard, 1990; Anetzberger *et al.*, 1994). However, certain questions remain unclear; these have been summed up by Anetzberger *et al.* (1994):

- Does alcohol render individuals prone to abuse infliction by its ability to remove inhibitions and increase impulse response, including aggression?
- Does prolonged alcoholism foster a dependency between adult children and their elder parents, which distresses and disturbs both, leading to the occurrence of abuse?
- Do individuals with tendencies toward alcoholism turn to increased alcohol consumption in an attempt to cope when frustrated with elder care?

At present, it is therefore not clear whether alcohol abuse arises before abuse is inflicted upon an adult or as a potential consequence of the stress of caring.

Intergenerational transmission of violence

This much-quoted risk factor consistently arises in the literature on child abuse and domestic violence; however, in the six case control studies no evidence for this factor could be found. It may well be that the methodologies utilised were not sensitive enough to discriminate satisfactorily; further studies focusing on this factor should inform the debate. In two studies, evidence of longstanding abusive relationships continuing into later life were found (Homer and Gilleard, 1990; Grafstrom *et al.*, 1992). The study by Grafstrom included commentaries, including a statement from one wife that:

> her husband had been an evil husband, now she was paying him back (Grafstrom *et al.*, 1992, p. 244).

A second wife stated that she had been abused herself, and a third complained that she had been subject to:

> sexually demanding behaviour from the husband throughout their lives (Grafstrom *et al.*, 1992, p. 245).

With the above evidence in mind, it has been suggested that for that proportion of elder abuse that occurs within longstanding mutually abusive relationships:

> Among married couples they may be seen as the elderly graduates of domestic violence (Homer and Gilleard, 1990, p. 1361).

Similarly, in connection with possible risk factors of abuse, Biggs *et al.* propose that:

> it may be pertinent to suggest at this point in time that although inter-generational transmission of violence cannot be stated as a risk factor, 'graduated domestic violence' perhaps can (Biggs *et al.*, 1995, p. 45).

Dependency

This particular risk factor continues to cause heated controversy amongst both researchers and practitioners. For example, within a recent US text, Steinmetz and Pillemer take polar positions on the dependency debate (in Gelles and Loseke, 1993). Their particular stance is noted in the relevant chapter titles – Pillemer: 'The abused offspring are dependent: abuse is caused by the deviance and dependence of abusive caregivers'; Steinmetz: 'The abused elderly are dependent: abuse is caused by the perception of stress associated with providing care'.

However, within the six case control studies considered here, no evidence arose suggesting that the victim was dependent. Moreover, in the study by Pillemer, victims of abuse were found to be less impaired than the control cohort for activities of daily living. In addition, perpetrators were found to be dependent on the victim for finance and living arrangements (Pillemer, 1986). Pillemer sums up the position on dependency thus:

> It is interesting to note that there has been the most debate over the one issue on which we have the clearest data. Simply put, all of the more vigorous studies of elder abuse have failed to find dependency of the victim to be a primary characteristic of maltreatment situations (Pillemer, 1993, p. 246).

Stress

This particular risk factor has its basis in the premise that carers, most of them female, who care (albeit sometimes reluctantly) for an older person are driven to abuse because of continued pressure and stress from caring tasks.

The stress factor hypothesis is also closely linked to the dependency debate. However, certain basic facts require consideration. Firstly, caring is a highly stressful occupation; in one survey of 3,000 carers,

88 per cent of women stated that they suffered from stress through being a carer as well as working, whilst 44 per cent of male carers describe feeling stressed (Opportunities for Women, 1990). The prevalence for abuse is, however, very low, at between 2 and 5 per cent, so no direct correlation can therefore be made between stress and abuse. It is therefore likely that factors other than stress are also involved.

As a risk factor, stress appeared only in the work of Grafstrom *et al.* (1992), with the abusive group themselves reporting that their health was worse than expected; they also had a higher level of psychotropic drug use than did the non-abusive control, and in a few cases had been victims of abuse themselves. As with dependency and intergenerational transmission of violence, further research is required before we can be certain about the exact nature of stress as a risk factor.

Social isolation

Evidence from the case control studies for social isolation is rather mixed. Two studies found that the victims and perpetrators were socially isolated (Pillemer, 1986; Grafstrom *et al.*, 1992). The studies by Phillips (1983a) and Homer and Gilleard (1990) found no evidence of isolation, however. Clearly, it will be necessary to consider the type of population studied, random population samples *vis-à-vis* groups receiving health and welfare support, and whether these groups feel isolated from family and friends, community or professionals.

From the evidence presented above, it is clear that evidence exists to suggest that mental health problems and alcohol abuse are risk factors for abuse, and that victims are often dependent on the abuser. The other risk factors must still be considered tentative in the light of no or conflicting evidence. Finally, the fact that only one of the case control studies was completed in the UK brings us back to the discussion about research travelling culturally. Clearly, more UK data are necessary, with some degree of urgency, if professionals are to be assisted in their work with individuals affected by abuse, whether they be the victim or the perpetrator.

Conclusion

It is clear that since 1989 elder abuse and neglect has re-emerged in the UK as a further form of mistreatment discovered in the private world of family affairs. Mistreatment can be seen to traverse the life course, victims and perpetrators being of all ages. The range and type of mistreatment inflicted upon individuals can be noted at three levels: macro, mezzo and micro. However, the absence of the voices of older people themselves, which might suggest at what level older people view the existence of elder abuse, means that concern has been limited.

The level at which mistreatment occurs suggests different perpetrators, but, much more importantly, the remedy at each level is likely to require differing solutions. Mistreatment at the macro and mezzo level is structurally bound in the institutional ageism found in society, and seen in reality with the age-segregated social policies of health and welfare provision. Mistreatment at the micro level, between two actors, is seen mainly within the dynamics of the domestic setting of the family within local communities. The area of concern surrounds those older people who are abused or exploited by strangers, often because of vulnerability. These victims do not find themselves within the accepted definitions of abuse, whilst their younger counterparts do. This omission needs serious attention and re-examination.

The relative lack of knowledge surrounding later life, and certainly the dynamics of care in later life, also suggest that interpretations based on US risk factors may be misleading service providers in their quest to alleviate elder abuse and neglect and to provide solutions. An urgent reappraisal of the knowledge base in the UK is needed, alongside an urgent validation (or repudiation) of the known US risk factors in the UK. It is appropriate at this point, however, to stretch out from the UK and travel conceptually more widely. The next chapter will focus on a framework concerning family violence in more general terms in order to provide one of the contextual bases from which elder abuse and neglect can be more fully considered.

2

Dimensions of Family Violence

Introduction

As documented in the previous chapter, there has been, in recent years, a growing international knowledge and awareness concerning elder abuse. This development to an extent mirrors the development in earlier decades of concern and knowledge about other areas of interpersonal violence, in particular child abuse and domestic violence. The focus of this chapter, therefore, is to consider the similarities and differences between elder abuse and other forms of familial violence. Consideration will also be given to some of the causative factors that are considered to be of importance within the development of situations of familial violence. This will provide valuable contextual information for the reader from which the rest of the book then develops.

The development of family violence

Recognition of the phenomenon of family violence in the UK is some 10 years behind that in the US. Since the mid-1980s, there have been in the US further developments within the field of interpersonal violence more generally so that there are now texts that include, for example, contributions on date and acquaintance rape, abuse between siblings, abuse by grandparents of grandchildren, and abuse of parents by their (adolescent) children (see, for example, Cornell and Gelles, 1982).

The further development of the knowledge base concerning elder abuse means that there are likely to be issues emerging that share common themes with other forms of intrafamilial violence. What will be needed, therefore, is an appreciation and understanding of how far these commonalities can assist in the development of our understanding of elder abuse as well as other types of familial violence.

It is also necessary to try to determine whether the phenomena (specifically child, adult and elder abuse) are entirely encapsulated and distinct from each other or merely points on a continuum of broadly similar forms of abuse that might perhaps be profitably considered as part of a continuum of interpersonal abuse found in both the private world of the individual or the public domain. In addition, some consideration needs to be given to how far the differences between various types of abuse may add to our knowledge and understanding and whether these differences are in fact of more importance than the similarities, or vice versa. It would appear unlikely at present that answers to all the above questions exist or will be found in the very near future: this is clearly a task that will take some time and which in fact may never be wholly completed due to the ever-changing nature of the field of enquiry. It will also depend on the nature of the questioners, be they theorists, practitioners, researchers or policy-makers.

Similarities between elder abuse and other forms of family violence

It is apparent that many agencies attempting to deal with elder abuse have looked for guidance to the experiences learned from colleagues in the child abuse/child protection arena. Indeed, following the 'discovery' of elder abuse in the US in the late 1970s, it would seem that in many areas it was claimed by experts in family violence. The reasons for this were logical. Elder abuse has certain characteristics in common with other forms of family violence, and it is worth considering these similarities before moving on to consider why the comparisons may not be entirely appropriate.

When considering the situation, it is evident that the ideological and methodological debates within elder abuse have, in the main, paralleled those which occurred in the child protection arena and to a lesser extent the area of domestic violence between adults (spouse abuse). To date, there has been very little thought given to the most appropriate conceptual models that might be relevant within elder abuse; many of the research studies (apart perhaps from within the feminist arena) until now have drawn on concepts more widely applicable within the field of family violence generally.

The theoretical frameworks that have been developed to try to determine the possible causes of abuse are similar, as attempts have been made to apply the models proposed for other forms of familial violence to elder abuse. There have been rather uncritical assumptions made that the theoretical frameworks and explanations from both psychological and sociological disciplines are comparable and transferable between different forms of abuse. The main frameworks concerning theories of causation will be presented later in this chapter.

Family violence is currently conceptualised and accepted as that violence which occurs within 'familial situations' and is perpetrated against powerless and otherwise vulnerable people (Finkelhor *et al.*, 1983). In somewhat broader terms, violence may be viewed as an aggressive act (whether this be verbal, sexual or physical aggression) by a more powerful individual, group or institution towards those who are less powerful. As Hughes perceptively noted, abuse between two people occurs:

> only if a power imbalance exists between them: one person believes himself, and is perceived by the other, to be more powerful; the other believes himself, and is perceived, to be relatively powerless (Hughes, 1995, p. 133).

With regard to abuse occurring at this micro/individual level, Hughes suggests that the perception of power imbalance need not necessarily be at a conscious level; it develops from the patterns of interactions between individuals from which relative positions in terms of power are then secured (Hughes, 1995).

Membership of certain groups in societal terms may also confer status with regard to power on individuals, whilst others may experience disadvantage with regard to power due to the structural inequality experienced through membership of a weaker group. This broad framework certainly includes many, if not most, situations of elder abuse, perhaps in particular because of the structural disadvantage experienced by older people within society. Additionally, heightened vulnerability of many older people as individuals may also have an effect in this type of situation (more on this aspect later).

There appear to be strong similarities in the characteristics of those individuals who commit abusive acts. Research has indicated that such people often have alcohol and/or drug misuse problems or histories of psychiatric or personality difficulties and associated relationship problems (Pillemer and Wolf, 1986). There are also rather more tentative suggestions that those who perpetrate elder abuse are likely, as in other forms of domestic violence, to have been subjected to abuse within the family setting at earlier stages of their lives (Pillemer and Suitor, 1988, and later this chapter). This area is likely to require further careful attention, especially in the area of research, to try to establish the veracity of some of the statements made (or even to refute them).

With regard to what is known about risk factors for elder abuse (as detailed in Chapter 1), some similar mechanisms would seem to exist in other types of familial violence. In particular, conditions of social isolation, poverty and extreme stress (both internal and external) within families appear to be common within all forms of domestic violence. Families in which elder and child abuse occur have been found to be more socially isolated and have fewer financial and social resources available to them than 'ordinary families' (Pillemer and Wolf, 1986). Familial roles can appear to be distorted and disturbed within such abusive families, and clarity of roles between individual family members may become less distinct or more blurred (Korbin *et al.*, 1989). There is some evidence that the dynamics of role reversal (Steele, 1980) and 'generational inversion' (Steinmetz and Amsden, 1983) may operate within some abusive situations. The dependency of those who commit abuse (whether this be emotional, physical or practical) may also have an effect in these types of situation.

The effects of different forms of abuse on victims also appear to show some degree of correspondence (even allowing for individual differences in terms of reactions to abuse). Such effects can include attitudes of self-blame and stigma, a lowering of self-esteem and a reduction in the general coping skills of the person. Other effects of note may be depression, sleep disturbances, a sense of isolation and despair and an increase in feelings of dependence. This type of effect can be seen in victims of virtually all forms of familial violence across the lifespan (although they are not found in every situation).

It is possible that this may well relate to the structural issues of inequalities of power within relationships, which, as suggested above, may in any case be an essential prerequisite to the development of abusive situations. Additionally, it may be that it is the perception of the parties involved as to the power relationships that is critical in this respect: if the perceptions between individuals are of inequality and skew in the distribution of power within a particular relationship, reactions will inevitably be based on this. It could also be possible that individuals who perceive themselves to be at a disadvantage in terms of power may use violence and abuse as a means of restoring personal power within a situation. An example of this might be that of an adult child who is dependent on an elderly parent for accommodation and finance who uses violence to redress a perceived powerlessness on their part.

Within situations involving child abuse and also within heterosexual domestic violence, as they are currently understood and conceptualised, the phenomenon which occurs most often is that of male violence, largely physical in nature, directed towards females (Birchall, 1989; Johnson, N., 1995). A parallel situation prevails in elder abuse, where the majority of victims are also female. With regard to the gender of those who abuse, whilst some women do abuse children and male partners, the greatest amount of abuse is perpetrated by men.

Difficulties have been encountered within all the differing forms of family violence, in terms of establishing appropriate strategies of intervention. There is a societal stigma surrounding abuse (of all types) and this will in all probability lead to a reluctance on the part of those involved in abusive situations to accept or to seek assistance in their predicament. Clearly, those individuals who are abusing another may resist seeking assistance because of the likely ascription of a label and of the stigma resulting from this action. On the other hand, however, victims are not infrequently both intimidated by and fearful of their abusers. Their powerless positions (and the associated perception of this) can make it difficult to empower them sufficiently to leave or change an abusive situation. In addition, within some abusive situations, there are levels of attachment and affection that the parties concerned do not necessarily wish to alter.

It may be difficult to reach a point at which the existence of abuse is readily acknowledged by all parties; even gaining appropriate levels of access can be very hard for professionals to achieve on a sustained and consistent basis. The continued delivery of services and monitoring the safety of individuals may also be problematic in association with this. To achieve a successful and lasting outcome to a protection plan can require a great deal of effort and commitment from all concerned in the process.

Within the area of family violence, elder abuse has been compared with child abuse more often than spouse abuse. This would seem to be due in part to the level of similarity that can be found between the two forms of abuse. It is perhaps also due to the increased attention and priority given to child protection within health and welfare agencies compared with the wider issue of domestic violence. As is apparent,

there are a number of legislative requirements of health and in particular social care professionals with regard to children and their welfare,
which means that precedence is given to work in this area. This may
mean that more attention has been paid to comparisons between child
abuse and elder abuse than between elder abuse and domestic violence.

The lack of attention and research in this area is clearly an issue of
concern, which needs to be redressed. What is also worthy of some
note, however, is that both child abuse and elder abuse have their
origins (in terms of initial recognition of the problem) within the
medical domain and have thus tended to be 'medically constructed'
(Kingston and Penhale, 1995a), whilst domestic violence has its
antecedents in the feminist movement of the 1970s and is thus seen as
a social problem rather than a medical one.

Differences between elder abuse, domestic violence and child abuse

Despite the similarities between the differing forms of abuse, there are
some important differences, and these should not be overlooked. The
differences between elder abuse, child abuse and situations of heterosexual domestic violence occur on a number of different levels. The
way in which these levels (between macro, mezzo and micro, as
outlined in Chapter 1) interact suggests that it is very important not to
underestimate both the type and extent of these differences when
considering elder abuse. In particular, this aspect is crucial when
dealing with the micro level of individual situations of elder abuse.

What is not known yet is the extent of the exact applicability and 'fit'
of the family violence model to situations of elder abuse; it is evident
that more work is urgently needed in this area. In addition, there are
ever more complex and complicated forms of familial violence that are
being 'discovered' and are subject to attention in America: abuse by
grandparents of grandchildren, abuse between siblings and abuse of
parents by their children (in particular by adolescents of middle-aged
parents) to name but a few recent examples. The following section
looks at some of the differences between elder abuse and other forms of
familial violence in slightly more depth.

Societal aspects

Societal expectations and attitudes towards young and old people are important here. It is likely that children and younger adult women are viewed as being far more vulnerable and in need of protection than older people who are stereotypically seen, in Western society, as being burdensome. The abuse of children and younger women may therefore be considered by many people to be more serious crimes, and because recognition and intervention in child abuse situations has been with us now for several decades, statutory agencies are far more aware of the problems of child abuse than any other form of abuse. This means that, when potential signs and risk factors are present in a family setting with young children, professionals are more likely to suspect abuse, but not necessarily to perceive any need for intervention with regard to domestic violence (DOH/SSI, 1996). Child abuse is accorded a higher priority than is elder abuse or domestic violence in both health and social care agencies. The latter situation is, of course, due also to the legislative and statutory responsibilities held in relation to children and the dearth of such systems for the protection of older people or younger adult women.

It is also necessary to remember that the social situations of children, young adult women and older people are in fact quite different. Elderly people, as adults, have far more legal, economic and emotional independence than is possible for children. Young women, although adult, may be kept in a subordinate and dependent position by their male partners (particularly financially). The economic independence of many elderly people may make them vulnerable to a type of exploitation and abuse that is rarely seen in other forms of family violence.

Individual aspects

A number of significant differences in the development of abuse can be seen at the micro level of abuse. Firstly, the potential causes of the abuse may be quite different. A number of victims of elder abuse are mentally and/or physically frail and dependent, while abused children, although dependent, do not necessarily have any disability (although children with a disabling condition have been found to be at greater risk of abuse). Younger adult women may be neither dependent nor disabled (or alternatively may be both!).

Secondly, the abuse of elderly people can be far more difficult to detect. Older people do not, generally, lead such public lives, and there may be a lack of contact with external agencies or indeed with anyone other than the abuser. They do not attend school, work or have routine medical examinations. There are well-established developmental norms and standards with regard to young children, and any undue deviation from these may result in at least a medical investigation of the cause (Bennett, 1990); however, with older people, the situation is far more complex. The absence of established comparative norms contributes to the differing extent and presentation of acute and chronic illnesses in old age. It can be very hard to ascertain, medically, the difference between an accidental fall and a deliberate injury (see Homer and Gilleard, 1990). Within potential situations of elder abuse, it is generally difficult for doctors to be categorical about many of the situations that are presented to them. Therefore medical definitions of what constitutes abuse can be somewhat misleading to people without a medical background.

Many of the carers of older people may themselves be elderly and have poor health and/or disabilities (Lau and Kosberg, 1979). It is not uncommon, given recent demographic trends, to find carers in their seventies caring for parents in their nineties. It is also necessary to acknowledge that at least some elder abuse seems to be dual-direction in nature: the older person may either respond to or perhaps even provoke the abuse (McCreadie, 1991). This phenomenon is referred to by Froggatt (1990) as 'old age abuse'. Research by Homer and Gilleard (1990) appears to confirm this tendency. Victims of child abuse or domestic violence may not directly initiate the abuse to the same extent.

Elder abuse can often involve relationships of many years' duration. Abusive situations may arise as a result of very longstanding difficulties within a relationship (Fulmer and O'Malley, 1987). Within situations of child abuse and some instances of domestic violence, the relationships are generally much 'newer' and of more recent origin, although some situations of domestic violence may endure for many years (Pahl, 1995). Longstanding difficulties of many years' duration may be highly resistant to change. A further difference of perhaps critical importance between those particular groups who are vulnerable to abuse is that whilst some protective measures may be necessary, it is important not to infantilise either older people or women who experience abuse.

Elder abuse would seem to consist of a number of related, but quite distinct, types of abuse that may be compared with different forms of familial violence. For example, it may be preferable, and indeed more profitable, to compare abuse occurring between spouses/partners irrespective of the ages of those involved or the length of time over which the abuse has occurred (i.e. to compare spouse or partner abuse between elderly people with that occurring between younger couples). Indeed, research findings by Pillemer and Finkelhor (1988) strongly suggest that the majority of abusive situations with which they were concerned consisted of abuse by partners that was in some instances undoubtedly of many years' duration. Homer and Gilleard also found that a history of longstanding relationship difficulties between family members appeared to be a factor within some abusive situations (Homer and Gilleard, 1990).

It is possible, however, that some abuse and abusive situations between partners only develop in later life. This may perhaps be as a result of what had always been a difficult relationship being 'overloaded' due to other problems and difficulties (financial, health and so forth). An inability of the individuals within the situation to manage additional difficulties in addition to an already problematic and dysfunctional system may lead to abuse occurring where none previously existed. The possible existence of this type of situation does not, however, necessarily negate the desirability of comparison with other forms of adult abuse rather than with situations of child abuse.

The abuse of vulnerable older people by their adult children may perhaps be considered as more comparable to the patterns observed within many situations of child abuse. This may be of particular relevance when there is an established history of interpersonal violence within the family as a learned response to stressful situations and disagreements. An additional motive of revenge on the part of the adult children (or indeed even the previously abused spouse) may also occur if the older person was abusive towards his children or spouse in an earlier developmental phase of the family; here there may be elements of the 'fallen tyrant' scenario. There is some evidence to support this from the study by Grafstrom *et al.* (1992; mentioned in Chapter 1).

There is a need to consider whether a further form of abuse, that of adult children by their elderly parents, should be considered comparable or even an extension to what is usually considered to be child abuse. This may also link to the situation noted above, of violence as a learned response within the family system, particularly if the abusive behaviour was of a longstanding nature. An abusive situation may possibly occur which was established when the adult child was a child, consisting of a pattern which has continued into adulthood.

It has been common knowledge for many years that certain families use violence as a means of dealing with conflict within the familial setting. It is perhaps not too surprising, therefore, that conflict between generations in later life may equally be considered to be dealt with by violence as a learned response to dealing with stress and conflict within the family. With regard to relationships that have been difficult in the early years, it is possibly somewhat unwise to believe that in later life they will improve. As already noted, Homer and Gilleard (1990) found that in many of the abusive situations in their study, there was a lengthy history of relationship difficulties between the parties involved. Pillemer (1986) found that 60 per cent of the cases of elder abuse were actually cases of spouse abuse. Indeed, there is strong evidence from the field of domestic violence which suggests that abusive relationships can last over periods of many years (Dobash and Dobash, 1992; Pahl, 1995).

Should there be suspicions of an injury, questions not just about the causation of the injury but also concerning family relationships should be asked. It is possible that the relevant questions are not always asked. An example could be determining what support or help is necessary instead of asking about the state and nature of the relationship between individuals. This may be in part because of a reluctance to ask personal questions about private lives. It may also be because practitioners do not really wish to hear the possible answers to the question as they might then need to respond in some other way that they would rather avoid. The public airing of what are essentially considered to be private matters is a difficult area for some individuals to approach and manage successfully.

Societal and professional attitudes

Within the field of family violence, and in particular with regard to elder abuse, attitudes, knowledge and values of both the general public and professionals working in these areas will affect both awareness of the problem and views concerning strategies for intervention. Penhale (1993c) has discussed some of the broader, societal barriers to identification and intervention within situations of elder abuse, which include societal views about ageing, family life, conflict, use of violence and the perceived role of the state in intervening in familial settings (Penhale, 1993c).

With regard to professional attitudes towards abusive situations and violence, one of the determining features is the evidence concerning attitudes and judgemental practices by health and social care professionals. It has been suggested that some nurses are ageist (Kingston and Hopwood, 1994) and assume that older people naturally have health deficits due to their age. This may affect the assessment of an older person. There is also some indication that knowledge about gerontological care of older people in general terms is marginal within nursing and medicine.

Ageism is also apparent within social care and social work and is reflected in the existence of lower levels of status, qualification and pay for many care staff working with older people (Biggs, 1993). Jack (1992) referred to the existence of 'institutionalised ageism' – the routine discrimination against older clients on the basis of age by local authorities – within Social Services Departments. Qualified social workers have consistently tended to prefer work with children and perceived work with older people as both less stressful and more oriented towards practical provision (Stevenson and Parsloe, 1978; Borsay, 1989; Hugman, 1994a).

Within the wider domain of adult abuse and domestic violence against women, professional commentators have also suggested that the attitudes of nurses to violence denies the magnitude of the problem. For example, Ingram (1994) suggests that:

> domestic violence is on the one hand denied and on the other hand accepted as something that happens in our society' (Ingram, 1994, p. 143).

It is likely that these and similar views may also be shared by other professionals and also by the wider general public. There also appears to be a quite widely held view within nursing that abuse is often a 'one-off occurrence'. This suggests that nurses are not aware of the repetitive nature of much abuse and are ignorant to the complex dynamics of family violence.

In a perceptive analysis of the social work response (or lack of it) within situations of domestic violence, Lloyd suggested:

> social workers' responses to domestic violence are determined by the workers' own value systems and their perception of women's roles within the family... Their responses are also the result of adhering to stereotyped images of women who experience domestic violence and the beliefs of individual social workers about why it occurs (Lloyd, 1995, p. 159).

There is some evidence, too, that nurses display a tendency to 'victim blame' and believe that a battered woman can simply leave an abusive situation (Bokunewicz and Copel, 1992). Stereotypical attitudes by nurses and other professionals may also lead to assumptions that mental illness is the cause of much of the abuse, thus excluding the fact that men without a mental illness may also be potential abusers. There can also be a view that women victims of violence are masochistic (Bokunewicz and Copel, 1992) and that the violence is 'normal' and 'not very serious' (Ingram, 1994). Attitudes within society generally concerning violence may not assist in this regard; ambivalence towards violence and what might constitute acceptable levels of violence is clearly likely to be of influence here (Browne, 1989).

Attitudes and values, on both an individual and a professional basis, are also likely to affect both the likelihood of detection of abuse and whether intervention is proceeded with within abusive situations. Their existence may also affect such matters as interprofessional communication, which has been found to have been influential within child abuse tragedies (Reder *et al.*, 1993). The inquiries set up to determine what went wrong in such situations determined problems in communication between professionals as a key factor within several such tragedies. It is also possible that confusion between professionals concerning respective roles and responsibilities will affect how adequately situations are dealt with. It has been suggested that unresolved interprofessional conflicts concerning such issues as these account for some of the difficulty in identifying and responding to situations of abuse (Phillips, 1989).

The existence of such attitudes is understandable in part because of the lack of education within professional training courses of nurses and social workers which is necessary in order to understand family violence (McCleer and Anwar, 1989; Kingston *et al.*, 1995). This also appears to be the case with medical students. Smith *et al.* state that:

> Medical students in Leicester receive only one session of teaching about violence in the family, psychologists give this lecture... there is no protocol for dealing with victims of Adult Domestic Violence (ADV) in the hospital; this contrasts with arrangements for victims of child abuse (Smith *et al.*, 1992).

This lack of knowledge about family violence clearly needs urgent rectification, with a readjustment of medical, nursing and social work curricula to encompass the whole spectrum of family abuse (see also Kingston *et al.*, 1995).

Doctors also display ageist attitudes and practices. This would also seem in part to reflect their training, with wide variations in terms of curriculum content concerning older people in medical schools and perhaps even fewer providing teaching time concerning elder abuse (Kingston *et al.*, 1995).

The existence of ageism, the fact that nurses (and perhaps other professionals) are morally evaluating patients, allied to the fact that physicians also say they feel less comfortable caring for older people, must be vigorously challenged and alternatives developed to counteract these attitudes and behaviours.

Elder abuse as a separate entity?

There is a need to determine whether elder abuse should be considered separately and distinctly from other forms of family violence or as part of the broader phenomenon of family violence.

As Steinmetz suggests:

> Unlike other forms of family violence, it is the age of the victim, not the act or the relationship between the victim and the perpetrator, that defines elder abuse. For example, is the spouse who has been physically abused during the marriage now, upon reaching 60, a victim of elder abuse? (Steinmetz, 1990, p. 207).

Some writers have suggested that elder abuse is not or should not be afforded a separate status from other forms of family violence (see Crystal, 1986; Callahan, 1988; DOH/SSI, 1992). This tends to be based on a view that to treat older people separately from other adults is an ageist response and that services for adults in general terms should be better designed in order to meet the needs of older people more effectively (Crystal, 1987). This view is also seen in Chapter 5 concerning legal issues, where some commentators have rejected specific legislation for older people on the grounds that it would reflect ageism and would deny elders full adult status (Slater, 1994). This is further expounded by McDermott, who stated:

> We did not want to perpetuate an artificial and ageist notion that family discord and violence, including violence between spouses, is of a completely different nature if it involves elderly people (McDermott, 1993, p. 5).

Such views would seem to acknowledge that elder abuse occurs within a social context, that familial violence occurs throughout the life course and that the responses that are developed to deal with these problems (in terms of both policy and service provision) should more adequately reflect this.

Other commentators, such as Finkelhor and Pillemer, argue persuasively that elder abuse should have a separate categorisation. The reasoning behind this view is premised on particular characteristics of older people, which, it is suggested, have a strong bearing on the types of abuse to which older people are subject and the increased vulnerability of many older people to abuse (Finkelhor and Pillemer, 1988). A slightly different perspective is that the lowered social status and general lack of resources for older people is indicative of a need for elder abuse to be considered separately from other forms of family violence. Furthermore, specific services should be developed in order to protect older people appropriately.

The discrimination and lowered social status experienced by older people, the routinised devaluation that older people experience from living in an ageist society, can exacerbate any vulnerability that may already exist due to deterioration in physical and mental health. The risk of abuse may thus be increased for individuals. In addition, factors such as the wider oppression and marginalisation of older people, and structural concomitants, such as the poverty facing many older people in our society, are of some importance within these considerations. Indeed, these factors may also combine with the general lack of resources for older people to either avoid or prevent abuse and lead to an exacerbation of the problems encountered by what is likely to be a significant number of older people.

It is apparent, too, that all of the above may be seen to interplay with individual circumstances and any pre-existing psychopathology on the part of both the older person who is subject to abuse and the person who is perpetrating the abuse. It is this potential interplay of individual and structural and societal circumstances that leads to the pervasive and somewhat intractable nature of many of the abusive situations experienced by individuals in whatever setting the abuse occurs.

Furthermore, concern about elder abuse has arisen over the past 7 years in the context of specialised services and professionals working with older people (see Penhale and Kingston, 1995b, for a further discussion of this). It is within this particular context that responses and interventions to alleviate abuse appear likely to develop: elder abuse is thus viewed as a problem with its own distinctive characteristics which set it apart from family violence more generally.

The setting in which elder abuse occurs is towards the end of the lifespan, the end-stage of relationships rather than the beginning or earlier stages. As suggested elsewhere, such relationships are often subject to stresses related to later life more generally, such as dependence, ill-health and disability (Marin and Morycz, 1990). Of importance also within the field of elder abuse are the societal views and attitudes that are commonly held concerning older people. The structural concomitants of abuse warrant further attention in terms of the extent to which these aspects perpetuate abusive situations and militate against their resolution.

There is a very real sense in which the wider marginalisation of older people within an ageist society is likely to hinder attempts to prevent and alleviate abusive situations and may actually exacerbate those which occur. It is possible, for example, that the current emphasis on community care for elders may mean additional areas of difficulty for carers, which, if not alleviated via appropriate service provision (perhaps because of a lack of resources), may lead to the development of elder abuse where none previously existed or of a worsening of a pre-existing situation (Penhale and Kingston, 1995a).

What is needed over the coming years with regard to elder abuse in particular is some elucidation of the extent of the similarity to and difference from other forms of family violence. Research should help to clarify some of the following issues:

- how much elder abuse of different types occurs (spouse abuse or abuse by adult children);
- whether abuse is most often a longstanding behaviour pattern or a new response to an unmanageable problem (or one perceived as such);
- the degrees of risk associated with different types of dependency (of the victim or the abuser);
- the nature and extent of the relationship between elder abuse and other forms of interpersonal violence: the degree of fit between them.

Elder abuse is similar to and yet very different from other types of family violence. The nature and extent of the differences strongly suggest that it should currently be considered separately, although not in isolation from the totality of family conflict. The spectrum of elder abuse, if viewed as a continuum, encompasses both spouse abuse and child abuse, and many variations in between. It also encompasses abuse that occurs within institutions, as can be seen in Chapter 3, due either to the regime within the institution or which occurs directed at an individual in that setting (from a relative, paid carer, volunteer or indeed another resident). Whilst not denying that abuse occurs within institutions that provide care for children and adults with disabilities, this form of abuse does appear to be different from other types of abuse that are considered within the broad domain of family violence. It is perhaps a further indication of the especial status that currently needs to be accorded to elder abuse.

Social factors and abusive situations

Much of the early theorising and conceptualisation of family violence appears to have been strongly based on a psychopathological model of behaviour. Social factors were largely discounted, and the causal explanations of violence within families (for both child abuse and domestic violence) were viewed as being firmly rooted within the personality disorders, psychological difficulties and mental health problems of those who abuse. There are several difficulties with a reliance on such an approach. Firstly, most of the studies from which such conclusions are drawn are small-scale retrospective studies of a limited number of cases. Secondly, cause appears at times to be muddled up with consequence in circular fashion: those people who abuse are mentally ill; the evidence that they are mentally ill is derived from the fact that they are involved in violent acts and must be ill to commit them! The abuse is both the behaviour to be explained and the main way of explaining it.

Part of the reason for the attraction of such psychological theories is that it is easier to contemplate abuse and an abusive situation when it is viewed as a terrible action (or series of actions) by a disturbed person who is different from 'normal people'. Psychological theories have developed further in recent years and are no longer as reliant on psychopathology, but within society powerful stereotypes still exist that continue to portray abusers as psychotic or extremely disturbed. This is nowhere more evident than within the media, who seem predominantly to report the sensational instances of abuse that tend to confirm the stereotypical view of the 'crazed abuser'. The relevance of certain social factors to abuse is still not wholly considered within such psychological perspectives, yet it is important that these be given adequate attention. The following section will therefore be concerned with such a consideration.

Social isolation

Evidence from the domain of child abuse has indicated that isolated families are more at risk of violence (Belsky, 1978). An ability to call on family and friends for help and support acts as a source of stress reduction and in some senses as an insulation against familial violence occurring. If a family is well integrated into the local community, there is less likelihood of violence taking place (Straus *et al.*, 1980). Clearly, older people can be even more socially isolated than children. Older people are not involved in education or employment markets; they are not subject to mandatory health tests at certain age junctures (only being offered a health screen at 75, see Homer and Kingston, 1991) and they may therefore be in less contact with others. Pillemer found that victims of elder abuse had fewer social contacts than did non-victims (36 per cent versus 17 per cent) and their relationships were less satisfactory (39 per cent versus 20 per cent) (Pillemer, 1986). Extreme social isolation of older people and their carers may lead to situations in which abuse not only occurs but is also perpetuated.

Stress

Research has indicated that homes in which there are high levels of stress (due to unemployment, financial problems, relationship difficulties or single parenthood) are also at high risk of being violent (Straus *et al.*, 1980; Gelles, 1989). This evidence suggests that stress is related to abuse that happens in the domestic setting (see also below, under social situational theories of family violence).

What also has an impact on the situation is the learned response by individuals or family units to the stressful situation and how to deal with it. The stress may be internal to individuals, for example personality or relationship difficulties, mental health or substance abuse problems. The stress may also be due to external factors such as unemployment, poverty or overcrowding. In addition, there are suggestions that an accumulation of a number of stresses can lead to overload, with abuse resulting as an outcome, the so-called pressure cooker effect.

In relation specifically to elder abuse, there is limited research evidence to support the idea that too much stress results in abuse. The study in Sweden mentioned earlier does seem to indicate that internal (psychological) stress was linked to dependency and abuse, but to date it is the only study to do so (Grafstrom *et al.*, 1992). With regard to external stressors, Pillemer's early work included consideration of external stress factors and determined three specific stressors that appeared to have a bearing on abusive situations. These were a person getting arrested (not necessarily in connection with abuse), a person leaving a situation and a person moving into a situation (Pillemer,

1986). In the absence of any of these specific factors, external stress did not appear to be linked with abuse in any causal way.

Although the research evidence is limited, there are indications that there is still a very widespread view that stress, and specifically the stress of caring for an older person, is related to abuse. This is despite the fact that there are many thousands of people in caring situations where abuse does not occur. Although stress may be a factor within some abusive situations, it is likely that there are other important factors that will also have an effect within abusive situations. This may well include such factors as the perception of stress (Steinmetz, 1990) or the nature and amount of ambivalence within the caring relationship (Pillemer, 1997). Clearly, more research is needed in this area in order to provide further clarification about the nature of stress as a factor within the development and continuation of abusive relationships and abusive situations.

Social characteristics

Despite common misconceptions, violence is not confined to those families of lower social classes. Additionally, family violence is not found evenly distributed across all strata of society. Rates of family violence appear to be highest in poorer urban families experiencing high rates of unemployment. For all forms of abuse, it would appear that for those cases which are reported, the majority of identified abusers are of lower socioeconomic status and are more likely to experience unemployment and social isolation (Belsky, 1978; Pelton, 1981; Finkelhor, 1991; Creighton, 1992). The research by Creighton indicated that early parenthood, poor marital relationships, criminality and large families characterised those people who abused their children (Creighton, 1992).

It is very likely, however, that more individuals who are poor, unemployed and from difficult social situations will come to the attention of authorities concerning violence of all types, which will obviously include situations of familial violence. Detection rates are therefore likely to be higher in areas where there are high levels of social deprivation. Additionally, such characteristics as those outlined above are also found in families where no abuse has occurred and where there may be few difficulties.

Whilst deprivation, unemployment, poverty and stress clearly do affect the parenting capacity of parents in some poor families, only a relatively small number of such parents abuse their children. Poverty is very widespread (Millar, 1993), yet not all children from poor families are abused. Social characteristics are likely to have a bearing on the development and continuation of abusive situations, but evidence of a direct causal relationship is perhaps unlikely.

Cycle of violence

The idea that individuals who are abused in childhood grow up to become abusive parents and violent adults has been widely discussed within the family violence and perhaps more particularly the child abuse literature (Gelles, 1980; Starr, 1988). The evidence concerning this notion is far from conclusive at present. A review of the literature and research findings suggests that the best estimate of the rate of trans-generational transmission of violence is around 30 per cent (plus or minus 5 per cent) (Kaufman and Zigler, 1987). This figure is less than the total number of abused children (within the US) but is more than the general rate of abuse found within the general population (2–4 per cent; Straus and Gelles, 1986).

A more recent study comparing rates of intergenerational transmission within situations of child abuse and elder abuse has indicated that whilst the experience of both groups of abusers of 'overall violence' in childhood was of similar amounts, those individuals who were involved in child abuse when adult were significantly more likely to have experienced 'severe forms of violence' as children than were those adults involved in situations of elder abuse (Korbin *et al.*, 1995). More research in this area would clearly be of benefit in attempting to determine how far childhood experiences influence actions and reactions in adulthood.

Whilst experience of violence in childhood may often be correlated with later behaviours which are violent, this is not likely to be the only determining factor involved within such situations. In general terms, such situations tend to result from a combination of complex psychological and sociological factors.

Gender differences

Outside the family, violent behaviour is much more likely to be the perogative of men than women. Much of the early research concerning child abuse indicated, however, that mothers were slightly more likely to be abusive to their children than were fathers (Gil, 1970; Parke and Collmer, 1975). Mothers do tend to spend more time with their children than fathers and additionally, in Western society, generally have more responsibility for the children than do their male partners. This was tested out in a study in which the amount of responsibility between men and women for their children was controlled. In this instance, men were more likely to be abusive than women (Margolin, 1992). Recent evidence from the area of child sexual abuse indicates that the majority of people who sexually abuse children are male (Finkelhor, 1991).

Within the wider sphere of domestic violence more generally, there has been much debate in recent years concerning the comparative rates of violence between men and women. Some researchers have suggested that the rate of female-to-male violence is pretty much the same as that of male-to-female violence (Straus and Gelles, 1986). Others have strongly argued that women are much more likely to be the victims of domestic violence (Dobash and Dobash, 1979, 1992). At present, it would appear that whilst a number of men are subject to violence from their partner, there are far fewer men who are victims than women.

More recent writing has suggested two distinct phenomena (Johnson, M.P., 1995):

- common couple violence, in which rates of violence between men and women are comparable and the violence may not be as extreme in its nature and effect;
- patriarchal terrorism, in which women are systematically terrorised by their male partners and where the violence may become very severe and persistent.

This distinction may prove useful in terms of the further determination of the nature and causes of domestic violence. An alternative view is that such distinctions are not wholly relevant as they do not address the central issues of concern, those of inequalities in gender relations and power within relationships between men and women.

Within the field of elder abuse, it appears that the majority of victims are generally also female. An exception to this was an early US study that found nearly equal numbers of men and women in their sample of victims (Pillemer and Finkelhor, 1988). When the figures were adjusted to account for the actual numbers of men and women in the total population of older people, the risk of abuse for men was twice that which existed for women. However, in terms of the severity of abuse, this tended to be greater for women (Pillemer and Finkelhor, 1988). There are a number of possible reasons why a higher number of women may come to the attention of professionals. It may be that women are more likely to seek assistance or to report abuse than men. Additionally, the populations surveyed may be made up largely of either women or of very elderly people, most of whom are female (O'Malley *et al.*, 1979).

It is also possible that more assistance is necessary for women due to the severity of their injuries, resulting in their coming to the attention of professionals, which then leads to the conclusion that the risk to older women of being abused is higher than the risk to men (Pillemer and Finkelhor, 1988). Abusive behaviour by women, which is more likely to be psychological or passively neglectful, may be much less likely to result in any treatment (of injury) for the male victim and may thus go comparatively unnoticed by professionals.

With regard to the gender of those who abuse older people, many of the early studies reported that abusers were also more likely to be female, usually relatives. Further analysis of these data, which separated physical abuse from neglect, discovered a statistically significant sex difference, in that men were more likely to use physical violence and women neglectful acts (Miller and Dodder, 1989). However, these researchers also proposed that because categories of reported neglect were very high in the studies they analysed, this went some way towards explaining why it had appeared that the perpetrators of abuse against older people were predominantly female. A later study by Pillemer and Finkelhor (1988) discovered that abusers were more likely to be spouses/partners than adult children or non-relatives. In most cases, those people who abused were close family members, usually living with the victim. There is a need for more research in this area in future in order to clarify further such aspects as these.

Theories of causation

The conceptual frameworks regarding the possible causes of family violence that have been developed to date include a number of distinct theories drawn from the disciplines of psychology, sociology and feminism. It is worth outlining several of these for the reader. Common themes that appear in all forms of family violence, albeit to differing degrees, include power, stress, isolation and diminished resources (emotional or physical) with which to counter such difficulties. It is

worth reiterating, however, that such theories have not as yet been fully
tested out to ascertain their applicability within the UK context. Clearly,
more work needs to take place within this area before it is possible to be
more certain about causative factors within the field of family violence.

In an overview of theories originally developed to explain physical
violence within families, Gelles and Straus suggested that there are
three main types of theory (Gelles and Straus, 1979a). These are:

- intraindividual theories, which view the cause of violence as due to
  flawed characteristics of individuals or the effects of alcohol or
  drugs (e.g. psychopathology, alcohol and drugs);
- social psychological theories, which focus on the interaction of the
  individual with others, and of the role of learning in developing
  violent behaviour (e.g. social learning theory, exchange theory,
  frustration–aggression theory and symbolic interaction theory);
- sociocultural theories, which emphasise the importance of social
  structures and institutional organisations within the development of
  violence (e.g. resource theory and conflict theory).

Gelles and Straus identified 15 theories which fitted within their broad
framework of the three main types (Gelles and Straus, 1979a). It is not
possible to do justice to all of these here, and in any case some are less
favourably viewed at present. However, it is useful to summarise some
of the main theories and explanations that have been developed with
regard to family violence and also, specifically, elder abuse. (The first
three theories are those in which specific application to elder abuse has
been attempted.)

Social situational theory

This explanation of the cause of familial violence suggests that the
immediate circumstances surrounding the individuals involved in the
abusive situation are of prime importance. In particular, two principal
factors seem to be crucial. The first of these is stress and the amount of
stress experienced by the family unit within a given situation. The
stress may be either internal or external stress for the family and/or the
individuals concerned, or a combination of these. Internal stressors
such as poor mental or physical health, personality characteristics and
the nature and type of a relationship can affect how a situation is dealt
with by the individuals within it. Stressful events (external stressors)

due to such structural factors as inadequate finances, unemployment, overcrowding or illness may exacerbate difficult situations. What is clearly of importance here is the effect of the stress on the individuals involved, how it is dealt with by individuals and also, perhaps critically, the perception of those involved as to the nature and degree of stress present within the situation and their capacity to cope and deal with this (see Steinmetz, 1990, for further details).

The second major factor within this theory concerns the cultural views and attitudes concerning violence and particularly the use of violence as a corrective force within families. Within a societal structure in which use of violence is normative, positive attitudes are linked to violence and any distinction between 'normal' violence and abusive 'abnormal' violence is difficult to maintain (Browne, 1989).

The theory proposes that when the societal and cultural norm is approving of the use of violence (in general terms), when levels of tolerance of violence within society and within a particular family setting are at certain points and when particular groups experience major stressors (or combinations of stressors) these groups and families are likely to use violence as a way of dealing with stress and resolving conflict.

Although this theory is attractive to practitioners in the field, there are few empirical data to substantiate it. Phillips (1986) examined available research data and determined little support from research for this type of theory in relation to elder abuse. Although in her view this was in part due to methodological and definitional difficulties within the research, 10 years later the research evidence still does not support situational theories.

Exchange/social control theories

This set of theories concern social exchanges between individuals and within families and the dynamics of power within such relationships. The principal tenet is that all social behaviour is based on a general principle of costs and rewards. Mutually satisfying and productive relationships, it is held, are based on reciprocity or mutual reward from interactions. Individuals are generally motivated to pursue rewards and to act in ways that minimise the costs of such actions and minimise the associated risks. Failure to achieve a balance of rewards between individuals may lead to conflict and even abuse.

Violence as an outcome is likely to result when the rewards of this type of behaviour are higher than the perceived costs (Gelles, 1983). It is argued that the possible costs of violence and abuse are lessened by such factors as societal views concerning the privacy and 'sanctity' of the family, and general reticence to allow state intervention in what are perceived as private matters. This is despite some evidence to suggest that the family is not the happy, safe and idealised institution that is presented daily via the media and politicians (Gelles and Straus, 1979b; Frost and Stein, 1989).

In any case, if the power of an individual (physical, emotional or fiscal) over another is not subject to control or sanction by society (police, courts, neighbours), the risk/cost to the abuser may be perceived by them as minimal. Consequently, the rewards derived from the continued use of violence may be viewed by the individual as outweighing the possible costs. Conversely, the potential rewards deriving from violent behaviour are increased by a cultural norm in which violence is accepted, condoned and legitimated.

Equally, the potential for imbalance in rewards may be higher in situations in which an older person is dependent and vulnerable and less able to contribute to the relationship in any positive way. This latter proposition assumes, however, that abuse is more likely to occur in situations in which the older person is more dependent, which, as has been seen earlier (Chapter 1), does not appear to be the case. In fact, as Glendenning states:

> researchers have failed to produce unequivocal evidence that abused elders are more dependent than non-abused elders (Glendenning, 1993, p. 25).

The theory develops in the following way. If the dynamic of the interaction can be altered so that the costs outweigh the rewards, violence is less likely to ensue or to continue to be used within the situation. The introduction of other individuals (for example, care workers) into the situation may be a sufficient alteration to affect the outcomes of such situations and to prevent or act as a deterrent to further abuse occurring. As suggested, there has been little empirical evidence to support this theory to date.

Symbolic interaction theory

This theory is concerned on a more global level with the way in which social life is established and developed through a series of interactions with others from the same social group (Rose, 1962). It is concerned with the meaning of actions, both for individuals and those which are shared, and also the expectations derived from the roles people hold. Individuals' actions are based on their perception of themselves and the others they relate to. Reality is not therefore a universal truth but will vary between individuals; the amount of agreement and consensus between individuals will depend on the extent to which the perceptions can be shared, negotiated and agreed upon by individuals concerning interactions (McCall and Simmons, 1966). Although relationships are the principal context within which life (and abuse) must be understood, it is the meaning of the relationship and events occurring within it that is crucial for the individuals concerned.

Within this type of framework, abusive situations and familial violence may thus arise and be maintained due to particular types of interaction occurring between individuals or within wider social institutions such as the family or institutions. Specific expectations arising from particular roles and the development of role strain if such expectations are not met may lead to disagreement, particularly if there is misunderstanding about the degree to which the perception is shared. Such disagreement, if not resolved, may lead to violence and abuse between individuals. Inability to renegotiate respective roles within relationships when necessary may lead to conflict or even the termination of the relationship (Hughes, 1995). Biggs *et al.* (1995) have considered such theories in particular relation to elder abuse, drawing on the work of Phillips concerning changes in perceptions of role and relationships due to ageing processes (Phillips, 1986). Within this framework, abuse is likely to result from conflict arising out of changing roles and identities between individuals as they grow older and an inability to successfully renegotiate these.

In recent years, the scenario that is most often considered within the field of elder abuse from an interactionist perspective seems to be that of two actors in a familial setting who are in conflict or dispute with each other. In addition, as Johns and Juklestad (1994) have suggested, the role of the witness to the abuse may be of major importance within this area. Johns views abuse as predominantly a social act that critically involves a witness in addition to the principal actors. It is the witness who is instrumental in labelling the act as abusive (or not) and whose role is to evaluate whether the act is 'legitimate' in terms of social mores (Johns *et al.*, 1991). It seems appropriate here to acknowledge that there may be multiple witnesses of elder abuse, including:

- those actors and key players within abusive situations who may also observe the interaction;
- witnesses and audiences who observe the acts from their unique and differing perspectives;
- practitioners who observe from a professional perspective and who wish to assist via their specific interventions;
- researchers whose specific remit is to analyse the phenomena;
- politicians, policy-makers and legislators;
- the media, who report acts of abuse and construct a 'reality' for the wider public.

Finally, there is the wider public who witness these complex and difficult situations and have their own perceptions, attitudes and definitions of what constitutes abuse and what (if anything) should be done about it.

Although the theory offers some attraction in its consideration of the meaning of acts for individuals and of a necessary concern with attitudes and behaviours, it may be difficult to substantiate through empirical research.

Resource theory

This theory proposes that all social systems, particularly the family, are based on the use of force or threat of its usage in order to maintain the *status quo* and order. The main proponent of this theory, Goode, has suggested that the more resources (economic, social or emotional) an individual has, the less likely it is that there will be an overt display of violence (Goode, 1971). There are parallels to be drawn with the previous section on exchange theories (Gelles, 1983). The dominant position in a family may need to be established and maintained through the use of violence by the person who has lower status and education and lacks social skills. The resolution of differences and conflicts may be achieved through the use of force by those individuals within the family who have few other resources available to them. A variation on this theory suggests that it is the use and misuse of power relationships that critically determines the potential for violence within families (Finkelhor *et al.*, 1983).

Ecological theories

This set of theories derives from the work of Garbarino in the field of psychology and the genesis of child abuse. An alternative title could be the 'human development approach' (Garbarino, 1977). Essentially, the central tenet of this theory is that abusive situations arise from a mismatch between the family and their community, or even the wider environment. The risk of violence occurring is seen as being highest when family functioning (critically, that of the individuals involved) is limited by developmental problems. Thus, children with disabilities (physical or learning difficulties, or emotional problems) are perceived as being at an increased risk of abuse compared with 'normal' children. Adults who have their own personality or mental health problems or who experience major life stresses are at a higher risk of perpetuating abuse and abusive situations. If the social interactions within the family increase the stress or worsen the pre-existing problems of the individuals, the potential for abuse is heightened even more. And if there is a lack of supportive agencies in the community to assist families, the risk of violence and abuse may be raised even further.

Social learning theories

These theories have developed within a social psychological framework and emphasise the role of social learning within abusive relationships. Attention is also given to the role of family relationships in shaping the future behaviours of individuals and patterns of family life. Currently used psychological theories, such as these, appear far more complex than previous theories developed to explain violent behaviour that focused on the psychopathology of the individual or frustration–aggression arising from poor parent–child relationships (specifically mother–child relationships).

Social learning theories emphasise that family life is the arena where individuals learn about roles and role sets, where they learn how to be husband, father, wife, mother or child and where patterns of behaviour are established and perpetuated (O'Leary, 1988). Families are also where people experience and learn how to deal with stress, pressures and frustrations of different sorts. Steinmetz and Straus described family life as a 'training ground for violence' (Steinmetz and Straus, 1973).

Home life is often the place where individuals experience violence first hand, and both learn how to use violence and also how to justify its usage. For example, physical chastisement of children may be described by the parent inflicting the punishment as being for the child's own good; the physical abuse of a woman may be explained in the same way by a husband or partner; an older person may be abused by a carer ostensibly acting in the best interests of the older victim. Such psychological explanations of abuse focus very much on individuals, and there is little emphasis on the role that social factors might play within such situations.

Domestic violence theories

The previous theories all tend to suggest that families and the individuals within them are responsible for violence and abuse. Thus there may be a tendency to pathologise individuals and to apportion blame. The catalyst for the abuse is perceived as being the stress of different factors that individuals are unable to manage or deal with. From the field of sociology has come a valuable contribution emphasising the social and structural factors that may result in violence. The feminist perspective focuses on the role of gender and power within domestic violence in particular. Specifically, certain social and economic processes within society are viewed as supporting (both directly and indirectly) a male-dominated, patriarchal societal and family structure, to the detriment of women (Dobash and Dobash, 1979; Johnson, M.P., 1995).

The central thesis is that such a patriarchal structure leads directly to the subjugation and subordination of women (and children). Within this framework, violence (of different types: physical, psychological and emotional) is used in order to maintain men in their position of power within society and within familial and partnership relations. Physical and psychological forms of coercion are used by men, usually in ways that are harmful, in order to control women and to maintain dominance and power over them.

Some support for the view that inequalities in gender relations between men and women leads to violence in certain situations has been forthcoming from research within recent years (Ptacek, 1988; Ferree, 1990; Jones and Schechter, 1992). Such research has used different methodologies and different theoretical approaches and focused on differing aspects of violence against women, yet the findings have been quite similar.

Critics of the feminist approach (such as Gelles, 1993) suggest that what has been developed is an approach that uses a single variable (patriarchy) to explain violence. The phenomenon of familial violence is, however, in the view of such critics, multivariate and complex, and feminist theory is therefore flawed by its reliance on a singular approach.

In a useful counterargument, Yllö states that patriarchy is not conceptualised by feminists as a single discrete measurable variable but is multidimensional and complex in interaction (Yllö, 1993). Furthermore, sociological theories such as exchange or resource theories would benefit from the inclusion of gender analysis within their frameworks. Two further areas of concern are raised by Yllö. These are, firstly, that psychological explanations of violence should not develop as excuses of why abuse occurs, and secondly, that a clear focus on domestic violence as a social and political problem (not just an individual one) be retained and reaffirmed. Finally, Yllö acknowledges the potential contribution to be made by other perspectives, in particular from the sociological field (Yllö, 1993). It is unfortunate that there has, as yet, been comparatively little attention paid to the areas of child abuse and elder abuse from the feminist point of view, although Leeder (1994) and Whittaker (1995) have provided preliminary analyses with regard to elder abuse; future developments are both hoped for and expected in this regard.

Integrated theories

In recent years, there has been a move to develop more integrated theories of the causation of family violence. These attempt to combine social, structural, cultural and psychological theories in order to develop more coherent explanations of why abuse occurs and is perpetuated. Such theories propose that the development of familial violence is affected by both situational (internal) stressors and structural (external) stressors (Gelles, 1987; Browne, 1988). The chances of the combination of stressors resulting in violence will be further affected by and depend on the nature of the relationships and interactions between the individuals involved in the situation. As Browne has indicated:

> A secure relationship between family members will 'buffer' any effects of stress and facilitate coping strategies on behalf of the family. By contrast, insecure or anxious relationships will not 'buffer' the family under stress and 'episodic overload', such as an argument, may result in physical or emotional attack (Browne, 1988, p. 22).

Additionally, any violence that occurs will be likely to have a negative effect on the existing relationship and will thus reduce any potential buffering effects, either then or in the future. Although Browne was writing specifically about child abuse, it is possible that similar mechanisms might operate within other situations of familial violence; however, this needs to be considered further and perhaps empirically tested. Such a theory may assist in developing an understanding of episodic violence but seems much less effective in explaining phenomena such as child sexual abuse. Sociological and feminist explanations that emphasise the role of socialisation processes and inequalities in power within relationships are likely to be of more value for such phenomena.

Elder abuse has been described as 'elusive, ambiguous and multi-dimensional' (Filinson, 1989, p. 26); the whole arena of theoretical issues has been perceived as difficult and problematic. The theoretical approaches presented above have limited support from empirical research (some more than others), and there has on occasion been some confusion concerning theoretical frameworks, likely causative agents and risk factors. As McDonald *et al.* perceptively noted:

> Much of the literature does not make the important distinction between theoretical explanations and causal factors related to elder abuse and neglect. For example, a theory provides a systematic explanation for observed facts in the form of interconnected propositions regarding the relations between specific variables or factors. However, in the literature, specific factors such as stress and dependency are often treated as theoretical explanations when these are merely factors that may be incorporated into one of a number of theories that attempt to explain elder abuse and neglect (McDonald *et al.*, 1991, p. 23).

In presenting their summary of the main theories developed concerning family violence, Gelles and Straus stress the importance of complementarity and the way in which theories interrelate and potentially integrate with each other (Gelles and Straus, 1979a). Within the continuum of elder abuse and neglect are found many different types of behaviour. It is unlikely that any one theoretical perspective will be developed which will account for every type of abuse. The aim is surely to reflect more accurately what is likely to be 'a complex and multi-layered structure' (Sprey and Matthews, 1989, p. 57).

If this is so, a variety of different conceptual frameworks and explanations will be necessary to account for specific but different phenomena within the continuum as a whole.

Summary and conclusions

Violence within the family has been viewed as being a relatively rare phenomenon, yet research has consistently shown in recent years that family and other close interpersonal relationships contain high levels of violence. Far from the commonly accepted view within Western society that families are warm, nurturing, safe environments, it is apparent that family life can be very dangerous indeed, especially for women and children (both of whom appear from the evidence to be particularly at risk of abuse), and increasingly for older people. Different forms of violence – by adolescent children towards their parents, date and acquaintance rape and violence between siblings – have been identified in recent years; other forms may yet be recognised. The issue of men being subjected to violence within the home (or other close relationships) remains somewhat controversial. Whilst it is apparent that some men are abused within such settings, the number involved is small in comparison with the numbers of abused women.

Traditionally, violence within the home has been viewed as occurring due to highly disturbed individual members: the psychopathological model prevailed. It is evident, however, that social factors play a significant part in the causation and continuation of violent patterns of behaviour. Familial violence occurs across the social spectrum but appears more likely to happen in homes where there are very high levels of external (or social) stress, such as poverty, unemployment and social isolation. Additionally, men tend to be the most physically violent members of families. The harm caused by physical violence is not just physical in nature: there may be emotional, cognitive and social effects on the individual concerned and the family.

Other forms of violence, such as psychological abuse, sexual abuse, even neglect and financial abuse of older people, can and often do have longlasting and personally devastating effects on individuals and are thus included within the spectrum of family violence. In attempting to ascertain the causes of elder abuse, it would seem appropriate to consider the range of possible theories: from those which focus on individuals and the dynamics of interpersonal relationships to those which focus on inequalities in power, social factors (including social attitudes) and the role of different types of oppression within society. It is also apparent that any theory concerning elder abuse needs a clear focus on the effects of ageism, marginalisation and sexism within the development and perpetuation of abuse.

Similarities and differences between elder abuse, child abuse and domestic violence more generally occur on a number of different levels. Differences appear at both macro (societal) and micro (individual) levels. Due to the nature of the interaction between these levels, it is essential to consider both the nature and extent of these differences when considering elder abuse. In particular, this is important when dealing with individual situations of elder abuse and attempting to find resolutions to these.

It is also apparent that more work is needed in future on the wider applicability of the family violence model to situations of elder abuse and how far the fit extends. As outlined above, a number of theories concerning the possible causes of familial violence have been developing in recent years. It appears unlikely that any one cause will be identified which would be applicable to all forms of abuse, and a number of different theoretical approaches are helpful in this regard and may assist the practitioner in the search for solutions.

Elder abuse is both similar to and very different from child abuse and should currently be considered separately, distinct from a more generic adult abuse focus. It is germane to suggest here that, in the view of the authors, our current knowledge and understanding of elder abuse strongly indicates that, despite the evident differences, the phenomena should be considered as part of a wider continuum of family violence rather than an entirely separate entity. This contextual background is an important prerequisite to moving on to our next chapter, which is concerned with the abuse that occurs in institutions, for it is equally important to develop as clear an understanding as possible of abuse that is not necessarily familial violence but is occurring in institutional rather than domestic settings.

3

Institutional Dimensions

Introduction

The previous chapter looked at elder abuse in relation to family violence in more general terms. Notwithstanding this perspective, it is important not to lose sight of the fact that there are a range of environments in which elder abuse and neglect are found. This depends, in part of course, as we have seen in Chapter 1, on the types of definition of abuse that have been adopted and the forms of abuse under scrutiny. Traditionally, considerations concerning elder abuse have focused on either abuse found within the domiciliary setting (most often the elderly person's own home) or institutional abuse (usually located within some form of residential or nursing home setting). There have also been numerous scandals within the National Health Service (NHS) continuing care sector, including services for people with mental health impairments, learning disabilities and services for older people (Martin, 1984; DOH, 1992; Kingston and Brammer, 1997). The range of abuse and neglect found encompasses acts and omissions, due to either the regime within the institution or abuse directed at an individual in that setting, from a relative, paid carer or indeed another resident.

The aim of this chapter is to present a distillation of the current state of knowledge concerning the abuse and neglect that occurs within institutions: what is known and what is not known; the outcomes of some of the enquiries into abuse that has occurred in institutional settings; and some of the research findings concerning abusive situations that can occur. It will also be necessary to explore the changing nature of continuing care and to consider how it will be necessary to monitor the quality of service provided in a future health and welfare sector driven by a market economy and based on a pluralistic statutory/independent/voluntary sector mix.

Institutional care: the background

There has been a well-established tradition within the UK of creating large institutions designed to accommodate and provide care for some of society's most vulnerable members. The roots of this tradition undoubtedly rest in the Poor Law and the workhouse but are seen elsewhere in modern society. Such a tradition is not restricted to the Victorian notions of 'deserving' and 'undeserving' recipients of benefaction and philanthropy but also to some of those individuals at opposite ends of the social spectrum. An example of this is the provision of private boarding school education for those of a higher social class status or the provision of a prison regime for those whose criminal activities have resulted in a period of incarceration.

The provision of residential and nursing home care for frail older people, and the historical development of such services and current status of such care, has been adequately explored elsewhere (see, for example, Phillips, 1992; Allen *et al.*, 1992). What is of interest is the extent to which views of adequate and appropriate care have been imposed on society as a whole. The view that institutional care is a desirable outcome for older people in later life has thus been created and is perpetuated within the wider society. In fact, it is by far the minority of older people who experience such provision: only 5 per cent of the population of those aged between 75 years and 84 years are likely to enter residential care, and a smaller number live out their lives in nursing homes, although this rises to 21 per cent for the age range beyond 85 years (DOH, 1996). However, the perception of many, if not most, people is that it is entirely normal and appropriate for older people to receive care in an institution at some point towards the end stages of their lives and that by far the majority of older people do so. There is equally a view that institutional care is a one-way process, almost invariably ending with the death of the individual. The notion of rehabilitation or of short periods spent in institutional care (apart, perhaps, from acute hospital care) is not seen generally as being of relevance to older people.

This perception may, of course, be very different for those from the current cohort of older people. For this generation of older people, those over 75 years of age, notions of institutional care centre around images of the workhouse. These images are extremely powerful, pervasive and difficult to dispel. Those individuals of subsequent generations who cannot physically recall a workhouse, and who have only experienced the shame and associated stigma at second or third hand, may have a totally different set of attitudes and aspirations. This group may well approach the notion of such care very differently (Nolan, M., personal communication, 1994). Indeed, such perceptions may well be superseded in any case by the comparatively recent set of attitudes concerning community care.

Political reasons for the development of such policies apart, such statements as those contained in government guidance concerning the desirability of individuals remaining in their own homes and communities of origin for as long as practicable and feasible may also in the longer term affect notions about institutional care for individuals. Given that the provision of institutional care is fluctuating in this latter part of the century and looks likely to continue to do so over the next decade, an alteration in the public perception of such provision may well be necessary in any case.

The notion, for example, of continuing care in NHS hospitals for the frailest and most dependent elders who are in need of constant nursing care may well disappear altogether. This will particularly be the case if the small amounts of this provision that continue to survive in 1997 diminish still further into obscurity over time. The demise of such facilities may be met with somewhat mixed views, especially as some of the worst forms of institutional abuse have undoubtedly occurred in such provision. Managers may have little option but to close such wards rather than to attempt to refurbish them with appropriate equipment, care and attitudes, given the magnitude of the task (Rowe, J., personal communication, 1994).

However, the notion of NHS care to be 'provided free at the point of delivery', rather than means tested, is a central tenet of the welfare state, which, despite the attempts of successive governments over the past two decades to dismantle it, continues to be widely held by the public at least. The point is made succinctly by Pitkeathley, who argues that, in the absence of any public debate concerning long-term care, policy changes appear to have been made by stealth.

The issue of policy change by stealth is an important one to note, and this form of subtle, incremental change without public debate continues. The continuing reduction in NHS beds for long-term care has led to political debate surrounding continuing care for older people; in 1995 the English Department of Health asked all Health Authorities/Commissions to produce draft local policies suggesting eligibility criteria for meeting continuing health care needs (as opposed to social needs) following consultation on a local basis.

Such local guidelines were formalised for use from 1 April 1996; after that date, Health Authorities also had to incorporate, as part of this process, proposals for independent review panels to arbitrate when an individual or carer considered that eligibility for free NHS inpatient care on a longer-term basis had not been correctly applied. This set of circumstances led Saper and Laing to comment that:

> The entire process of defining eligibility criteria is something of a novel departure in British health policy, since it asks Health Authorities to lay down explicit criteria for rationing access to 'free' NHS long-term care services – something the NHS has so far studiously avoided doing for acute medical care (Saper and Laing, 1995, p. 22).

The provision of means-tested private residential and nursing home care for older people is also a comparatively recent phenomenon and, it is suggested, one which is economically driven. Traditionally, only those older people with independent means could afford to purchase care in such provision. It was the tendency for care provided by the state, in effect by Local Authority Social Services Departments, to be used by those individuals without financial means who, although they were financially assessed, usually contributed little more than their state pension towards the cost of their care.

From the early 1980s, there was a shift of emphasis from the traditional view that only people with means could afford to enter private care. This was produced by the provision by the Department of Health and Social Security (DHSS) of payments to individuals to assist with the cost of such care. This resulted in a rapid increase in the number of people exercising their right to choose such care and to enter private care homes. The result was an escalating bill for government running into billions of pounds of payments via the DHSS for care.

Suspicions were raised on the part of government that the majority of older people entering private homes did not require that level of care. This view was not, however, borne out by research (see Allen *et al.*, 1992, for further exploration of this). However, as eligibility for DHSS assistance was based purely on assessment of income with no assessment of care needs, the view that more control of the situation was necessary emerged and held sway.

This was operationalised via the implementation of community care reforms so that Local Authority Social Services/Social Work Departments became responsible, from April 1993, for the assessment (financially and in terms of care needs) of people in need of social care. This situation has particularly applied to all adults in need of assistance via public funding for residential or nursing home care; it has arguably had most effect on older people (since higher numbers of older people than other adult groups use such care facilities).

The Wagner Report, published in 1988, focused on the problems arising from public funding of private residential care by DHSS and the apparent perverse incentives available to older people to enter residential care and obtain assistance with funding. The attitude of government towards care for people at home has no doubt been affected by the cost of public funding for such residential provision, with a view that it is cheaper to maintain people in their own homes.

This also reflects a shift in perception about the desirability of institutional care for individuals that dates back over three decades to the work of Goffmann (1961) and others. A view has emerged that institutions are in some ways inherently abusive in themselves, especially if they serve to marginalise groups of older people from the community in which they have lived most of their lives (Basaglia, 1989, p. 255).

At the same time as this shift in political and economic thought, the field of social welfare was in any case seeing the development of concepts concerning deinstitutionalisation. The restrictive and dehumanising effects of institutions, in particular those concerned with mental health services, had been recognised and well documented over a lengthy period both in the UK and the US (Szasz, 1961, 1973; Laing, 1964; Goffmann, 1968; Scull, 1977).

These aspects were reiterated again in the Griffiths Report (1988), which discussed the need to assist people to remain living at home and for there to be a new system for funding private residential care from the public purse. The development of real alternatives to institutional care was argued for within the report. Additionally, there were strong statements that government policies and state provision of welfare should shift from resource and service-led provision to needs-led provision, in effect that individuals and their carers should be offered more choice and flexibility of provision within the community.

What is becoming clear, since the implementation of the community care reforms, is that the provision of care for people living in their own homes is not a cheap option. For these groups of dependent people with complex care needs, the provision of adequate care may not be possible on economic grounds (too expensive) or practical grounds (for example inadequate accommodation to allow for a live-in carer). The choice to stay at home may be a false choice for individuals in situations such as these; there may not, in reality, be such a choice. Certain forms of institutional care may thus be necessary for these individuals.

Additionally, there are some older people who wish to be looked after in later life and who request residential care, perhaps as much for psychological and emotional reasons as any need for assistance with physical care. This has led some commentators to propose that there should only be one form of care for individuals and that admission to care should be limited to those whose dependency needs indicate a necessity for such care (see, for example, BASW, 1992). The argument runs that, for those individuals who require residential care or some form of group living scheme, what should be developed further are assisted living schemes and sheltered housing on the model provided by the Abbeyfield Society. Institutional care would then be utilised solely for those individuals whose primary need was for intensive levels of physical and/or nursing care and supervision. It follows, too, that the current division between nursing home and residential homes should cease to exist and that there should be one type of care for individuals in need. This would then obviate the difficult situation arising whereby individuals may have to move from one type of home to another as their need for care increases.

It has already been suggested that many individuals in residential care are in fact in need of nursing care, which is placing an unnecessary burden on community-based nursing staff as residential homes usually have neither trained nursing staff working in them nor adequate access to community nursing staff (RCN, 1993). If this change does take place, it will be necessary to check that adequate levels of nursing care are provided in the single registration homes. This may be particularly necessary when there may a perverse incentive to employ a skill mix heavily tilted towards unqualified health care assistants.

In addition, it should mean one system of inspection and registration for homes, and hence a simplification of existing systems. In 1997, should a home wish to achieve dual registration as both a residential and a nursing home, this still involves registering with both the Health Authority and the Local Authority Social Services Department and inspection from both authorities (except where Authorities have collaborated to provide joint registration and inspection units, which is as yet a useful, if rather rare, phenomenon). Attempts have already been made to lobby politicians on the matter of the single care home with joint initiatives between the British Association of Social Workers (BASW) and Royal College of Nursing (RCN) (BASW/RCN, 1994). Hopefully, a favourable response may be forthcoming from government, who indicated that there would be further examination of the idea, perhaps linked with the notions of deregulation popular with conservative politicians. Subsequently, a consultation document was produced concerning the possible deregulation of residential and nursing home care (DOH, 1996), as well as a report commissioned by government concerning options for change.

Elder abuse and neglect in institutions

The spectrum of abuse and neglect found within various types of continuing care spans a remarkable range:

- lack of basic standards of privacy (Counsel and Care, 1991);
- physical care and quality of life (Hughes and Wilkin, 1989);
- the erosion of individuality in the care of older people in hospital;
- resistance to change in geriatric care (Smith, 1986);
- physical working conditions in hospitals (Millard and Roberts, 1991);
- nursing staff burn-out (Heine, 1986; Schaufeli and Janczur, 1994; Duquette *et al.*, 1995; WHO, 1995);
- organisational factors leading to low standards of care (Wiener and Kayser-Jones, 1990);
- fraud in nursing homes (Halamandaris, 1983);
- various types of restraint (Marks, 1992; Brungardt, 1994; Liukkonen and Laitinen, 1994; Mapp, 1994; Sullivan-Marx, 1995; McDonnell, 1996);
- the taking of life in old people's homes (Dissenbacher, 1989).

Needless to say, the spectrum is increasing, with other forms of abuse being considered on a regular basis; these include sensory deprivation, inadequate dietary provision and deficient nursing care in the terminal stages of illness.

Abuse may occur at a number of different levels, for example an older person may be abused or neglected by a paid member of care staff, another resident, a voluntary visitor or relatives or friends who visit. An abusive or neglectful relationship between an older person and their carer may not necessarily cease on admission to institutional care; sometimes the abuse may equally continue to take place within a different setting. The existence of abuse is not necessarily dependent on the setting; just because the setting has altered, this does not mean that the abuse will automatically cease as other contextual and situational factors are likely to be important in connection with this. The abuser is, however, usually known to the victim, and the abuse generally takes place within the context of a relationship, even if it is an abusive relationship.

There is, equally, a distinction to be made between individual acts of abuse or neglect inflicted upon individuals and institutionalised abuse, in which the regime of the institution itself may be abusive (Gilleard, 1994). However, in reality, within an abusive or neglectful institution it is often difficult to define whether the reasons for abuse are caused by individual acts or omissions, or are due to intrinsic managerial failings within the institution: both are often found in the same institution.

These acts or omissions may be due to.

- a lack of staff training/education about caring for elders;
- work-related stress and professional burn-out;
- the organisational structure or culture, including attitudes;
- the personal psychopathology of individual staff members;
- the personal characteristics of victims;
- a lack of adequate resources to provide good-quality care.

An assumption that an abusive or neglectful situation arises only in poor-quality homes may not, however, be entirely accurate. The differences in quality of care between different types of institution may not be very great. A key finding from an examination of reports of inquiries into scandals into residential care suggested that the change required to alter an acceptable or good care practice into an abusive practice was not very large and could occur rapidly with only a slight, perhaps barely detectable, change in the situation (Clough, 1987). Potential warning signs of abuse occurring within such settings are listed as: run-down establishments; the existence of a 'closed institution'; multiple complaints about the establishment; staff stress; evidence of alcohol consumption by staff; and too much staff autonomy (Clough, 1987).

It is also apparent that an individual establishment with a poor quality of care may have individual members of staff who are trying (often in very difficult circumstances) to improve the quality of care (Sone, 1995). It is no coincidence that organisations like Public Concern at Work, Freedom to Care and Action on Elder Abuse have emerged within the last 5 years, charged with a remit to help the whistleblower who seeks improvements in care.

There is a lengthy history of mistreatment and neglect of elders in long-stay hospitals, Poor Law institutions and old people's homes in the UK (see Townsend, 1962; Robb, 1967). The enduring nature of this form of abuse and neglect is clearly alarming; a quick recourse to a

letter published in *The Times*, 9 November 1965 suggests that it could
have been written 30 years later and still be accurate:

Sir,

We, the undersigned, have been shocked by the treatment of geriatric patients in
certain mental hospitals, one of the evils being the practice of stripping them of
their personal possessions. We have now sufficient evidence to suggest that this is
widespread. The attitude of the Ministry of Health to complaints has merely reinforced our anxieties. In consequence, we have decided to collect evidence of ill-
treatment of geriatric patients throughout the country, to demonstrate the need for
a national investigation. We hope this will lead to the securing of effective and
humane control over these hospitals by the ministry, which seems at present to be
lacking.

We shall be grateful if those who have encountered malpractices in this sphere
will supply us with detailed information, which would of course be treated as
confidential.

Yours faithfully,

Strabolgi, Beaumont, Heytesbury, Brian Abel-Smith, Edward Ardizzone, Audrey
Harvey, John Hewetson, Barbara Robb, Bill Sargeant, Daniel Woolgar O.P.
10 Hampstead Grove, NW3.

There have also been a number of official inquiries into scandals and
abusive practices within residential care homes. Of the situation at the
now infamous Nye Bevan Lodge, a Local Authority-run home in
Southwark, South London, one commentator wrote:

when elderly, often confused residents are made to eat their own faeces, left unat-
tended, physically manhandled, forced to pay money to care staff and even helped
to die, something is seriously wrong (Vousden, 1987, p. 19).

In an analysis of long-stay hospital wards in 12 consecutive Health
Advisory Service reports, which was reported at a national conference
on elder abuse held in 1988, Horrocks (cited in Tomlin, 1989) found
the following instances of institutional abuse:

- Wards were large, open, unhomely, impersonal.
- Overcrowding was common and beds too close together.
- Furniture was 'dilapidated' with no carpeting.
- There was excessive use of restraints.
- Catering was poor, with little choice.
- Meals were served to suit the needs of the institution (the last meal
  of the day often being at 5pm).

- There was a lack of individual care plans for patients.
- Policies on the management of continence were absent in half the units inspected.
- Staffing ratios were poor.
- Privacy was lacking (for example group bathing, open toileting and washing).
- There was a total lack of mental stimulation for patients.

As Tomlin perceived, 'These examples reflect passive abuse on a massive scale' (Tomlin, 1989, p. 12). In a review of the literature on institutional abuse, Glendenning suggests that:

> There is chilling evidence that these elderly people are more likely to be at risk than the 95 per cent or 91 per cent who live in the community (Glendenning, 1993, p. 1).

From one US study comes the claim:

> Abuse is sufficiently extensive to merit public concern and may be a common part of institutional life (Pillemer and Moore, 1989, p. 318).

It appears that continuous reference to abuse and neglect seems to be reported in a variety of forms. This ranges from the reporting of local scandals in the media and press, through to local scandals of such significance that the DOH demand an enquiry, to reports from registered homes tribunals or, finally, through to occasional reports either from registering bodies, for example the UKCC, or of the publicly available results of enquiries into scandals.

However, systematic research reporting either prevalence or risk factors is noticeable by its absence in the UK research. This is perhaps largely due to the difficulties of asking sensitive questions about the caring process within the institutional sector. Research in the US appears to have managed to utilise the telephone survey to avoid the difficulties of face-to-face questions of front-line health and social care workers. Such one-to-one interviews often seem to lead to socially acceptable answers in these highly emotive areas of concern, although observational studies within institutions over a period of time may provide additional forms of evidence.

Evidence from US research

In an observational study of one nursing home, Foner found that psychological abuse was most common and that physical abuse was comparatively rare, although physical restraints were used by staff (Foner, 1994). Similarly, a multisite, descriptive and exploratory study using observational techniques and semi-structured interviews of individual residents within three different nursing homes found no incidents of overt physical abuse such as kicking, hitting or punching, but instead instances of 'covert' psychological abuse such as isolation, lack of personal choice for residents and thoughtless care practices by staff (Meddaugh, 1993). Additionally, Meddaugh found that there were differences between aggressive and non-aggressive residents in terms of their treatment by care staff. Aggressive residents were isolated more often than non-aggressive residents and were not given choices concerning their bathing or in the selection of clothing following personal care routines. They were also more likely to be labelled by staff as 'bad' (Meddaugh, 1993).

The research on which the statement that abuse was a common part of institutional life was made utilised data from 577 nurses and nursing aides (61 per cent nursing aides, 20 per cent licensed practical nurses and 19 per cent registered nurses) working in long-term care facilities in the US (Pillemer and Moore, 1989). The staff were randomly chosen from the staff lists of intermediate care facilities and interviewed by telephone.

Both groups were asked whether they themselves had committed abusive acts, defined as both physical and psychological. The group was also questioned about observing physical or psychological abuse in their work environment. In order to define physical and psychological abuse, the definition of Straus was utilised; aggression or violence was broadly defined as:

> an act carried out with the intention of, or perceived as having the intention of, hurting another person. The injury can be either symbolic, material or physical (Straus, 1979, p. 77).

In order to operationalise this definition, questions were based on the Conflicts Tactics Scale (Straus, 1979). The behaviours were prefaced with 'Sometimes when conflicts occur with patients, the staff may find it difficult to respond in ways they are supposed to'. Indicators of physical abuse included excessive use of restraints, pushing, grabbing, shoving or pinching a patient, throwing something at a patient, slapping or hitting a patient, kicking a patient or hitting with a fist, and hitting or trying to hit a patient with an object. Indicators of psychological abuse included the carer isolating a patient beyond what was needed to control him or her, insulting or swearing at a patient, yelling at a patient in anger, denying a patient food or privileges as part of a punishment, and threatening to hit or throw something at a patient.

The frequency of each of these behaviours was rated on a scale of never, once, 2–10 times or more than 10 times in the past year. Within the preceding year, 36 per cent of the nursing staff had observed physical abuse and 81 per cent psychological abuse. Additionally, 10 per cent of the nurses admitted committing one or more physically abusive act and 40 per cent admitted to psychological abuse in the past year. These figures suggest a very disturbing picture of abuse, both physical and psychological, committed on a frequent and regular basis. Given that there is a tendency to underreport anti-social behaviours in order to report socially desirable behaviours, these figures are all the more alarming.

Perhaps more importantly than prevalence studies are insights into the predictors of maltreatment of patients in nursing or residential homes. Data from the same sample of 577 nurses and nursing aides interviewed in the research were analysed to identify predictors of physical and psychological abuse (Pillemer and Moore, 1989). The 13 independent variables identified included: ownership of facilities (non-profit or profit); number of beds; rates of charge; age; education and length of experience of staff; staff position; negative attitude to patient (using a 4-point Likert scale); staff burn-out; frequency of staff–patient conflict; and finally a series of different aggressive actions.

Predictors of psychological abuse

Of the 13 variables identified, only staff burn-out, patient aggression, staff's negative attitude towards patients and staff age were found to be statistically significant (at the $p > 0.05$ level). As staff age increases, the risk of psychological abuse decreases; the lower the level of staff burn-out, the less probability of psychological abuse; as patient aggression increases, the probability of psychological abuse by staff increases.

Predictors of physical abuse

Three variables were found to be significant predictors at the $p>0.05$ level: staff burn-out, patient aggression and conflict between staff and patients.

Clearly, it is necessary to be sure that these factors 'travel culturally', and would also be predictive of forms of physical and psychological abuse found in institutions in the UK; research is necessary to validate this. It is, however, worthwhile looking in more depth at staff burn-out as a particular variable.

Staff burn-out

One of the major hazards of working in stressful environments is that of burn-out. Burn-out is often characterised by physical, psychological and spiritual exhaustion and can lead the individual to have little concern for the safety and well-being of the client group being cared for. The phenomenon has been well documented, and numerous strategies now exist to prevent it. No single factor taken in isolation can be considered as a factor for burn-out and individual employment circumstances allied to the traits and personalities of individuals must be taken into account. There are, however, a series of factors that should at least be taken into consideration in the event that burn-out is indicated (WHO, 1995):

- role or case overload;
- institutional disregard for the needs of patients in favour of administrative, financial and bureaucratic needs;
- inadequate or inappropriate leadership, supervision or both;
- a lack of training and orientation specific to the job;
- a lack of sense of impact on and control over one's work situation;
- a lack of social interaction and support among staff;
- caseloads consisting predominantly of extremely difficult patients;
- a majority of time spent on administration and paperwork tasks.

Most of the above factors are amenable to modification, given an environment that allows the expression of views and empowers the workforce to offer constructive advice for change. The following have been identified as potential promoters of healthy work environments (WHO, 1995):

- reduction of staff–client ratios (or workload);
- availability of time out periods;
- limitation of the number of hours of stressful work;
- flexibility from hiring (effectively matching the proper person with the job as a preventive measure) to job growth and change;
- job-related training (to improve work-related skills, including how to work effectively within an organisation/bureaucratic setting), continuing education and training for staff.

The above factors are taken as extracts from the WHO Guidelines for the *Primary Prevention of Mental, Neurological and Psychosocial Disorders: Staff Burnout*. These guidelines sum up succinctly what is required from management:

> Management should aim to foster innovation and creativity, promote lines of communication where constructive critical feedback from supervisors and subordinates can be exchanged, and provide a sense of success through rewards, appreciation and recognition of task completion (WHO, 1995).

Whilst a similar prevalence study and predictors for psychological and physical abuse have not yet been completed in the UK, evidence from the UKCC indicates that:

> Cases [of nurses appearing before its Professional Conduct Committee] involving practitioners working in the nursing home sector have been rising, as a total of the cases, each year. The statistics also show that for the year ending 31 March 1994, nursing home cases were almost 100 per cent greater than any other area of practice (UKCC, 1994, p. 1).

The UKCC document sets out in the summary a series of issues that arose during consideration of certain of the cases. Staffing issues arose because of the enormous variation in size of homes; difficulties sometimes arose when rostered staff did not turn up for duty and staff were called in at short notice. In smaller homes, the qualified member of staff might have been in charge for excessively long periods of time, with potential effects on standards. Part-time work forces, necessary, it is argued, for flexibility, often result in a lack of continuity of care for individuals within homes.

Difficulties with induction of new staff were also encountered, alongside employment of new staff who had either only recently qualified or who had not practised for many years. This lack of in-service education might affect such aspects of the running of the home as the safe administration of medicines.

Other factors included care assistants afraid to take matters further when they suspected commissions or omissions for fear of retribution by not only qualified staff but also proprietors. It is possible that, if any members of staff were sacked because they attempted to alert the authorities to acts or omissions, they could have their reputation questioned. In small distinct geographical areas where the proprietors all know each other, finding alternative employment may be impossible.

Commercial pressures can also prove to be problematic, with inadequate equipment, aids and domestic materials, whilst at the same time a bed occupancy rate of 100 per cent is always the aim for maximum profit. The emerging issue of excess provision in certain geographical localities is also causing concern to small family-owned residential and nursing homes who clearly cannot compete with the larger homes of over 100 beds and tend to be owned by large corporations.

The final two areas that are emerging in the literature as areas of concern are the adequate safeguard of residents' finances (see Langan and Means, 1995), and accurate and safe record-keeping. All the above areas of concern are covered by the UKCC document, with a series of recommendations in its final section. It is noticeable that many of the factors suggested as causes of burn-out, particularly lack of education and training for staff, are similar to those found in the UKCC report.

Counsel and Care

More recent evidence that abuse continues to occur within institutions is also available but rarely widely reported. The organisation Counsel and Care has been influential in its attempts to raise the profile of the topic, and has published a series of reports on related issues. These include the following: *Not Such Private Places: A study of privacy and the lack of privacy for residents in private and voluntary residential and nursing homes in Greater London* (1991); *What if They Hurt Themselves: A discussion document on the uses and abuses of restraint in residential care and nursing homes for older people* (1992) and the latest in the series, *Care Betrayed* (1995), which specifically focuses on issues of abuse in institutions and addresses such aspects as the potential role of loyalty, fear and power within institutional settings and within the abusive situations that can arise in such settings.

The general thrust of the findings of the report *Not Such Private Places* suggests that invasions of privacy, often justified by concerns about the safety of the residents, happen on a regular basis within the residential and nursing care sectors. However, blanket rules over safety are often made using the 'lowest common denominator mentality', that is that safety and security are based on the most impaired resident, not the most able, and there are therefore unnecessary restrictions on many able, capable and autonomous individuals. A disturbing factor that emerged was the residents' own low expectations of privacy; this is perhaps indicative of the insidious forms of institutionalisation that take place in residential and nursing homes. And, of course, privacy is only one factor to be taken into account when considering the values that should underpin the provision of residential and other forms of care (DOH/SSI, 1989). The other values are dignity, rights, fulfilment, choice and independence.

Restraint

The discussion document *What if They Hurt Themselves* explores the reasons why staff often resort to the use of restraints. Firstly, it is necessary to understand the dimensions of restraint and to be aware that physical restraint is just one manifestation of the phenomenon. The document offers a wider discourse:

> Restraint should be seen in a broad context as embracing individual physical restraint on movement, physical restraints to circulation within and beyond a building, the use of certain drugs, excessive supervision and observation, some institutional, professional and cultural attitudes, and allowing situations to exist in which residents have insufficient money to afford reasonable mobility (Counsel and Care, 1992, p. 32).

The obvious examples are physical restraints in the form of straps, harnesses and bars on chairs, tight blankets, 'cot-sides' (the infantilisation message being blatantly apparent, although this term is not used in the Counsel and Care document) used to restrain and restrict individuals. There are, however, more insidious forms of restraint that may be used, for example unwritten rules suggesting staff territory and resident territory, or the use of Health and Safety regulations to restrict residents inappropriately from certain places, such as food preparation areas. Obviously, certain residents may be in danger, given certain types of equipment in such areas, whilst others may wish just to share a conversation over food preparation. Examples of this type suggest that 'blanket rules' are often used without thought to the needs of individual residents. This may evidence the existence of an abusive type of regime within an institution.

The use of locked doors (including the use of baffle and other security type locks) constitutes a clear denial of freedom, as does controlling environments by heating, for example turning off of the heating in certain rooms, thereby causing *de facto* restriction; this is sometimes used in bedroom areas during the day time as an economic measure but could stop older people using their own bedrooms as they wished. Other forms of restraint include the use of practices that restrict movement or freedom of action, for example tightly tucked in bed-clothes, the use of chairs with fixed tables (such as the notorious Buxton chairs) or other use of furniture to restrict action.

A report by the SSI following a series of inspections of Local Authority Social Services Department residential homes established standards and criteria on restraint usage, risk-taking and abuse as part of the inspection process (DOH/SSI, 1995b). The report recognises that, with respect to the use of restraint and risk-taking in more general terms, a balance has to be found between the needs, wishes and freedom of choice of individual residents and their relatives, and the organisational requirements of the home (such as those concerning health and safety). Involving residents and relatives in making decisions about acceptable levels of risk was considered to be an essential part of this process.

The general standard to be employed within Social Services-run establishments should be that physical restraint should never be used except in the most exceptional circumstances. In such instances, the use of restraint must be considered essential in order to protect the individual, other members of the group (for example other residents) or members of staff. The use of restraint was considered very much as a last resort within situations, effectively when all else had failed to work. Medication was never to be used as a means of restraint or social control (DOH/SSI, 1995b).

Additionally, the report strongly recommended that staff, residents and relatives should be aware of the policy of the organisation concerning the use of restraint. This should include knowledge of the circumstances (if any) in which restraint might be considered and/or used, who could authorise the use of any form of restraint, what forms of restraint might be used, and how residents and relatives would be consulted and involved in decisions about use of restraints. Restraint should be used only for very short periods of time (as short as possible) and was to be subject to stringent monitoring and review. All decisions about restraint usage should be recorded; records should include full details about the reasons for the use of restraint, the method of restraint used, who authorised the usage and the timescale of usage, including reviews. Alternatives to restraint use should always be considered as part of the decision process surrounding restraint usage (DOH/SSI, 1995b). Although the report focused on residential settings, the recommendations could equally be applied to other institutional settings, including day care provision.

Electronic tagging

Rather more controversial areas of concern surrounding restraint include electronic tagging and the use of closed circuit television for monitoring and surveillance purposes (themselves forms of social control and restraint). The politics of tagging are inherently bound to the economic nature of long-term care, as Parkin suggests:

> Funding changes have highlighted the economic pressure to deliver the service at a cost that is within the means of either the resident, the relatives, or the funding authority, particularly as the development of purchaser and provider relationships is accompanied by a general decline in continuing care within the NHS. The availability at reducing prices of improved systems of security, surveillance and control may make their use attractive as a means of reducing the costs of running such facilities... (Parkin, 1995, p. 431).

The RCN (1994) has produced guidance which includes both the potential advantages and disadvantages of the use of tagging:

Advantages
- It is an alternative to locked doors.
- Patients are free to move in a limited safe area.
- It is unobtrusive and discreet.
- Nurses have more opportunity for uninterrupted periods of patient care.
- There is less chance of potentially serious accidents/incidents.
- It maintains the good reputation of ward or unit because patients do not wander away.

Disadvantages
- Patients and relatives may object as it is undignified and interferes with their civil rights.

- Similar systems are used for criminal offenders.
- Freedom is still curtailed as there are limits on movement.
- It is ineffective in wards or units with large numbers of people who wander.
- There can be an argument for cutting back on staff/patient ratio.
- It is not necessarily time saving, as nurses still have to leave caring for other patients to attend to those who wander.

The main issue in the debate surrounding electronic tagging and camera surveillance is surely 'intentionality'. If this type of equipment is seen as an adjunct to high-quality care, and is used to decrease the chance of falls, accidents, tension between agitated residents and other forms of concern, its use may be justified. Conversely, if their presence reduces the quality of care, by allowing lowered staffing levels, decreasing staff–resident communication or impinging on quality care in any other way, their use is surely unacceptable.

The discovery of more insidious forms of restraint are also of concern; many of these types of either restriction or coercion are found in the areas of personal values or lifestyle orientations, for example pressure being brought to bear on an older individual to vote for a particular political party in conflict with the personal and lifetime values of the individual. Similar examples could include having to watch television programmes with 'relatively' explicit sexual or violent scenes that disturb or shock the older person.

Sexuality and residential care

The issue of sexuality and later life, in particular within residential care settings, is another example of the conflicting stereotypes and attitudes carried by society in its attempt to understand the postmodern phenomenon of growing older. It comes as no surprise that sexuality causes major difficulties in attempting to provide a quality of life that is as congruent to the personal needs of the resident as possible. Tensions can become apparent when the sexual needs of individuals are taken into account within institutions.

The care staff often become embroiled in arguments and disagreements around such issues as 'The sexual needs of older people – do they exist?' or 'How do we allow individuals to fulfil their sexual needs, and with whom?' Further areas of concern surround aspects such as how to ascertain if there is mutual consent within a relationship and whose rights (if anyone's) should take precedence within these situations. There are, of course, immense difficulties when consent and competence become issues, especially when the competence and capacity to consent of an individual is in question. It is necessary to address these issues, and one way of moving forward could be to be explicit about the facilities and the degree of privacy that are available to individuals before they consider moving into residential accommodation.

As far as sexuality has been considered, often inadequately, it has been approached from a heterosexual perspective. The concept of homosexuality and later life remains hidden within the literature, although it is now beginning to emerge (Friedan, 1993, p. 280). What is totally absent is any forward thinking to develop long-term care facilities that could cater for gay and lesbian lifestyles. Curtis (1993) recalls that, whilst she was a co opted member of the Women's Committee of the Greater London Council, a paper was presented to the forum on the special interests of older women, lesbians and older women with disabilities:

> Older lesbians argued, for instance, that those responsible for older people's homes should recognise the need for single sex homes and take into account the realities of lesbian family life (Curtis, 1993, p. 196).

Clearly, thinking in this area has not advanced as far as it should; new debates are necessary around the residential needs of lesbian and gay service users and also their needs in other areas of health and community care.

Additionally, the needs of individuals who may have been subject to abuse and abusive relationships should be taken into account within residential settings. It is possible, for example, that a woman who had been the subject of domestic violence in previous years might be wary of a mixed-sex, small-group living arrangement and might prefer either a larger unit or even a single-sex setting in terms of institutional care offered. In commenting on a single-sex unit living arrangement that developed in one residential home, Davis indicated that the majority of women in that particular unit had been victims of domestic violence and did not wish to live with men (Davis, S., personal communication, 1996). Although the home had not been set up along these lines, when it transpired that this group of women wished to have a 'women-only' unit and the reasons for this became clear, appropriate arrangements were made.

It is apparent that those individuals who have special needs in terms of residential, nursing home or day care requirements should have those needs addressed and met within institutional settings. This should be the case whatever the reason for those special needs, whether it be due to vulnerability, culture, disability, lifestyle, sexual preference or past experience. Care service providers, purchasers and policy-makers must also be cognisant of the range of needs that exist and take appropriate action to ensure that these needs can be met within care settings. When social workers and care managers, as purchasers, assist individuals to find suitable accommodation, they must also be aware of such needs and provide appropriate advice and guidance for individuals and their families.

Possible remedies to abuse and neglect

Any attempt to explore remedies to what appears to be an endemic problem within certain residential and nursing establishments needs to be realistic within the contemporary health and welfare climate. It must also be predicated on an understanding of the history of the phenomena. Nevertheless, a greater combined effort is required in order to place the issue of institutional abuse on the political agenda; for too long this issue has only been considered as 'any other business' on the health and welfare profile.

Furthermore, the patronising comments found in certain circles that suggest that 'it is a small minority of homes where abuse and neglect is found', and that it is 'not very common', not only deny the magnitude of the problem but also falsely lead the public to believe that the scandals that do emerge are because of the adequacy of the registration system in policing a few unacceptable homes or centres. It is perhaps nearer the truth to say that what reaches the public domain in the form of scandals and enquiries is the tip of the iceberg, mainly due to the 'closed' nature of most institutional care.

Given the historical consistency of institutional scandals and the monotonous regularity with which they continue, it is sometimes difficult to be optimistic about prospects for change. The political will adequately to police this sector is also in question (Nolan, M., personal communication, 1994). There are, however, a number of different approaches that should be attempted to try to lessen the chances of abuse occurring and of yet another enquiry being held. These include developing a more open environment in institutions (more open visiting, more open management, more open culture), the increased use of complaints procedures and inspection units, and the increased monitoring of establishments.

Furthermore, consideration should be given to the increased development of advocacy schemes within institutional settings (Ivers, 1994; Dunning, 1995) or the UK equivalent of the US ombudsman scheme in which an individual 'ombudsman' visits an establishment on a regular basis. It would appear that, in part because they are not part of the formal registration and inspection process, such ombudsmen pick up more information over time concerning the quality of life and quality of care issues of residents and relatives. It is also their remit to receive, investigate and resolve complaints about such issues. More training for staff about caring issues, dealing with stress and abuse, coupled with more support for and supervision of staff, would also assist in lowering the incidence of abuse, if not totally preventing it. This smörgåsbord of ideas does not arrive without a cost, and it is important that a debate emerges in political, professional and academic circles that starts seriously to address the nature of Seedhouse's discourse on the inherent tensions found in amalgamating 'health care values' and 'business values', and their effect on the quality of health care (Seedhouse, 1994).

Registration and inspection units

Inspection and registration units also, however, have a potentially important role to play in protecting vulnerable people in residential or nursing home care. This may be by use of their regulatory process but also by inspectors acting as an independent monitoring system of homes by examining what is happening within the institution (to act as an extra pair of eyes within a situation). It is possible, however, that inspectors, although well able to deal effectively with situations once identified, may have more limited success in the prevention of abuse. The development of ombudsman systems, such as those operating in the US where an ombudsman links regularly with particular establishments and visits on a fairly frequent basis, thus establishing relationships with residents and staff, might assist in this regard.

The following potential signs of abuse may be identified within institutions and may be picked up by inspectors. Although some inspectors, in particular in the nursing home sector, may have to limit their visits to those prescribed within the Registered Homes Act 1984, concerning the annual inspection process, or to investigate complaints, many inspectors do manage to visit homes on a regular basis at times other than for pure inspection purposes. This can then allow for the inspector to provide advice and guidance, where necessary, but also perhaps more critically it allows the inspector to ascertain other factors such as the overall atmosphere within a home on a more regular basis. Many of these indicators of possible abuse may be evidenced within the records of the home (for example, daily log, medication records and accident records), which will only be inspected as part of the inspection process. Other indicators, however, are likely to be observed through visits to homes and could thus be detected by lay people, relatives and non-inspection Local Authority staff.

- *Physical abuse:* Unexplained falls and injuries, burns and bruises; old and new bruises at the same time; accidents happening in unexpected places or at unexpected times; signs of neglect; poor standards of hygiene; excessive repeat prescriptions or underusage of medication.
- *Psychological abuse:* Individual residents appearing anxious, agitated, withdrawn or fearful; isolation of individuals; evidence of unkempt residents; problems over access to residents (proprietor or staff insisting on being present or denying access).
- *Exploitation:* Missing belongings or money; inability of residents to buy essential items; misappropriation of personal allowances of residents.

Inspectors are, of course, not the only people who may identify potential abuse in homes, but through their regular contact with particular homes they may well detect early untoward signs that may trigger concern about possible abuse and neglect and may act to try to resolve these at an early stage. Obviously, the presence of any of the above signs is not absolute evidence that abuse is occurring but should serve to trigger concern and raise the index of suspicion within such situations.

Should an allegation concerning abuse be made to a registration unit, one of the functions of the unit should be to assess how and whether the incident is being adequately handled and to refer onwards if necessary to another agency such as the police. The unit should conduct its own investigation, however, concerning whether any breach of registration has taken place, and this will be the principal focus for them. It may involve interviews with individual residents concerning the situation. The specific use of the regulatory and legal process surrounding registration and the role of inspectors within homes may assist in the protection of residents. Extension of this type of process to domiciliary and day care settings has been increasingly advocated since the implementation of the NHS and Community Care Act in April 1993, increasing concern being expressed about the need to protect vulnerable people living at home.

The DOH/SSI report following a series of inspections of Local Authority Social Services Department residential homes established standards and criteria on abuse as part of the overall inspection process (DOH/SSI, 1995b). The general standard advocated was that individual service users should be protected from abuse (whether this be physical, sexual, financial, emotional or racial) from whatever source (DOH/SSI, 1995b). The report propounded a clear view that members of staff must be aware that abuse can occur in residential settings and that it may be committed intentionally or unintentionally. Additionally, staff should know what to do about situations of abuse through the existence of clearly defined policies and procedures relevant to the particular setting.

Through the course of the inspection process, it became apparent that only a minority of authorities that were inspected had effective and relevant policies that were supported by adequate operational procedures and guidance documents. Generally speaking, authorities had policies and procedures that applied throughout the Social Services Department, and there was some confusion by the staff of homes (including the managers) over how a generic policy might be applied to their specific setting. Racial abuse, sexual harrassment and emotional abuse were often not covered in those policies which existed (DOH/SSI, 1995b).

The report noted that during the inspections which took place, no evidence of physical abuse of residents by staff was observed by inspectors. A number of instances of abuse of staff by residents were observed. These were predominantly situations of physical abuse, racial abuse or sexual harrassment. Night staff were considered to be particularly at risk of abuse occurring from residents, but this was very much seen by staff as part of the job. Several instances of abuse occurring between residents were also noted.

Incidents of comments of a sexual nature from residents to staff were also observed during inspections. These did not always appear to be handled or dealt with effectively, although similar situations arising between residents were considered by the inspectors to be more likely to be handled appropriately within the setting. The report recommended increased training for staff in the recognition of possible situations of abuse and concerning what actions should be taken if abuse is suspected, witnessed or experienced. The need for support from managers was also clearly indicated, both in terms of the acknowledgement of the difficult and stressful situations with which staff have to deal within residential settings and also in terms of the need for managerial support of staff who report actual or potentially abusive situations (DOH/SSI, 1995b). As noted earlier in the section on restraint, the findings of this report could be utilised within all institutional settings and should not be restricted to publically provided residential care settings.

Legal shortcomings

The legal provisions that can be used to counteract situations of institutional abuse and neglect are in fact quite limited. Private residential and nursing homes are licensed to operate under the Registered Homes Act 1984, and action is usually taken within the Act. Registration can be refused on three different grounds:

- 'fit person', including the attitudes and values of individual;
- 'fit premises', including physical accommodation, staffing, equipment and the state of repair;
- underlying philosophy: the aims and objectives of the establishment and how care is provided within this.

The annual inspection should aim, as part of its remit, to be a review of the registration criteria (i.e. are all three elements still complied with?). Failure under any of the criteria can be used in the determination of cancellation of registration. There are two main ways in which this is achieved, either through an emergency closure order (which uses Section 11 of the Act and is only used in extreme circumstances) or via a longer-term route to cancellation (using Section 10 of the Act). These will be outlined briefly below.

Under Section 10 of the Registered Homes Act 1984, an application for registration of a home may be refused or registration cancelled if a person or premises are considered 'unfit', or if the underlying philosophy is no longer appropriate. If an inspection by the registration unit highlights a problem, attempts should be made by the inspector to work with the owner to rectify the situation (unless an emergency closure is warranted under Section 11; see below). This will require the owner to be given legal notice of the problem, through a Regulation 20 notice in a letter, and of what steps should be taken to resolve it within a given time period. If the home owner persistently fails to comply with regulations or to rectify identified problems within a set time, their registration licence may be revoked, or there may be prosecution in a Magistrates' Court of an owner concerning a specific problem that does not necessarily result in cancellation of the registration. If cancellation is effected, there are rights of appeal by the owner against cancellation to local councillors and to Registered Homes Tribunals who can uphold either the appeal or the cancellation of registration.

A number of criticisms of the 1984 Registered Homes Act have been made (Brammer, 1994). Firstly, within the Act itself the term 'unfit' is not defined. Some remedies to problems have been suggested (Brammer, 1994). For example, with regard to the 'fit person criteria', Brammer suggests that a statutory definition of 'unfitness', alongside a checklist of factors to be considered in determining 'fitness', would help.

Secondly, in situations where there is a 'serious risk to the life, health, or well being of residents in a home', a magistrate may make an order cancelling registration with immediate effect (under Section 11 of the Registered Homes Act). Application to the magistrate is usually made by the registration authority; it can be made '*ex parte*' without the owner knowing about the intended action beforehand.

This type of emergency action does, however, mean that the home can no longer operate. The effect is immediate closure and the residents have to move to other accommodation, with all the resultant trauma and potential mortality. Whilst this somewhat draconian action may be in the best interests of the residents in the long term, an alternative temporary solution would be to allow the registration authorities to place a temporary manager within the home. The remit of this person would be to improve the standard of care to the required level. The salary of this temporary manager would be paid by the home until the required standard had been met; clearly, this would provide an incentive for the home owner to cooperate and improve standards sooner rather than later. This might also help the registration authorities who sometimes appear to consider that closure is the only alternative but are aware of the difficulties of transferring perhaps more than 100 residents to alternative accommodation and may therefore require very high levels of proof prior to taking action regarding closure.

It is also necessary to acknowledge that inspection units must work closely with other agencies when there are allegations of abuse within homes. An inspector will generally only conduct an investigation concerning a possible breach of registration criteria (although this may concern an abusive regime within the home). A parallel police investigation may be necessary, for example, concerning an assault of an individual resident. In addition, in some areas, it is likely that reports of alleged abuse of an individual will be passed to a district social work/care management team to assess and deal with, as the registration unit will only be concerned with those aspects which concern them (i.e has a breach of the registration criteria occurred?).

Thirdly, it would appear that the area of financial considerations in the running of private care homes is bound to become more complex as the tension between 'business values' and 'health care values' becomes ever more complex (Seedhouse, 1994, p. 181). It is suggested that the tension between the two values arises when the two dominant beliefs conflict: 'business values', dominant in a belief 'in the overriding importance of financial profit', and 'health care values', dominant in the belief 'in the fundamental importance of helping other people achieve as much of their potential as possible' (Seedhouse, 1994, p. 181). For Seedhouse, when these two beliefs are combined only two truths emerge:

1.   'Health care values' and 'business values' are always different.
2.   Some 'health care values' and some 'business values' are
      commensurable, others are not.

The inherent danger occurs when either value dominates, to the relative exclusion of the other. For example, Brammer cites the case of Wassell *v.* Wolverhampton Borough Council (1991) decision 161, where the tribunal was unconvinced that the expenditure of £800 on a bath hoist was justified, even though the purchase would clearly have given a greater choice for some residents to bathe, let alone save potential injuries to staff! This conflict is further emphasised by Nazarko (1995), who suggested that:

> Nursing homes are run as businesses with the aim of maximising profits by reducing costs. They are labour-intensive businesses and their greatest cost is staff wages. Many nursing home proprietors seek to maximise profits by paying below the Whitley Council Scales (Nazarko, 1995, p. 57).

The issues that arise from this statement are indicative of how society values (or rather devalues) our ageing population. That proprietors are, in fact, prepared to pay lower salaries to staff working with older people than with other age groups is indicative of society's ageist attitudes. Furthermore, in an attempt to maximise profits, inadequate staffing levels are sometimes found. These are often a potential recipe for abuse:

> Although there is no direct connection (between high volume work and low staffing levels), I believe a relationship exists. And by ensuring a dependency-led

service sensitive to need, greater attention will automatically be paid to issues of staff exhaustion, low standards and patient abuse (Carter, 1995, p. 58).

Fourthly, the rights of residents are insufficiently stressed within the Act and are written in paternalistic terms. Brammer suggests that residents 'are limited to reporting to the registration authority', and if the registration authority does take action:

> it is possible that residents will be called as witnesses to the tribunal. In such a situation they will be unrepresented, subject to coercion and powerless (Brammer, 1994, p. 434).

Whilst it is possible to obtain recourse through the criminal law or law of tort, difficulties include obtaining legal aid and advice, and facing delays in the procedure. One improvement would be a greater use of 'contract law' before entering the home, with specified contract relating to service and standards (Brammer, 1994). It is also suggested that it is timely to retrace the legal situation with regard to residential health and social care, including the promotion of effective use of complaints procedures. In connection with the provision of private domiciliary care, the debate is only just beginning to emerge around the role of quality assurance and policing a 'mixed economy of welfare'. Pressures have been building in recent years to provide adequate regulation of domiciliary care provision, including police checks on care workers employed in such situations.

Whistleblowing

The concept of 'whistleblowing' re-emerged when it was again brought to the attention of the health and welfare services by Graham Pink in 1991. There has now developed a wide literature around the topic (see for example Carson, 1988; Tattam, 1989; Kaye and MacManus, 1990; Pink, 1994; Francis, 1995; Hunt, 1995; Lunn, 1995; Sone, 1995). The true reality of life after whistleblowing suggests that few individuals are equipped with either the prerequisite energy or motivation to be unaffected by the trauma. Perhaps an apt reminder of what it is like to take on the establishment should be reserved for Pink himself:

> 'Truth', wrote Emily Dickinson, 'is such a rare thing, it is delightful to tell it'. I cannot agree. Telling the truth of what I witnessed and was unwillingly party to has been a wretched, distressing, and costly business (Pink, 1994, p. 1700).

The climate in which health and social care is provided is often not conducive and receptive to criticism and often responds with what has been described as a 'knee-jerk, defensive reaction' (Kaye and MacManus, 1990). There are also particular dangers for unqualified carers working within the private sector. It is extremely stressful to make an approach and complain about standards, acts or omissions, sometimes above the head of the manager of the particular home. To do so is often to risk dismissal. However, loss of a job does not necessarily stop there; word of the 'deed' finds its way through the private sector grapevine. Inevitably, offers of positions in other residential or nursing homes start to diminish because the individual is considered a potential 'trouble-maker'.

The dangers for qualified individuals appear to be just as great, with clauses within contracts suggesting on occasion that all concerns should be dealt with internally. There have also been developments within Local Authority Social Services Departments recently which suggest that the insurance companies that are the agents providing cover for the departments may have certain levels of influence and power over the release of material and information that may possibly be viewed as incriminating. This may not bode well for NHS Trusts and other agencies who may potentially be in similar situations at some point. It is possible that the only effective way forward is via legislative changes and legal protection for the whistleblower.

Conclusion

Institutional abuse is an enduring feature found throughout the whole range of continuing care facilities: residential and nursing homes and hospitals, even day care centres and day hospitals. Scandals and enquiries continue to occur with almost monotonous regularity. The development of community care has also seen the virtual recreation of mini-institutions in people's own homes, with multiple service providers and personnel involved in helping to maintain individuals at home. The political will to police and regulate all care sectors at times appears to be virtually absent. Yet due to changes occurring largely as a result of the implementation of the NHS and Community Care Act, those residents who currently enter continuing care settings are more frail and may be increasingly vulnerable. It is time for a complete review of all continuing care provision and services; only a re-assessment and sufficient will to move forward at the turn of the century can assist in the cessation and hopefully the prevention of elder abuse and neglect within institutional settings.

The previous chapters have provided an overview and the range of settings and types of abuse that occur. In order to equip the reader with as full a picture as possible of different aspects of elder abuse and neglect, it is now time to consider some of these particular aspects from differing professional perspectives: we begin in the next chapter with a consideration of the medical dimensions of abuse.

4

Medical Dimensions

Introduction

The previous three chapters have aimed to provide an overview and general framework concerning elder abuse. For the reader in this chapter, the various threads that constitute a medical perspective are woven together. These include some points around demography, the current medical knowledge base, and issues concerning ageing as well as formal elder abuse protocols. The chapter explores the core of professional education, the role of the medical model (continuing medical education) and changes occurring at undergraduate education level.

Contextual information

The demographic changes occurring in the world today are quite unparalleled in human history. Not only is the total number of individuals increasing but also, more importantly, those individuals are living much longer. The positive viewpoint is to see this change as a validation of all the social and health measures that have contributed to the increase in longevity. The social changes that have occurred include better housing, sanitation, employment and a degree of prosperity (although the first two of these concern the arena of public health). Significant medical advances include the role of antiseptics, antibiotics, safe anaesthesia and increased knowledge about the most common 'killer' diseases such as cancer and atheromatous heart disease. It is arguable that social changes outweigh medical advances in terms of the degree of impact on the total population.

The percentage of the total population now living to be old is rising and is a global phenomenon. In Europe (especially Scandinavia and

Britain), some districts have 25 per cent of the population over the age of 65. On average in these countries, the percentage is approximately 16 per cent, being only slightly less in North America (Grundy, 1992). Comparisons may help to put the issue in context. In 1900, 1 per cent of the world population was aged over 65. By 1992 this had increased to 6.2 per cent, and by the year 2050 20 per cent of the total human population will be aged over 65 years. Some countries such as China will then have more older people than the entire US population (as it currently stands). India will have an even greater percentage of older people within the total population (Olshansky *et al.*, 1993).

A rather negative viewpoint is to concentrate on the impact this demographic tidal wave will have on the social and health care structures present in each country. Many countries, including the UK, are experiencing a complete review of systems of health care delivery. In the UK, this review concerns some of the basic components of the welfare state. In the field of health care, the government has split the total service into purchasers and providers of that care. There has been increased emphasis upon the creation of an internal market within the health service. This has involved the management of change with a 'managed' health service being set business-type goals. The language of change dominates a new cultural thinking on health, with an emphasis upon efficiency, consumers/clients, contracts, purchasing, providing and fund-holding.

There is little doubt that within this market-led health economy, older people are viewed negatively. Despite a greater consumer bias and the use of government Charters, older people fare badly in a free market, as they tend to be perceived as frequently suffering from chronic and multiple conditions that are expensive to treat. This is shown by examples where older people have been removed from general practitioner registers. The covert reason of expense for a fund-holder is not acknowledged. Older people feel marginalised, and this viewpoint is supported by decisions in some areas of medicine to determine treatment using age as one parameter. We have also recently seen well-publicised medical examples of older people denied access to coronary care, intensive care as well as physiotherapy.

In response to the UK government's document *The Health of the Nation*, certain clinicians felt the report inadequate to the challenge of an ageing population (Grimley Evans, 1992). In his response to the document, Grimley Evans pointed out that in some preventable diseases, such as cancers and stroke, incidence shows a powerful relation to age; in proximal femoral fracture, the relation is exponential

(Doll, 1971; Grimley Evans and Caird, 1982; Rees, 1982). He also stressed the need for further research and a balancing of emphasis on quality of life rather than just quantity of life.

The changes in health care in modern societies have a direct bearing upon sociomedical issues such as elder abuse. Unless specialising in paediatrics or obstetrics, all health care personnel will be dealing with adults, of whom a large proportion will be older people. Within many specialities, for example general medicine, general surgery (and hence anaesthetics), orthopaedics, ophthalmology, ENT, rheumatology, psychiatry and general practice, the main client group will be over 65 years old and an increasing proportion over 80 years old.

Professionals will be involved in implementing the new health care changes, including an emphasis on moving away from hospital care to management in the community. Hospital stays will be in the order of a few days, and many procedures will involve day care only. There is currently a marked shift away from hospitals providing respite and continuing care (free at the point of source), and the great debate concerning this fundamental change in NHS policy has yet to be made truly public. Increasingly, the vast majority of older people who need 'nursing' care on a permanent basis obtain it within the private sector (and pay for it from either savings or sale of property) after a means-tested assessment of their finances. This is an area of contention and change, however, with developments concerning insurance cover for long-term care and announcements from government concerning the possibility of older people retaining property rights even when in residential or nursing home care.

These changes are occurring at the same time as the knowledge base concerning the complex issue of ageing is growing rapidly. There has never been so much information available to health and social care workers to help them to deal more holistically with the needs of older people. Information abounds about the formal and informal networks that are crucial to enable frail older people to remain living in the community with successful management of their care needs in those settings.

Discharge policies should ideally cover every older person leaving hospital. The role and needs of any carer(s) should be investigated and acted upon, and packages of care should be available to all who need them. Such packages should incorporate care from health and social services. The reality for many older people is a care package that is affordable to the care manager (budget holder) rather than a true needs-assessed package. Resources for pump-priming innovative schemes remain scarce. Patient and carer have to carry on as best they can. If the situation deteriorates into an abusive one, the same realities prevent intervention and help.

Knowledge about elder abuse

The knowledge base concerning elder abuse is in a constant state of change as information from research and experience in the field updates current thinking. The US leads the way in the volume of research being conducted, but many other countries are beginning to see the vital need to test out some of the findings for themselves and indeed answer new questions. Increasingly, we in the UK are gaining our own expert knowledge base through the experience of health and social care workers. One of the main difficulties now is how to channel that expertise successfully to meet the challenge of the demographic changes and to alter if necessary the philosophy of health and social care.

A summary of the present general knowledge base followed by a review of the medical components within this subject will hopefully set the situation in perspective.

Case reports concerning elder abuse appeared in the UK literature in 1975 (Baker, 1975). There was no attempt to research this issue scientifically in this country for another 15 years, with only limited upsurges of media interest coinciding with institutional scandals and the efforts of individuals (for example Mervyn Eastman) in trying to keep the topic alive. In the US, however, the subject quickly became a social and political issue. Indeed, the media interest and the emergence of data from research rapidly transformed elder abuse into a social problem perceived as requiring government action. The history of this transatlantic difference in progress has been summarised elsewhere (Bennett and Kingston, 1993).

One difficulty facing researchers everywhere has been the lack of accepted and standardised definitions (as indicated in Chapter 1). This has resulted in a wide range of statements describing physical violence, psychological or emotional abuse, material exploitation and sexual abuse. There has also been debate over the question of neglect and whether it is included within definitions or not. There have been further problems concerning questions of intentionality. Numerous authorities in the field over the past 17 years have all redefined the various parameters of abuse with greater or lesser degrees of commonality and acceptance between them (see for example Block and

Sinnott, 1979; Lau and Kosberg, 1979; O'Malley *et al.*, 1979). Others have sensed an air of pragmatism and called the whole subject 'inadequate care' or 'elder mistreatment' (Fulmer and O'Malley, 1987; Johnson, 1991).

The only UK random sample community-based epidemiological study of elder abuse to date took place in 1992 (Ogg and Bennett, 1992).[1] The UK survey (Ogg and Bennett, 1992) also allows for some cautious projections concerning abuse and the British population. Using 95 per cent confidence limits, if the entire adult population were asked the same questions, up to one million older people could be at risk of verbal abuse and up to half a million at risk of either physical or financial abuse. The figures for adults reporting abuse would be up to three million potential verbal abusers and half a million physical abusers in this country. In the US, a figure is quoted of between one and two million older Americans experiencing mistreatment annually (US Congress House, 1991). The potential reality of these prevalence figures should focus the minds of professionals.

All surveys suggest that although the prevalence is low, abuse of older people by family and close relatives exists. As stated before, the knowledge base on both sides of the Atlantic is now considerable, yet in contrast to other forms of family violence, especially child abuse, interest from the medical and nursing professions remains limited at best. There have so far been no surveys of the medical profession in the UK to assess their awareness of elder abuse or, as importantly, their ability to be part of either prevention or intervention strategies.

In the US, one might expect medical awareness to be on a par at least with the other forms of domestic violence considering that the issue has been a recognised social problem for over a decade. In addition, most health care professionals in America are subject to mandatory reporting laws. In essence, these laws compel the professional to report the incident to an investigatory body, Adult Protective Services, when alerted to a case of possible elder abuse. Adult Protective Services then coordinate and handle the case. The research findings are disappointing, however, studies showing that doctors in particular are unfamiliar with mandatory reporting and are less effective than other health care groups in identifying cases of elder abuse (Wolf, 1988; Clark-Daniels *et al.*, 1990; Blakely and Dolon, 1991).

In the UK, anecdotal evidence suggests a similar situation, with all other professional groupings highlighting the medical profession as not only having the least awareness concerning the issue of elder abuse but also allowing that ignorance to hinder prevention and intervention work by other health and social care workers. The knowledge base actually available to clinicians has never been greater and has been summarised by Lachs and Pillemer (1995) based on the original work by Jones (1990). Presentations, accompanied by examples, are described that may suggest elder abuse and/or neglect:

1. Delays between injury or illness and seeking medical attention – examples include lacerations healing by secondary intention, X-rays revealing healed but misaligned fractures, decompensated chronic disease presenting *in extremis* where the carer has been monitoring the patient.
2. Differing histories from patient and abuser – examples include different mechanisms of injury offered and a different chronology (timings) of injuries.
3. Implausible or vague explanations provided by either party – for example fractures that are not explained by the mechanisms of injury.
4. Frequent Accident and Emergency Department visits for chronic disease exacerbations despite a care plan and available resources – for example chronic obstructive airways disease or chronic heart failure due to lack of medicines or their administration.
5. The functionally impaired patient who arrives without the main carer present – an example is a patient with advanced dementia who presents to the Accident and Emergency Department alone.
6. Laboratory findings are inconsistent with the history provided – for example sub-therapeutic drug levels (e.g. digoxin) despite carer-reported compliance. Toxicology may reveal that psychotropic agents have not been administered.

One of the prerequisites to making a diagnosis is being aware that the possibility of such a diagnosis exists. Many clinicians have diagnosed a condition without ever having seen it before. Facts obtained from the history and examination build into a composite picture and recognition of a pattern occurs. Currently, many physicians do not diagnose abuse because it is not part of their knowledge base and hence does not even enter into their list of differential diagnoses.

Linking elder abuse and domestic violence

One way of enabling a 'higher index of suspicion' may be to link domestic violence with elder abuse, whilst also accepting that elder abuse is manifested in forms other than domestic violence. To link the two phenomenon together allows the medical profession to use effectively the expertise they have generated in dealing with domestic violence.

For example, there is clear evidence that domestic violence in later life is a factor in the Accident and Emergency Department: McCleer and Anwar (1989) found that in an Emergency Room population of 412 cases of battered women, 18 per cent were over 61 years of age. In a study in Leicester, UK (Smith *et al.*, 1992) found 5 per cent of the population of 59 years and older attending the Accident and Emergency Department to be victims of domestic abuse; furthermore, 14 victims were male and only 2 female, clearly indicating that elderly men are also victims of abuse.

Chez (1994) suggests that certain myths, for example the view that family violence is more prevalent among the lower classes, have hindered nurses' recognition of domestic violence. This may also be the case for other forms of abuse including elder abuse and neglect.

This lack of knowledge, and abundant myths and stereotypes, about family violence and elder abuse clearly needs urgent rectification, with a readjustment of medical/nursing and social work curricula to encompass the whole arena of family abuse.

There is also evidence that knowledge about gerontological care of older people in the Accident and Emergency Department in general is marginal. The entire July 1992 edition of the *Annals of Emergency Medicine* considered 'Geriatric Emergency Medicine'. The author, Sanders (1992), suggested that:

- Little attention is being paid to the special needs of elderly persons in emergency departments [EDs].
- Health care professionals feel less comfortable caring for elderly than for non-elderly patients.
- The social and personal concerns of the elderly frequently are not addressed in ED encounters.
- There is a paucity of research and education in geriatric medicine.
- Psychosocial issues such as elder abuse, depression, suicide prevention, and substance abuse are not commonly addressed in an ED encounter.
- Most EDs do not have protocols for detecting and dealing with elder abuse... 27 per cent only reporting a protocol.

Although this paper related to findings in the US, it is pertinent to ask whether this set of circumstances is also equally applicable to the UK.

More recently, Jones (1994) in the US has again made a plea that Emergency Department staff contribute to the identification of elder abuse and neglect; their contribution should include more research with the Society for Academic Emergency Medicine identifying elder abuse as a priority grant area. Identification should also be helped by the American Medical Association (quoted in a paper by Sanders, 1992) urging all physicians to:

> ask their older patients routinely whether anyone at home has ever hurt, scolded, or threatened them; whether they are alone frequently; and whether they are afraid of anyone living in their home.

It is also suggested that some nurses are ageist (Kingston and Hopwood, 1994) and assume that older people naturally have health deficits due to their age. There is also evidence that they are not the only profession to devalue elders, (see Greene *et al.,* 1986; Adelman *et al.,* 1990; Thomasma, 1991; Cohler, 1993). These stereotypical attitudes may affect the evaluation process. A recent study (Grief, 1994, pp. 271–4) suggests that emergency nurses impose a system of moral values on patients, as evidenced by comments such as:

> I expect people to take control and responsibility for their lives... I do not tolerate well those who continue to be fat, smoke, not take their meds, drink, and otherwise abuse their bodies.

Excellent examples from the domestic violence arena of how to communicate with potential victims of abuse and what questions should be asked exist and could be transfered to elder abuse and neglect. Examples given by Jezierski (1992) and Snyder (1994) include:

- The injuries you have are like bruises and lacerations people get when someone hits them. Did someone hit you? Are you afraid?
- Sometimes patients tell me they have been hurt by someone close to them. Could this be happening to you?

In addition, Breckman and Adelman have produced protocols consisting of a number of different questions that can be asked of older people and their care-givers. These are undoubtedly difficult and sensitive areas to explore with individuals; the guidance produced is welcome (Breckman and Adelman, 1988).

More recently, Grunfeld *et al.* (1994) have suggested that the triage nurse should consistently ask questions about domestic violence. Again, although focused on women, it is potentially useful in cases of elder abuse. In a 5-day study period, all triage nurses were instructed to ask the following (or a paraphrase of this question):

> We know that violence is a problem for many women in their lives. Is this a problem for you in any way?

This research project found 6 per cent of the population disclosing abuse, of whom 50 per cent requested help. Replication of this study as soon as possible would be useful in the UK.

If the interview produces evidence that abuse is taking place, a discussion should take place with victims on whether they wish a social worker to attend to either help them make decisions about the abuse, including any actions to be taken, or to involve other agencies as requested. It is clearly important that when older victims are competent to do so, they should take their own decisions and their wishes be followed. There may, however, be a need for support and advocacy from nursing personnel for the individual. This is clearly potentially an important area of need that should not be overlooked. If this cannot be provided by nursing staff, attempts should be made to obtain it from elsewhere. There are, for example, a growing number of advocacy schemes for older people (see Ivers, 1994, for further detail on this).

The existence of ageism, the fact that nurses and other Accident and Emergency Room staff morally evaluate patients, allied to the fact that physicians themselves say they feel less comfortable caring for older people, must be vigorously challenged; the design of elder abuse protocols is one way forward.

Elder abuse protocols

This situation is certainly changing in the US, where many medical organisations are now using formal elder abuse protocols to improve their detection rate. These not only act as an *aide-mémoire* (so that unexplained injuries or implausible explanations are not overlooked or malnutrition and dehydration questioned when a main carer is present) but also allow retrospective findings to be analysed. Jones reviewed 36 cases of abuse identified by use of such a protocol in an Accident and Emergency Department in the US (Jones, 1990). Neglect was the most commonly found manifestation of abuse, with obvious dehydration and malnutrition. The most common physical injuries identified were unexplained bruises, cuts, head injury or fractures. Lachs and Pillemer stress that other clinicians are in fact more likely to encounter the less dramatic forms of abuse, for example psychological/emotional, and their task is made even harder by such things as the amount of chronic disease (multiple pathology) present in this age group and the altered presentation of disease in older people (Lachs and Pillemer, 1995).

These facts have been championed by British geriatricians for about three decades. They have been the basis for a separate knowledge base concerning illness and older people. Diseases may present classically in old age (and are likely to be recognised by all clinicians), but, crucially, in the most senior and frail they usually do not. These different presentations were termed 'the geriatric giants' by Isaacs *et al.* (1972) to indicate their importance to the health care of older people. Any disease process can present as:

- confusion
- incontinence
- immobility
- falls
- pressure sores.

Despite this important message being championed for so long, many clinicians and certainly the majority of the public associate the above features with old age – regrettable but unavoidable. Few see beyond the presentation to the ill older person behind, who can usually be restored to better if not full health. It is likely to be inevitable that as the education process concerning elder abuse reaches a wider medical audience, another information gap will become apparent and the presentation of ill-health will mimic some aspects of abuse and hence lead to false positive diagnoses. This process will only be minimised if all health care workers become aware of both sets of issues.

These formal elder abuse protocols are holistic and multidisciplinary, and hence they should prove less daunting to those health care workers already dealing mainly with older people. Work within the specialism of 'care (or medicine) of the elderly' within health care has pioneered many of the good practice systems that are now part of mainstream medical practice. This includes information-gathering that is as comprehensive as possible (hopefully including patient, carer, medical, nursing, social work and home care personnel). More than one assessment may be necessary, and the complexity of many of the cases will probably require mental as well as physical evaluation. The views and needs of the carer(s) are important, as is early and comprehensive preparation for discharge in terms of providing appropriate packages of care. Assessment includes medical and nursing aspects, activities of daily living, possibly predischarge home visits (if the person is in hospital) to check physical capabilities and observing potential areas of conflict and any other risk factors of abuse.

This holistic approach within the speciality of health care of older people has evolved into the formation of highly specialised teams with numerous resources to call upon. These include the use of day hospitals, day centres, memory clinics, out-patient clinics, in-patient assessment beds, domiciliary visits and a pool of colleagues with individual expertise. All of these help in the evaluation and management of complicated health and social problems, including elder abuse. The situation in the UK is highly sophisticated, with its tradition of primary health care on the one hand and specialist training for professionals dealing with older people on the other. It is much more difficult for health and social care workers who only deal intermittently with older people to have access to and use the available resources appropriately.

The formal elder abuse protocol has been pioneered in the US and includes many techniques and the general holistic approach that have been developed in the UK. Lachs has reviewed the protocols, including the one used at the Mount Sinai Medical Centre in New York (Mount Sinai Project, 1988). He has highlighted some of the common components of the protocols, indicating for the clinician which are the most important elements to 'target' and what the assessment should include.

'Target' – include in the assessment

1. *History from the older person:* the patient should be interviewed alone. There should be direct enquiries about physical violence, restraints or neglect. Precise details about the nature, frequency and severity of these events. Include a functional assessment (independence with Activities of Daily Living, ADL). Note who is the main carer if ADL impairment is present.
2. *History from the alleged abuser:* the alleged abuser should also be interviewed alone. This can be a highly demanding situation and is usually best carried out by someone skilled in such interviewing techniques. Confrontation should be avoided in the information-gathering stage. Interview other sources if possible.

Enquire about recent psychosocial factors (bereavement, illness, unemployment, financial hardship). Check the carer's understanding of the patient's physical or mental health (care needs, prognosis) and ask for the carer's explanations for the injuries or physical findings.

3. *Behavioural observation:* look for any withdrawal, infantilisation of the patient by the carer or the carer who insists on giving the history.

4. *General appearance:* note the patient's state of hygiene, general cleanliness and appropriateness of clothing.

5. *Skin/mucous membranes:* note skin turgor[2] and other signs of dehydration (note that skin turgor can be a misleading sign in older people). Check for multiple skin lesions in various stages of evolution. Note bruises and pressure sores and record how such lesions have been treated. Note that many older people bruise easily (senile purpura[3] and the transparent skin syndrome/ photoageing) and that pressure sores are one of the 'geriatric giants' and hence in addition to implying neglect can indicate underlying disease (Bennett and Kingston, 1993).

6. *Head and neck:* look for traumatic alopecia[4] (distinguishable from male pattern alopecia on a basis of distribution), scalp haematomas (raised, blood-filled bruises), lacerations and abrasions.

7. *Trunk:* examine for bruises, welts, weals: the shape may suggest an implement used (for example an iron or belt).

8. *Genitourinary:* examine for rectal bleeding, vaginal bleeding, infestations, evidence of trauma, pressure sores. Recent suspected rape needs the expert examination by clinicians used to dealing with such cases and obtaining the appropriate specimens.

9. *Extremities:* wrist or ankle lesions suggest the use of restraints or immersion burns (glove/stocking distribution).

10. *Musculoskeletal:* examine for occult[5] fractures, pain. Observe the gait.

11. *Neurological/psychiatric:* this needs a formal and thorough neurological examination to ascertain the focal site of any lesion. Anxiety and depressive symptoms should be assessed. Where symptoms are indicative, formal testing using depression rating scales should be carried out or referral made to a psychiatrist.

12. *Mental state:* formal testing should be carried out usually using the Mini-Mental State questionnaire (Folstein *et al.*, 1975). Cognitive impairment suggests that either delirium (acute confusional state)

or dementia (chronic confusional state) is present. This then needs
further assessment to rule out treatable causes but also indicates a
question over the decision-making capacity. Psychiatric symptoms
may include delusions and hallucinations.

13. *Imaging:* the tests ordered will derive from the clinical evaluation.
14. *Laboratory:* again the tests ordered will be indicated from the
     history and examination and may include, drug levels, albumin,
     blood urea and electrolytes, haemoglobin and occasionally
     toxicology.
15. *Social and financial resources:* document the social networks
     (formal and informal) available to assist the patient. Record all
     available financial resources. This information may be crucial if
     interventions are considered later which include alternative living
     arrangements and/or the provision of home services.

Although this final point relates particularly to the US as the protocol
was developed there, it is increasingly the case in this country that
older people are financially assessed for contributions towards the cost
of care provided at home as well as for residential/nursing home care.

Professional education

The implementation of training programmes for various professional
staff concerning elder abuse is at a comparatively early stage in the
UK. This challenge of education has been taken up in some areas and
by particular professional groups (for example, social workers). One
such training strategy for elder abuse/inadequate care has been
described by Zlotnick (1993). In her paper, she describes the model
initiated for one London borough. The initital objectives were to:

1. acknowledge the existence of cases of elder abuse;
2. define elder abuse and inadequate care;
3. help members of the health and social service staff to begin to
    tackle areas of policy and procedure.

Zlotnick created a learning framework based on a combination of
teaching methods using adult learning theory, which was then applied to
communicate the complex issues related to elder abuse. The formula
used incorporated the work detailed in an article by Douglass discussing
three methods of adult teaching (Douglass, 1991). The three methods are:

- pedagogy – relies on the teacher as the source of control for all aspects of learning;
- andragogy – has the teacher as facilitator in the learning process;
- synergogy – encourages learners to take full responsibility for their own learning.

Applying the learning theories allowed Zlotnick to modify the original objectives of:

1. creating an awareness of elder abuse/inadequate care;
2. developing a working definition, for example a definition that could be used in day-to-day work so as to direct individual efforts appropriately;
3. using available skills in working with clients, carers and staff in addressing the problems in the light of the present lack of statutory policies, guidelines and so forth.

There are comprehensive training packs available aimed at Social Service staff incorporating written and video material that have been developed (Phillipson and Biggs, 1992; RCN, 1995). However, there is currently no educational material available specifically aimed at the medical practitioner. Elder abuse as a topic has not been found in most textbooks of geriatric medicine at either undergraduate or postgraduate level, with a few notable exceptions (Bennett and Ebrahim, 1995). This situation is changing in the late 1990s, with the major postgraduate textbooks incorporating chapters on elder abuse (Brocklehurst *et al.*, 1997; Pathy, 1997).

Within postgraduate medicine, a revolution is occurring with respect to continuing medical education (CME). General practitioners have evolved a CME scheme, allowing financial compensation, that encourages doctors to attend postgraduate lectures, seminars and conferences. Elder abuse is beginning to appear as a topic within this education framework, but it has a very low profile. Junior doctors pursuing hospital postgraduate careers initially have to pass a postgraduate examination, for example to become a Member of the Royal College of Physicians (MRCP). The health care of older people does not feature highly within most examinations, so it is not surprising at this time to find that elder abuse is missing. The British Geriatrics Society organises and examines for a Diploma in Geriatric Medicine (aimed primarily at doctors who will enter general practice); the topic of elder abuse is not yet on the syllabus.

CME has been introduced for hospital staff at consultant level. The Royal Colleges are all bringing out guidelines to encourage the voluntary participation of consultants within such a scheme to encourage ongoing updating not only in their own specialised subject but also of the wide range of new issues that have emerged. Elder abuse must be placed on the curriculum of medical courses (Kingston *et al.*, 1995).

Undergraduate education has also undergone many changes in the last few years in a response to General Medical Council guidelines. Medical student education has been a bastion of the apprenticeship/ teacher-centred approach. The topic of medicine was hospital based as well as discipline based, with the student as information-gatherer. The wind of change within education has incorporated the changes that are happening within the practice of medicine itself. Courses are now student centred, and the training is systematic and integrated with the various disciplines. Learning is problem based and aimed at a community context rather than hospital.

Wider views of medicine are encouraged by the use of elective periods spent in the UK or abroad studying the different approaches to health care problems. The undergraduate curriculum for medical students now involves the use of stated learning objectives for each individual component. A proportion of study is via self-directed learning (SDL), where the student is encouraged to approach a problem using their own initiative, perhaps involving the use of books or information technology. The most recent SDL aid is the study guide, a tutorial in print. The guide incorporates key information and core facts, often helped by bullet points, areas for more detailed reading, help with clinical skills and examples of extended matching items (EMIs) and objective structured clinical examinations (OSCEs) for that particular subject. Appraisal has also changed with greater emphasis upon assessment evaluation. Multiple choice questionnaires are being replaced by EMIs (Case and Swanson, 1992) and clinical tests are incorporating OSCEs (Harden *et al.*, 1975).

Within this changing education initiative, the teaching of health care of the elderly (also known as medicine of old age or geriatric medicine) still competes poorly with the other disciplines. Not all medical schools have an academic department for the subject, and many undergraduate students are not examined specifically within their final examinations about the medical issues of older people. A recent survey of medical schools/colleges in the UK on whether elder abuse appears as part of the syllabus for student education within their qualifying curriculum indicated that the issue was being taught less at medical schools than on qualifying courses for either nursing or social work (Kingston *et al.*, 1995).

The potential for medical practitioner education about elder abuse in the US is much greater. The predominant legal framework in each State has the added result that resources have to be channelled into education of health care professionals. This is delivered in a variety of ways, including Elder Abuse Acute Care Resource Manuals (Chelucci and Coyle, 1992), video information and books, as well as seminars, study days and conferences.

What is often perceived as one of the main weaknesses in the US health care system (the lack of a comprehensive primary care network of doctors i.e. general practitioners) means that most US doctors lack the detailed client and family knowledge that particular tier of medical practice can produce. The UK is in a unique position with its comprehensive, accessible and organised system to implement education and training initiatives; elder abuse should be fully incorporated within the curricula of such initiatives.

Conclusion

Medical dimensions are an important element of the knowledge base for individuals to be aware of, even if they are not medically or health trained. Elder abuse is a complex, multifaceted field that requires input from a number of different disciplines, of which medicine, and in more general terms health, is but a part; it is therefore necessary for individuals to have an understanding and knowledge of what the different perspectives have to contribute to the field. Thus the health perspective is of use to the social worker, police or housing officer, just as an understanding of the law is useful to practitioners from a health background. Having considered the medical dimensions appropriate within the field, it is now necessary to move to a focus on the legal perspectives that are of relevance to the issue.

5

Legal Dimensions and Issues

Introduction

The previous chapter provided an overview of medical perspectives on elder abuse to give the reader a knowledge and understanding of the dimensions involved. The purpose of this chapter is to present a similar framework in relation to the law and elder abuse. Firstly, a synthesis of the current position with regard to the law and elder abuse will be presented, although a detailed analysis of the existing legislative framework will not be provided as this would be too complex in a generalist book of this type. In the event of the reader requiring more specific information, other documents should be consulted or legal advice sought (see ADSS, 1995, which contains a useful guide as an appendix; also McDonald and Taylor, 1993, and Ashton, 1994, 1995, for more general guides). It is useful to include a synthesis of the current position with regard to the law and elder abuse so that practitioners are aware of the broad nature and scope of legislation that is available and have an understanding of legal issues within this area. The legal provisions that exist in relation to residential care and abuse occurring within institutions will be covered in the following chapter .

The chapter then moves to a consideration of the possible problems in applying the law as it presently exists. Current and likely future developments will then be outlined, especially with regard to the English Law Commission's proposals and report concerning both the protection of vulnerable adults and issues concerning decision-making and mentally incapacitated adults. The particular emphasis in this chapter will be older people rather than the wider issues concerned with all vulnerable adults, given that we are considering elder abuse. A critique of the proposals will be followed by further discussion of the issues surrounding reform of the law, and suggestions concerning general legal principles with regard to older people and specifically in connection with the law and elder abuse. Finally, the set of linked issues surrounding rights, self-determination/autonomy and protection of older people will be raised and considered.

The existing legal framework

There is no specific or single body of law that exists which can be utilised in situations of actual or alleged abuse and which may necessitate protective measures for older people. There are a number of powers and duties contained in differing pieces of legislation that are available for usage; these cannot, however, be viewed as cohesive. There is an important difference between powers and duties, which are distinct legal terms: a power to act is in general terms permissive, whilst a duty actually requires action from the party and thus provides much less freedom. Linked to this distinction are implications in terms of legal redress, for example for the failure to comply with a duty to act. Specifically, the use of judicial review as a form of legal recourse (particularly with regard to the failure to act under a duty) is an important tool for individuals to be aware of.

It is important that health and social care professionals have an appreciation of the range of legal powers that exist so that they can assist older people who may have been subject to abuse (and their carers) to reach decisions about use of the law or equally appreciate the possible and likely consequences of abuse continuing and of possible legal remedies. In addition, it is essential that workers have an understanding of the responsibilities accruing to the different agencies involved in the application of the law and of the parameters that may limit the scope of intervention.

It is also necessary to appreciate that, as adults, older people are generally considered to be competent and responsible, and therefore the use of any intervention would require the person's consent as a necessary pre-requisite to any action being taken. The fact that no specific protective law exists in relation to older people may be seen as underlining the fact that the law does not currently discriminate on the basis of age and may thus be viewed as antioppressive in intent. As has been suggested with regard to legislation that exists in America concerning the mandatory reporting of elder abuse, such laws may in fact be perceived as discriminatory in the way in which they tend to infantilise older people (Salend *et al.*, 1984), potentially denying them full adult status. Whether the laws that exist are adequate for the purposes they are intended to serve is a matter for separate consideration. Decisions can usually only be taken on behalf of an adult if there is some finding of mental incapacity (see later); certain legal provisions exist that allow for this.

It is important to appreciate, however, as McDonald states, that:

> Different functions of the law: normative; protective and enabling; and different branches of the law: criminal law and civil law; private law and public law all need to be considered for their applicability to... elder abuse (McDonald, 1993, pp. 81–2).

Differences arise, too, when considering possible remedies for differing types of abuse, for example financial abuse, physical abuse or sexual abuse. The potential use of civil or criminal law will vary depending on the type of abuse and wrongful action that has occurred. Additionally, differences exist in terms of provision for those older people who are mentally impaired and incapacitated and those who, whilst vulnerable and frail, retain mental capacity (in a legal sense). The lack of agreement on definitions of capacity between different professional groups may also not assist in this respect.

Furthermore, the existence of differing professional attitudes and perceptions about the law and its application in relation to elder abuse may prove difficult to resolve. Differing definitions of what constitutes an abusive act or situtation may also come into the arena in this respect; lack of agreement on what constitutes abuse may well affect whether there is any consideration of possible legal remedy for the situation or not. In this context also, it is necessary to acknowledge that, by their very nature and construction, legal definitions tend to be tighter than those used by other professionals in terms of their everyday practice. Acknowledgement and a willingness to work with such differences is a necessary prerequisite for all professionals to successful work in this area.

General legislation

In terms of general legislation regarding the provision of services to older people, local authorities are enabled to make such provision under the Health Services and Public Health Act 1968 in order to 'promote the welfare of old people'. This statute links with other earlier pieces of legislation (for example the National Assistance Act 1948 and the

National Health Service Act 1946) regarding the provision of residential care, home helps and meals for older people. The Chronically Sick and Disabled Persons Act 1970 also relates to those older people who are either disabled or 'chronically sick' in terms of its general provisions. Under Section 2 of this Act, a duty was imposed on Local Authorities to provide aids to living, adaptations and other services for disabled people 'if satisfied there is a need'. The later Disabled Persons (Services, Consultation and Representation) Act 1986 did likewise, with rights to assessment and representation. It is necessary to note here that large parts of the 1986 Act remain unimplemented, with specific statements from successive Conservative governments that certain sections (for example those concerning assessment) have to a large extent been superseded by the NHS and Community Care Act 1990 and therefore do not need to be fully implemented. Certain Sections, however, such as those regarding the authorisation of a representative (as in an advocate) (found in Part I, Section 1 (1)) or statements of need (Part I, Section 7) would potentially be of use within abusive situations if implemented.

More recently, the National Health Service and Community Care Act 1990 requires local authorities (under Section 47) to conduct assessments of need where it appears that people are or may be in need of community care services. There is a duty under the Act for local authorities to carry out an assessment of an individual's needs in such instances. The original legislation, whilst advising consideration of the needs of a carer to a separate assessment, did not confer on carers any entitlement to an assessment. This has been rectified by the passing of the Carers (Recognition and Services) Act 1995 within the English Parliament (enacted April 1996). This new legislation established for carers the right to a separate and individualised assessment of their ability to provide care in conjunction with an assessment or reassessment of the older person.

Beyond the assessment process, however, the provision of services to meet the identified needs of the individual is a discretionary power (i.e. the Local Authority does not have to provide them as this will depend on the existence and operation of any eligibility criteria for the provision of services). The legislation concerning carers, mentioned above, may not necessarily result in any entitlement (of carers) to services either.

Clearly, those older people who are abused or who are at risk of abuse may well come within the category of those individuals who may be in need of services: it is likely that what may be necessary in such situations is for there to be a detailed and comprehensive assessment including the contributions of professionals from other agencies and settings. Any care plan that results as an outcome of the assessment and agreement of the individual (and hopefully their carer) should be the subject of careful monitoring and review, perhaps on the basis of continuing multiagency involvement.

Additionally, Section 48 of the Act allows for a power of entry to and inspection of any premises in which community care services are being, or may be, provided by a Local Authority. This refers to services which are being directly provided by the Social Services Department or by an independent agency with whom the Social Services Department has a contract. It does not apply, however, to residential or nursing homes that are registered under the Registered Homes Act 1984. This power of entry and inspection is limited to 'any person authorised by the Secretary of State' and may occur 'at any reasonable time'. It is possible that such a power might be used to gain access to an individual who was already in receipt of community care services provided by the Social Services.

The DOH, via the SSI, has been very clear in its guidance concerning elder abuse (DOH/SSI, 1993): that Local Authorities should develop responses to elder abuse (actual or potential) that are consistent with more general arrangements for assessment and care management within the existing legislative framework (of the NHS and Community Care Act 1990). What is apparent, however, is that whilst assessment should be needs led and holistic, it may also need, in line with the general legislation, to be *abuse-focused* (emphasis added).

Criminal law

Criminal law can be used in certain instances of elder abuse, most notably perhaps those involving physical abuse. As stated in their valuable document of 1986, Age Concern have been very explicit about this: 'physical abuse is a criminal act and... if there is sufficient evidence, prosecutions can be initiated' (Age Concern, 1986).

Criminal actions for assault can be initiated in such instances (Griffiths *et al.*, 1990). The Offences Against the Person Act 1861 remains the major statute governing such offences as wounding, actual or grievous bodily harm and assault. Common law offences such as murder, manslaughter, certain instances of assault and rape can also result in prosecution.

Other sexual offences (for example indecent assault, incest or buggery) are covered by the Sexual Offences Act 1956. Also contained within this Act are provisions (under Section 7) for prosecution of a man who has sexual intercourse with a woman suffering from 'severe mental handicap' (unless he does not know or has no reason to suspect that she is severely mentally handicapped). Section 1 of the Sexual Offences Act 1967 extends the provision to prosecution of a man for a homosexual act with a man who has 'severe mental handicap'. It is also an offence for the owner or manager of any premises to allow a 'severely mentally handicapped woman' to be on the premises for the purposes of having intercourse with a man (Section 27).

Criminal prosecutions are usually brought by the Crown Prosecution Service on behalf of the police, although it is technically possible for individuals to instigate a private prosecution under criminal law. It may be difficult, however, to obtain satisfactory evidence from older people who may be physically or mentally frail; attendance at court is required and evidence has to be given in open court (there is no provision for video evidence, etc). This should not deter those who wish to empower individuals by assisting them to use the existing law. It is perhaps too easy for professionals, and others, to make what are in effect ageist assumptions about the ability of older people to undergo the full judicial process and to exclude them from the benefit of utilising these on the basis of such assumptions. It is crucial to engage older people wherever possible in a full discussion and any decision-making process concerning whether or not to pursue a legal action, and for the decision to be meaningful for the individual concerned. Practitioners need to develop methods of enabling older people to withstand the possible rigours of court appearances and assisting them to do so.

Additionally, actions may be brought under the Domestic Violence and Matrimonial Proceedings Act 1976 and the Domestic Proceedings and Magistrates Court Act 1978, which provide primarily for civil remedies for those who have experienced domestic violence. There is no limit on the age of the victim. It is possible under these statutes to obtain ouster orders (1976 Act) or exclusion orders (1978 Act), either to exclude one party from the matrimonial home or to allow access for a person who has been wrongfully excluded. Magistrates may also make family protection orders that can have powers of arrest attached to them. Coupled with this are provisions for 'personal protection' and non-molestation orders for usage against real or threatened violence. In certain instances, powers of arrest may be attached to these orders.

This legislation can currently only be used in situations of marriage or cohabitation; it is not at present available to relatives living in the same household, although change may be forthcoming. Injunctions are available for use within such situations but only as an adjunct to other types of legal action, such as, for example, those concerning a civil action (tort) brought for assault. A recent report from the Law Commission proposed a number of alterations to the existing law, including an extension of the protective functions of the law to a defined group of close relatives as well as to present/former spouses and present/former members of the household (Law Commission, 1992).

This was translated into a Bill – The Family Home and Domestic Violence Bill 1995 – which proposed a unified code of protection for 'associated persons' (close relatives, members of the household and those with parental responsibility) and would extend the benefit derived from non-molestation orders that was previously limited to married or cohabiting partners only. This Bill passed its first reading in Parliament in early 1995, but then ran into difficulty in its later stages as it was considered to give too many rights generally to cohabitees. There was general agreement, however, from different lobbying organisations that this type of provision would be of benefit to individuals within abusive situations, including older people experiencing abuse within the domestic setting.

The revised bill, the Family Law Bill, contained several sections of potential benefit to victims of abuse. It combined clauses concerning domestic violence (from the previous failed Bill) with clauses concerned with the reform of divorce. Part three of the Bill covered the domestic violence aspects. Older people who had been or were at risk of physical abuse would be able, under the powers of this Bill, to apply to the courts for protection from members of the family and others with whom they lived. This would principally be through 'occupation orders', which would exclude an abuser from the home of the older person (if the older person was a tenant or an owner occupier) and gave rights to the older person to remain in the home. The abuser could be anyone sharing the accommodation provided the relationship was not primarily financial (as in a lodger, tenant or boarder). Only spouses, cohabitees or former spouses or cohabitees could, however, apply for an order for a property to which they had no legal claim.

Non-molestation orders would apply in the case of an older person living in someone else's house (with no contractual right to live there). Application to the court in this instance would be for an order to prevent certain specific types of molestation, or molestation in general. Such orders would be applicable to the same household members as those covered by occupation orders. Courts would have to attach powers of arrest to both types of order if the abuser had used or threatened physical violence unless the person applying for the order could be satisfactorily protected without such a power attached. The Bill also allowed for provision for the Lord Chancellor to issue regulations concerning which type of court should be involved with particular types of cases in an attempt to achieve consistency in the treatment of domestic violence. This Act was finally passed in late 1996.

Use of the domestic violence legislation is not without difficulty, however: the apparent reluctance of the police to become involved in 'domestic incidents' has been noted (Freeman, 1987; Barron, 1990). More recent commentators have suggested that this situation may thankfully be changing (Hague and Malos, 1993) following recent Home Office directives to police forces concerning the establishment of local Domestic Violence Units, in some cases known as Family Protection Units, in each district. In addition to this are situations in which victims may not pursue complaints, whether from fear, ambivalence, guilt or adoption of societal attitudes that the role of the state should be minimal in what are, or should be viewed as, private 'family' matters (Pleck, 1987). Again, recent changes to the actions that may be taken by the police in such instances (to pursue more formal action irrespective of the decision of the individual victim, particularly in situations of severe risk) may offer increasing assistance to individuals in such situations in future.

There is an additional area of difficulty in that use of the domestic violence legislation by a younger woman to oust her partner from the home may result in the man moving back to live with his parents (O'Loughlin, A., personal communication, 1996). An abusive relationship might then be established, if not re-established or even continued, between the man and his parents. In particular, there have been instances where a man has moved in with his mother who was living alone (perhaps through widowhood) but who was, additionally, a survivor of earlier domestic violence from her partner (O'Loughlin, A., personal communication, 1996). Clearly, such problems as these, with unintended and unforeseen consequences resulting from the use of legislation by one group of people to the possible disadvantage of another group, need further attention in future. In particular, there may be implications for the feminist movement in potential conflicts of interest between younger and older women. Associated with this may be difficulties in empowering both groups of women to live their lives free from domestic violence or risk of abuse.

Uses of civil law

An abused person may use the civil law to bring a private action against an individual. This would normally be to seek restitution via damages or a compensation payment or to effect an injunction to restrain an abuser. Consideration must be given to the potential cost of an individual bringing an action or to the availability (or otherwise) of Legal Aid. Civil law actions may be brought for the following types of situation and 'wrong':

- trespass: used as a generic term to include assault, battery and false imprisonment;
- assault: regarding reasonable fear of 'battery';
- battery: regarding actual application of force;
- negligence: regarding a breach of a duty to take care to avoid injury;
- wrongful interference: regarding harm caused by an intentional act;
- false imprisonment: regarding the restriction of movement without lawful authority.

This last action might be viewed as potentially applicable within residential care, for example (for a person admitted to care against their wishes). It is also possible that a civil action may on occasion (and subject to certain restrictions) be brought in addition to criminal proceedings or as evidence in a civil action (for example to assist the pursuance of a civil remedy like an injunction). A civil remedy may also be considered in situations when a criminal prosecution is not proceeding, perhaps when the available evidence is not likely to meet the standard of proof required for criminal prosecutions ('beyond all reasonable doubt') but may well meet the civil standard of proof, which is less stringent ('balance of probabilities'). Compensation may also be sought via the Criminal Injuries Compensation Board in certain situations.

Under legislation concerning housing, an individual who is vulnerable and threatened with homelessness may be considered as a priority for rehousing (Homeless Persons Act 1985, Part III). The code of practice produced in connection with the Act details those situations whereby individuals might be accorded priority. This includes those individuals without children who have experienced violence in the home or who are at risk of further violence if they return home. Application may be made by the individual to the relevant District Housing Department.

Protective legislation

There are a range of legal provisions that have a more specific protective function for older people which may be of some use and relevance within situations of elder abuse. It is important as a preliminary to distinguish between those older people who are 'mentally intact' and those who are cognitively impaired. The former group generally come within the jurisdiction of the National Assistance Act 1948 or the National Assistance (Amendment) Act 1951 whilst the latter come within the remit (if any) of the Mental Health Act 1983.

National Assistance legislation

The provisions of Section 47 of the National Assistance Act 1948 as amended provide for the compulsory removal from home of those meeting a particular set of criteria:

- suffering from grave chronic disease or being aged, infirm or physically incapacitated; and
- living in insanitary conditions; and
- unable to devote to themselves, and are not receiving from other persons, proper care and attention.

It must be established that removal is either in the 'best interests' of the individual (who is to be removed) or to prevent or remove either serious nuisance or injury to others. Application is made via a Community Physician's certificate, and a Magistrates' Court may make an order lasting for up to 3 months allowing for removal of the person to a 'suitable hospital or other place'.

Section 1 of the National Assistance (Amendment) Act 1951 allows for an accelerated emergency procedure, without notice being served on the individual concerning the order, if it is necessary to arrange for removal 'without delay'. This procedure is again instigated by the Community Physician, together with evidence from another registered medical practitioner that this procedure is necessary.

Whilst from the wording of the provision it is apparent that it is not limited to older people, it appears that this provision is used predominantly with older people (Griffiths *et al.*, 1990). This has lead to some criticism that it is an ageist piece of legislation (Age Concern, 1986). Although probably originally intended to deal with two main situations – where a person has become 'at risk' through longstanding self-neglect or where a person is seriously physically ill and refuses admission to hospital – this section could be used where abuse was occurring or carers were neglecting the person (Fennell, 1989). The provision does not generally appear to be used for those situations which are not insanitary, however; additionally within these provisions, the power to remove the person is not accorded to a social worker (the decision rests with a magistrate, the presence of the police being required to effect removal). The section does not provide for any legal representation and there is no right of appeal, although an application to revoke an order can be made 6 weeks after the date the order was made. This section also applies in Scotland.

Usage of this set of provisions is usually seen very much as a last resort when all other options have been pursued and failed. It would appear from research undertaken to discover the usage of these sections that the most frequent reason given for using the provision was that of self-neglect (Muir Gray, 1980). One of the clear recommendations from the English Law Commission as a result of their consultation process (see below) is that Section 47 should be repealed due to views that it is an outmoded and dated piece of legislation.

Mental health legislation

For those elders who are cognitively impaired, either through a progressive illness such as dementia or through some other mental disorder, the relevant legislation to consider in situations of actual or potential abuse is probably the Mental Health Act 1983 (or the equivalent Mental Health Act for Scotland; what will be referred to are the provisions from the English and Welsh Act). Whilst the Act makes it clear (in particular via Section 131) that informal admission to hospital should normally be appropriate for individuals who are mentally ill, compulsory powers for admission to hospital (of an individual unwilling to be admitted on an informal or voluntary basis) do exist within Sections 2, 3 and 4 of the Act. The only social workers who may operate the Act are Approved Social Workers (ASWs) who are appointed to act in accordance with the provisions of the Act (under Section 114). This is in addition, of course, to the need for two medical recommendations concerning compulsory admission.

With regard to those sections of the Act that might be of particular use in situations of elder abuse, the following are worthy of note. First is access by an ASW to a mentally disordered person (who is not living in a hospital) where it is believed that the person 'not under proper care' is covered by Section 115. Although this section allows for entry to and inspection of a premises, it does not provide for forcible entry to a premises. Under Section 129 of the Act, however, it is an offence for anyone to obstruct an ASW without reasonable cause. Additionally, Section 127(2) of the Act serves to protect all who come within the remit of its provisions from wilful neglect or ill-treatment by carers.

A power of removal of a person from premises exists within Section 135 of the Act, whereby an ASW can apply to a magistrate for a warrant authorising the police to enter and remove the person to a place of safety if there is reason to suspect that the person (believed to be suffering from a mental disorder) 'has been, or is being ill-treated, neglected or kept otherwise than under proper control'. It also covers those individuals who live alone and are unable to care for themselves. The provision lasts for 72 hours and allows for removal to a place of safety, usually a hospital. The police will usually be involved in serving the warrant and effecting the removal of the person. The section can only be effected if there is a view to making an application for admission to hospital under Part II of the Act.

Section 136 provides the police with powers to remove a person who appears to be suffering from a mental disorder in a public place to a place of safety for up to 72 hours, pending further assessment under the Act.

Other provisions that may be considered in connection with abuse are those contained within applications for guardianship (Section 7 of the Act), which are designed principally to provide some limited means of provision that fall short of hospital admission and to keep the person within the community. The Code of Practice to the Act, which was produced in 1990, encourages positive and flexible usage of guardianship. It also makes clear that the provision should not be used solely as a means of effecting the admission to residential care of an unwilling person as it was designed for use to protect and maintain individuals in the community.

There are certain sections of the Mental Health Act 1959 that are still in force and of note within the context of abuse. Section 128 makes provision concerning the prosecution of men who are exercising guardianship or running hospitals who have unlawful sexual intercourse with a woman subject to a guardianship order under the Act or receiving treatment for a mental disorder. Section 127 of the 1959 Act makes it an offence for anyone who is a member of staff of a hospital or mental nursing home to either ill-treat or wilfully neglect a patient.

Financial abuse

The use of the term 'financial abuse' (of older people) covers a very wide range of behaviours. This may extend from the theft of small amounts of money, perhaps the misappropriation of change from shopping done for an older housebound person, to the systematic cheating of large sums of money, property or possessions. It may also include the exertion of influence or pressure on an older person to leave property or money in a legacy or to otherwise gift it to an abuser. The current safeguards that exist to reduce the occurrence or risk of such abuse are limited, as outlined below.

For those mentally competent to take their own decisions, but possibly at risk of exploitation, there are several options:

- provision through a will, deed of trust or advance directive;
- provision through appointment of a Power of Attorney for an attorney to deal with finances and financial arrangements on behalf of the person;
- provision through appointment of an Enduring Power of Attorney (EPA; from the Enduring Powers of Attorney Act 1985), which continues to have effect after the person is incapacitated, provided it is registered with the Court of Protection. This also acts as a safeguard from potential abuse of the donor by the attorney. The legal test of capacity to assent to an EPA has been established via a number of test cases which indicate that the donor must understand the 'nature and effect of the power' at the time it is made; there does not have to be a continuing understanding over any particular time period. The English Law Commission in their proposals for reform recommended the creation of Continuing Powers of Attorney to replace the current bifurcated system (Law Commission, 1995).

Arrangements may also be made in connection with Social Security benefits:

- An agent may collect benefit payments for those people who are able to take decisions but need another to collect benefit on their behalf. Responsibility to inform the Department of Social Security (DSS) of changes rests with the claimant.
- An appointeeship may be used for those people unable to make their own decisions. Application is made to DSS for a named

individual (often a relative) to become an appointee and to collect benefits. The responsibility to notify the DSS of changes rests with the appointee; however, appointees are not subject to regular checks or auditing of how the money is spent (whereas attorneys have to provide annual accounts to the Court of Protection for inspection purposes).

Additionally, under Section 142 of the Mental Health Act 1983, payment of certain pensions (of people who fall within the jurisdiction of the Mental Health Act) may be made to a carer or relative.

Part VII of the Mental Health Act 1983 deals with provisions for the Court of Protection, which deals specifically with the management of property and financial affairs of those people who are impaired mentally and unable to deal with their own affairs. A receiver is appointed by the Court to be responsible for the day-to-day management of the person's financial affairs. The receiver may be a relative or other person approved, or an officer of the Court. Perceptions of those using or who have used the Court are variable (National Audit Office, 1994). Some view it as efficient and flexible, others as expensive (due to management charges by the Court), lengthy and insensitive. Criticisms of the process include the following (National Audit Office, 1994):

- It is not always possible to obtain a speedy decision on expenditure.
- Matters concerning welfare and personal care are not part of the court's remit.
- Decisions may reflect a desire to maximise resources (and inheritance) rather than allow for authorisation of expenditure to enhance quality of care.

A person is either outside the jurisdiction of the Court and therefore potentially vulnerable and at risk of abuse, or subject to the control of the Court, even in those areas where decisions by the individual might be possible.

In situations where there is reason to suspect that theft or misappropriation of finance or property has occurred, an investigation by the police may be appropriate, with the consent of the person to contact the police. This may lead to prosecution in a criminal court (the victim should be made aware of this at an early stage in the process). In relation to the possible fraud of DSS benefits, the local DSS office should be contacted; again the consent of individuals to do this on their behalf should be obtained if at all possible.

In Scotland, the following provisions exist which may assist in situations of financial abuse:

- Powers of Attorney which endure 'beyond capacity' may be appointed.
- Verbal mandates can be given by individuals authorising a person to deal with the individual's affairs.
- Social Security Appointeeship can be taken out.
- Powers of Incopax may be assigned to hospitals in order that they might deal with a patient's affairs.
- A 'Curator bonis' may be appointed by a court to handle a person's finances (this is an ordinary court rather than the Court of Protection).

In addition, courts may appoint tutors to handle the wider affairs of an incapacitated individual. This system derives from a 16th-century Scottish law; tutors may be either 'Tutors at law' or 'Tutors dative'. The former can deal with health, welfare or financial matters on behalf of an individual. This person must be the 'nearest male agnate' (blood relative) of the person. 'Tutors dative' can be a relative of either sex, but decision-making powers do not include the handling of finances and are restricted to health and welfare matters. There has been increasing use of 'Tutors dative' in recent years in Scotland.

Potential problems in applying the law

Generally speaking, social workers are trained in therapeutic rather than corrective methods (the old care or control debate in another context). Similarly, health care professionals are trained to cure and to relieve symptoms of ill-health rather than to punish those afflicted (despite current debates surrounding the rights of doctors to refuse to treat persistent chronic smokers, or dentists to treat those deemed to be responsible for their own excessive tooth decay). There may thus be a reluctance to use what legal remedies exist due to connotations about punishment and blame and whether it is appropriate to consider such concepts. In addition, for social workers in particular, questions are raised when considering matters of protection regarding child abuse and the development of both statute and services over the past 20 years or so.

The concept now in use regarding children is 'significant harm' (Children Act 1989, Section 31). Whether it is appropriate or even desirable to transfer such a concept to the context of older people is a debatable point. The term is, however, the one used by the Law Commission in their recent consultation documents (1993a, b, c) concerning 'mentally incapacitated and other vulnerable adults'. The clear view of the paper was that the concept could usefully be expanded to include vulnerable adults. Although there may be similarities between older people and children concerning vulnerability, assumptions that similar solutions can be applied should not be made. Nor do similar legal rights and duties exist regarding adults and children; there are important legal distinctions to be made and maintained.

In addition, with regard to children, the concept of significant harm may be viewed as the trigger for protective measures to be initiated. It does not provide automatic entitlement, however, to the provision of support or services. Such issues need to be acknowledged and addressed by professionals if they are to be successful in work in these complex and difficult situations.

Despite recent indications on the part of the Law Commission that some reform of the law may be necessary (Law Commission, 1993a, b, c; see below) and a consultation exercise conducted, any forthcoming legislative change is likely to take some years to place on the statute books. It is necessary therefore for practitioners to be mindful of this situation within their current working practices, and although it is desirable that they should be aware of the major recommendations of the Law Commission proposals, their practice must clearly reflect the current state of affairs rather than what might be.

Practitioners in this area of work should currently aim within their practice to assist individuals to use the existing law both wisely and properly in order to attain appropriate redress. Where possible, most health and social care professionals would agree that some measure of protection for vulnerable older people should be the aim of intervention from a legal perspective, rather than a criminalisation of abuse by an approach that advocates prosecution as the paramount consideration. Conversely, in some very serious situations, a criminal prosecution may be necessary in order not only to provide some measure of protection but also to acknowledge the severity of the situation and to indicate that such acts will not be tolerated within society. The notion of 'protective responsibility' as advocated by Stevenson and Parsloe may be of some use in this context. It is argued that practitioners need a good understanding of the circumstances in which they are required to act to protect a vulnerable adult and should act accordingly and responsibly (Stevenson and Parsloe, 1993).

On occasion, it is apparent that some professionals, in their desire to protect the vulnerable older person, may act somewhat paternalistically (or arguably, maternalistically) and deny the older person the right to take a decision on whether or not to seek recompense in a legal sense against their abuser. Many social and health care workers enter their respective fields through strong motivating factors such as a desire to protect, nurture and tend or care for individuals within their care. Such protective attitudes may be perceived as ageist in their outcome if not in the intent with which they were conceived. An assumption that an older person would not be able to withstand the rigours of a court appearance, cross-examination and so on without involving the individual in that decision is clearly somewhat problematic in terms of whether it can ever be justified in practice, and it flies in the face of equal opportunities and antidiscriminatory practice. Assumptions should continually be examined and tested out, and practice modified in the light of this.

Other workers, perhaps more predominantly (but not exclusively) within the field of social care, are more motivated by such notions as empowerment, client choice and self-determination, and feel more comfortable with concepts such as the individual's right to refuse intervention. The offer to a person of a potential legal remedy and of access to appropriate advice, from either the legal profession or local police officers, if the necessary good working relationships exist, may be sufficient for the person then to take his or her own decision, in due course if not immediately. Support for workers (from managers) may still be necessary if the person's decision is at variance with the worker's preferred option. It is important that individual professionals feel as comfortable as possible within such situations in order to be maximally effective: clear management support will clearly be of prime importance in such instances.

It is suggested that one possible effect of the current movement by Local Authority Social Services Departments to produce guidelines, procedures and policy statements in relation to elder abuse, as exhorted by the SSI in their 1993 document (DOH/SSI, 1993), may be to decriminalise abusive acts and to deny older people the right to redress in a legal sense for acts perpetrated against them. To subject individuals to the full gamut of procedures in terms of investigation and assessment may mean that criminal investigation is then precluded, or not even fully considered by workers in their attempts to operate the procedure properly. This is clearly not the case, however, with child protection matters, where one of the aims of procedures is to ensure that appropriate (statutory) legal action can be effected when necessary. It may be wiser in situations of elder abuse to involve colleagues from the police at the earliest stage possible, particularly perhaps when it is considered likely that a criminal act has been committed.

The alternative viewpoint, argued by Hugman, is that to criminalise abusive acts and to treat all such acts as criminal and subject to full legal processes, including police investigation and enquiry, is to miss the complexity and sensitivity of some of the situations in which there are a number of victims and not necessarily any criminal intent that can be proved (Hugman, 1994a). Hugman also suggests, however, that to label acts which in other contexts would clearly be seen as criminal (for example theft, rape or physical assault) as abuse is ageist and in some ways diminishes the older person's experience of the situation as these are not considered criminal acts.

However, as he also explores fully, the nature of the caring relationship may well be such as to produce higher degrees of ambiguity. It may be more profitable to attempt distinctions between 'criminal acts and abuse on the one hand and between conscious and unconscious abuse on the other' (Hugman, 1994a). The concepts of obligation to care and reciprocity within such relationships, in all their complexities, may mean that it is preferable to view events as abusive acts rather than events perpetrated with criminal intent, and for some individuals, decisions not to pursue investigation and prosecution may in any case be linked to reciprocity and familial relationships.

Inappropriate involvement of the police and criminal processes may lead to an exacerbation of the difficulties already inherent within such situations and less likelihood of eventual satisfactory resolution. However, conversely, to deny the person the right to obtain legal redress for a wrongful action against them because of fear of retribution and of making the situation worse is clearly just as inappropriate.

There may be situations in which there are no ideal solutions: no winners, no magic answers. Situations sometimes occur in which no action may be taken, in particular if older people are reluctant or unwilling either to initiate such action to be taken or to allow this to happen on their behalf. Penhale (1993c) has explored some of the barriers to identification of elder abuse, including a not insignificant reluctance on the part of many older people to report or admit to abuse having occurred (see Penhale, 1993c, for a further exposition of this). The possible reasons for this state of affairs are complex; it is not possible to consider these in any detail here.

One point does bear some examination, however. It is the perception of the general public that social workers, in particular, are often involved in the removal of individuals, often against their wishes, from a situation. This situation is often the family home, and the person who is removed is placed in another form of care, usually in an institutional setting. Legal powers accorded to social workers with regard to child protection and people with mental health difficulties obviously strengthen this view, but a not too dissimilar perception can exist in relation to older people. Social Services Departments are at times quite frequently contacted by concerned relatives or members of the public about the perceived need to admit an older person (not necessarily concerning an abusive situation) to a residential or nursing home, often with scant regard to the wishes of the individual. It is sometimes possible that the older person may not have fully articulated personal views on the matter and may appear acquiescent.

In fact, the legal powers that allow for this to happen are few (as seen in the section on legal framework above) and not frequently applied. Research carried out in 1980 and repeated in 1988 indicated that Section 47 of the 1948 National Assistance Act was being used approximately 200 times a year to effect the removal of older people from their homes, usually to a hospital setting (Muir Gray, 1980; Fear *et al.*, 1988). Whilst it is possible to view the research figures as indicative that the provision is not used very often, it is also possible to interpret the figures as usage of the section some four times per week across the country. This does not appear to be exactly infrequent, even given the discrepancies and variations in usage in different parts of the country (usage of the power is very variable across the country, with some areas appearing rarely to exercise it). It is possible, however, to view such usage as either rarely used or too frequently used, depending on the viewpoint of the individual!

Eastman in a small sample of practitioners found differences between groups of social services staff in their willingness to consider admission to residential care as an option to alleviate or resolve abusive situations (Eastman, 1984). Hospital social workers appeared more likely than field workers to consider usage of residential care from this survey, although this says nothing about the possible pressures on hospital social workers to move people out of hospital, nor of a perception by hospital staff that residential care may well be preferable to remaining in hospital any longer than is absolutely necessary!

A later piece of research, albeit small scale, by the SSI as part of their work on elder abuse indicated that practitioners saw the removal of an older person from the situation as very much a last resort, with great efforts being made to maintain people at home (DOH/SSI, 1992). The perception of the public, including elderly people, is nevertheless that powers to remove a person to residential care do exist and that older people are forced to enter institutional care against their will. The threat of removal to an institution to a person can, however, be very strong and very real and act as a demotivator for an individual to accept any offers of assistance, let alone to admit the need to effect any change to a situation.

In addition, for many older people, in particular those from the group who are very elderly (85 years and over), institutional care is not surprisingly associated with images of the workhouse and therefore something to be avoided at all costs. It has been seen in Chapter 3 that we have a long history in this country of scandals with regard to the levels of care given to older people in institutional care, which undoubtedly adds to the reluctance of many (if not most) older people to contemplate admission to such care unless absolutely necessary. This association is clearly most strong for those whose generation still recall the workhouse; nonetheless, perceptions of residential care held by many older people and indeed the general public are of institutions rather than homes, despite the efforts of such bodies as the SSI to counter these in such publications as *Homes Are for Living in* (DOH/SSI, 1989).

Other reasons may also exist with regard to a reluctance on the part of the older person to accept assistance in the resolution of a difficulty and/or prevention of the abusive situation continuing. This may, of course, include a choice on the part of individuals that they would rather continue with a known situation, perhaps with a combination of care given and abuse received on occasion, than risk the unknown quantity of life without that person (abuse and all). Elders may well weigh up all the associated factors and risks (or even choose not to do this) and determine that they wish to remain in the situation against all advice. They may also, however, be subjected to significant amounts of pressure and intimidation to resist intervention. Workers may need some assistance to acknowledge and live with or work with this fact and these situations; undoubtedly, it is easier for some people than others to accept. The reasons outlined above in terms of the underlying motivations of staff to work with particular client groups may account for the difference in attitude and approach by workers.

The Law Commission and the case for reform

One of the commonly held misperceptions at practitioner level about intervention in situations of elder abuse seems to be that appropriate legal remedies do not exist for older people and that the legal sphere does not need to be actively considered because relevant solutions do not exist. Moreover, the law as currently practised in this country fails to meet the needs of older people in general, and abused older people in particular. This view is obviously open to reconsideration and, as we have seen above, there are existing legal remedies that can be used to protect older people, even though practitioners may not be familiar with the range of available statute. There are also some indications of an opposing view that the law regarding older people (in this latter part of the 20th century), whilst perhaps not actively promoting the rights and needs of older people as fully as necessary, equally does not lead to injustices occurring and can allow for some measure of protection for the individual.

Notwithstanding this view, however, there has over a number of years been a growing amount of pressure concerning the need for reform of the law. The voluntary organisation Age Concern has lobbied since 1986 for an alteration to the existing legal system in relation to older people (Age Concern, 1986); the BASW, the RCN and other professional bodies have also lobbied intensively concerning abused older people and a reform of the law. As will be detailed more fully later, there is some debate between social work academics (namely Phillipson and Stevenson) over the legitimacy and utility (or otherwise) of such a view. It would seem appropriate at this point to consider the role and stance taken by the English Law Commission in recent years, and to acknowledge that a similar process was undertaken by the Scottish Law Commission.

In 1989 the Mental Health and Disability sub-committee of the English Law Society produced a discussion document concerning decision-making and mental incapacity (Law Society, 1989) and referred the matter to the English Law Commission to undertake a comprehensive investigation of this set of issues. The Law Commission included the topic within their programme for law reform and in 1991 produced a consultation document concerning the particular set of legal and ethical issues surrounding mental incapacity and decision-making and the need for reform. This document concerned all adults who were mentally incapacitated and was not confined to older people.

The consultation period extended over several months, and the response was far greater than originally anticipated by the Law Commission. Although the document was obviously concerned with the range of individuals who are or become mentally incapacitated (rather than solely older people), there were a large number of responses to the Commission regarding elder abuse and the possible need for some legal reform in order to protect older vulnerable people who were either being abused or who were at risk of abuse. This was in direct response to the appearance in the document of a statement that one of the policy aims within the whole area should be to ensure:

> that proper safeguards be provided against exploitation, neglect, and physical, sexual or psychological abuse (Law Commission, 1991, p. 110).

What most of the responses pointed out in connection with elder abuse was that there are likely to be a significant number of older people who may be in need of protection through their exposure to abuse or the risk of abuse who are not mentally incapacitated. Such individuals may be more appropriately considered as vulnerable rather than incompetent or incapacitated. A strong view was expressed that such people should not be precluded from any legislative changes that might be forthcoming, in particular since many of them were likely to be vulnerable if not actually impaired.

The Law Commission deliberated over the many submissions made to them and in 1993 published three documents for a further period of consultation. These documents covered those specific areas where changes were considered to be necessary. The documents were:

- *Mentally Incapacitated Adults and Decision-Making: A new jurisdiction* (Paper 128);
- *Mentally Incapacitated Adults and Decision-Making: Medical treatment and research* (Paper 129);
- *Mentally Incapacitated and Other Vulnerable Adults: Public law protection* (Paper 130).

The first of the documents concerned the domain of private (civil) law issues, such as the powers and responsibilities of carers. It contained proposals for key tests, such as the test of incapacity, and the main factors and criteria that should be taken into account when decisions are to be taken in connection with a mentally incapacitated person. The major proposal was for a 'new jurisdiction' (without any decision on the part of the Commission on whether this should be a tribunal or a court), which could act to authorise individuals to take decisions on behalf of incapacitated adults. Those decisions would include matters of property and also the person (i.e. care of the individual). One of the recommendations of the Scottish Law Commission on Mental Incapacity concerns the adoption of an attorney system in which the attorney can deal with financial, health and welfare matters, but with sufficient oversight of the attorney from a central court. This is similar to the recommendation from the English Commission concerning an extension to the Court of Protection for England and Wales.

The second document concentrated on issues surrounding medical treatment and research, more specifically decisions concerning consent to treatment. Also contained within this consultation document were the issues involved in advance directives, living wills and anticipatory decisions. A view was taken within the document that 'legislation should provide for the scope and effect of anticipatory decisions'. In this country, at present, despite extensive lobbying by such bodies as Age Concern, 'living wills' are not fully recognised as legal documents. In America, most States have enacted legislation allowing for anticipatory decision-making (with greater and lesser degrees of protection surrounding these documents drawn up by the individual). Whilst the general view in this country now appears to be that such a document would, if in existence, be considered valid, it would still not be regarded as a wholly legal document and might thus be open to some question as to its legitimacy (or otherwise).

The third consultation paper set out proposals for the protection, via public law, of incapacitated and 'other vulnerable adults' from abuse and neglect. Within this paper, a clear statutory framework was laid out concerning the potential roles and responsibilities of Social Services Departments in investigation, assessment and intervention in abusive situations. What is not considered within the consultation document was the possible resource implications of such a framework although views were invited on this aspect. At a meeting between the Law Commission and various professional groups (for example the Association of Directors of Social Services, ADSS; the Association of Metropolitan Authorities, AMA; BASW; the Association of County Councils, ACC; and the National Development Team, NDT, concerning learning disabilities), a clear view was expressed that whilst such a framework would undoubtedly necessitate resource usage, this should not mean that the changes should not occur as the legislative alterations were necessary. The fact that no commitment was given within the consultation document concerning resources was not seen as prohibitive. This latter paper is of most relevance within the field of elder abuse and is therefore the principal document which will be referred to in the following sections. What is also of some note, however, is that there are certain principles for action that are commonly applied across the different documents and which are of relevance more widely than in any consideration purely of elder abuse.

The consultation period concerning these proposals was 4 months in mid-1993. The number of responses to the proposals were, not surprisingly, considerable. In the spring of 1995, the Law Commission produced its report and final recommendations, which were laid before Parliament in the form of a recommendation for a single comprehensive piece of legislation, the Mental Incapacity Bill (Law Commission, 1995). Any legislative change is in a statutory sense, however, likely to take some long time to effect. It is worth briefly outlining the main recommendations that are of most relevance to elder abuse, in summary form.

Lack of capacity

- Lack of capacity is defined at 'material time' if the person is:
  a) unable to make a decision for him or herself due to mental disability, or
  b) unable to communicate a decision on that matter because unconscious (or for any other reason).
- Inability to make a decision is defined as occurring if the person is:
  a) unable to understand or to retain information relevant to the decision (including information about the reasonably foreseeable consequences of deciding one way or another or of failing to make a decision), or
  b) unable to make a decision based on that information.

Best interests

- The Act would establish a new general requirement to act in the 'best interests' of the person taking account of four statutory factors:
  a) the ascertainable past and present wishes and feelings of the person;
  b) the need to encourage and permit participation by the person in any decision-making to the fullest extent possible;

c) if practicable and appropriate, to consult any person named by the person, any person caring for or interested in the person's welfare, a donee of a Continuing Power of Attorney granted by the person, and any person appointed as manager by the court about views of the person's wishes and feelings of what would constitute best interests;

d) any intervention should be as limited as possible and least restrictive of the person's freedom of action.

General authority

- The Commission recommended the creation of a general authority to act reasonably in matters concerning personal welfare and health care of person who is, or is reasonably believed to be, without capacity.
- Within this framework, it would be lawful for an individual to do anything for the personal welfare or health care of a person without capacity (or reasonably believed to lack capacity) if it is reasonable for the person to do it and it is in the best interests of the person.
- Exceptions to the general rule do exist: no decision can be taken for the person regarding marriage, consent to sexual relations or voting rights.
- This general authority does not:
  a) permit the use of or threat of the use of force to make the person do something they object to;
  b) authorise the detention or confinement of the person (whether they object or not);
  c) authorise anything contrary to the decision or direction of an attorney or manager acting within scope of their authority;
  d) authorise treatment or medical procedure if an advance refusal applies, or a second opinion by doctor is necessary, or approval of court is required.

New criminal offence

- There was specific recommendation of a new offence for anyone to ill-treat or wilfully neglect a person in relation to whom they have powers by virtue of the Mental Incapacity Act.

New Court of Protection

- Recommendation was made for a new court to make decisions about the finances, health and personal welfare of people without capacity.
- The Court would have a central registry in London, and regional centres might be established.
- The Court could be used to resolve disputes concerning those without capacity.

Decision-making by the Court

- The Commission recommended the establishment of a single integrated statutory jurisdiction concerning decisions on finances, health and personal welfare matters of those individuals without capacity.
- The Court could make 'one-off' orders and 'declarations', or appoint a manager with powers of substitute decision-making for a person without capacity.
- The general principle recommended is that making an order is preferable to appointing a manager. The four factors used to determine 'best interests' should be taken into account here.

Public law protection

- A number of proposals for the protection of incapacitated, mentally disordered or vulnerable adults ('proper safeguards against exploitation, neglect and physical, sexual or psychological abuse') were specifically made.
- Section 47 was to be repealed and replaced by clearer and more appropriate powers for Local Authority Social Services Departments to intervene to protect individuals.
- A broad definition was established: 'A vulnerable person at risk... [is] any person who has attained the age of 16 and
    a) is or may be in need of community care services by reason of mental or other disability, age or illness, and
    b) is or may be unable to take care of himself or to protect himself against significant harm or serious exploitation.

- Social Services Departments were to be the authority responsible for investigation and initiating proceedings in relation to care and protection.
- There was a duty of 'authorised Social Services Department officers' to make enquiries, including gaining access to investigate and decide whether community care services (or anything to protect from 'significant harm') are required.
- There are specific powers of entry (via entry warrants), investigation and 'assessment orders', 'temporary protection orders' (a maximum of 7 days) and a duty to return home (as soon as possible if not at risk to do so).
- Powers may not be exercised where it is known or believed that the person objects or is likely to object unless the person is believed to suffer from 'mental disability'.
- A new offence of obstructing an 'authorised officer' in exercise of their powers was to be established.
- The Local Authority may assist a vulnerable person with advice or financial assistance in bringing proceedings under the domestic violence legislation.

Codes of Practice

- Recommendation was made that codes of practice should be developed (and kept revised) to provide guidance:
  a) on the assessment of the capacity or incapacity of an individual to make a particular decision;
  b) for those acting under 'general authority';
  c) for those acting as managers appointed by the Court.

A critique of the proposals

The specific proposals for legal reform made by the Law Commission have been subject to some criticism, not just with regard to the detail of the proposals but also more specifically at the level of the principles that the Commission proposes should be adopted. In a critical examination of the three papers, Carson strongly suggests that the proposals would disempower and further disable individuals (Carson, 1993). Carson outlines criteria for an effective and 'good' law concerning mentally incapacitated adults. In his view, such a law should promote dignity, enhance ability (rather than focusing on disability), be flexible and preventative in scope and action, and be inexpensive. Practical problems should be able to be addressed by such laws, and practical tests of such aspects as capacity and competence should be included. Any new law ought also to be properly monitored and satisfactorily enforced.

In a well-argued critique, Carson indicates that the tests, adequate concepts and underlying framework of the proposals fall some way short of the ideal, which should be of some concern as any reform of the law will be effective for decades (if not longer) and will thus also come to affect the view of the public about such matters. Carson argues strongly that the proposals do not prevent incapacity or lead to empowerment but may even serve to disable individuals. The point is made that the concept of disability should not be viewed solely as an attribute of the person but that it is dynamic and is very much affected by the views, attitudes and subsequent actions of others. Any law should seek to minimise disability and enhance competence. There might be a duty to maximise habilitation and rehabilitation for individuals (Carson, 1993).

A further criticism is levelled by Carson as follows. The presence of mental disorder as a fundamental test of capacity may be essentially flawed since a mentally disordered person is not necessarily always impaired in terms of capacity to make decisions. One of the reasons that his approach was favoured by the Law Commission appears to have been his view that a test of incapacity was not easy to define, establish or even apply. As Carson points out in a reasoned way, however, the difficulty of assessing one thing (i.e. incapacity) is not necessarily reason enough for developing this for another, especially if there is the potential that it may effectively be used as a substitute for a test of capacity.

Slater, in a balanced commentary of existing and possible future legal provision, is justifiably critical of the Law Commission's definition of 'vulnerability' including an association of old age with both disability and infirmity (Slater, 1994). Interestingly, however, he notes that the inclusion of older vulnerable adults with their younger counterparts may result in potential situations where protection from statutory powers might be available for an older person. The prospective statute is premised on the notion that an order could be made only if it is reasonable to believe that an individual would not object to an order being made: if it were known that the person was likely to object and the person was mentally capable of making that decision, no order could be made. Equally, this applied to the situation where an order was made being reasonably founded on that principle but it then transpired that the older person did object and wished to decline offers of assistance and intervention: 'If he is capable of making the choice, that is a choice he must be allowed to make' (Law Commission, 1993c). There may be a potential difficulty, however, revolving around emergency situations: how would any objection be ascertained in such circumstances? And perhaps more specifically, what safeguards would be necessary to adequately protect the individual from well-intentioned but potentially misguided social workers intervening unnecessarily? These are important questions that would need to be addressed prior to the enactment of any legislation.

Gunn, although writing primarily about younger adults with learning difficulties, is also critical of the Law Commission. The principal concerns raised by Gunn are firstly that the Commission focused too heavily on notions of disability and would therefore not empower disabled (or vulnerable) people, and secondly, that the proposed legislation would not be preventive in scope as it would not, ultimately, discourage the occurrence of abuse (Gunn, 1994).

The case against reform

There are some indications that a lobby exists which is not convinced that legislative change is necessary. These views bear some consideration in this context.

The suggestion outlined above, that there is insufficient legislation to adequately protect or serve the interests of older people, is directly countered by the view that the legal powers currently existing are perfectly adequate to protect older people. This view suggests that the problem lies with practitioners who view the law negatively and lack the knowledge to apply the law appropriately, resulting in an underutilisation of the law. What is apparent is that there is no piece of legislation to which practitioners may turn, but rather that existing law is found in a number of different statutes which may serve to confuse rather than to clarify matters. The potential difficulty of practitioner attitudes will be explored more fully in Chapter 6 (on intervention) but in essence consists of a view that legal interventions are juxtaposed to therapeutic interventions and should be avoided unless absolutely necessary. Such views do not encompass any notion that the appropriate use of legal powers and assisting individuals to use the law might be empowering for those individuals in addition to serving to protect them.

One of the keenest proponents of the view that the current law, if used properly, is satisfactory is Phillipson. In recent publications, he has also suggested that new powers might actually reduce the rights of older people and that existing powers are appropriate to both support and protect them (Phillipson, 1993). This view has also been vigorously propounded by the Alzheimer's Disease Society in recent publications (Alzheimer's Disease Society, 1993). Any reform of the law would only be likely to be successful, in any case, if it were to be accompanied by adequate resources (in both legal and social spheres) in order to implement it properly, and this may be unlikely within the current ethos of constraints on resources.

In addition, Griffiths *et al.* have indicated that some legal interventions such as prosecutions of the perpetrators of abuse may not be wholly appropriate, as in many situations it can be difficult to determine who exactly is the victim (Griffiths *et al.*, 1993). Both the abuser and the abused may be very much the victim of the situation that has developed over time, and criminalisation of the relationship difficulty that has become abusive may do little to repair relations (see also Hugman, 1994a, and above). From the legal perspective, there may be a further problem in that the notion of abuse is rarely conceptualised in any legal way. Differing and disparate definitions of what constitutes abuse, such notions as different types of abuse and differences in terms of those individuals involved, clearly do not assist in this respect (Griffiths *et al.*, 1993).

Caution in reform of the law has also been expressed by those who are concerned at any potential increase in the powers accorded to social workers and Social Services Departments (Alzheimer's Disease Society, 1993). In particular, legitimate concern has been expressed about the potential abuse of powers designed to protect vulnerable elders that might be used either against carers or, perhaps even more critically, against those cognitively impaired older people who may act aggressively towards their carers (both paid and unpaid). Vulnerable older people might thus be penalised (and labelled as 'abusers') rather than supported and protected. The experience of the US and the effect of mandatory reporting laws is also cited as indicating the need for caution in considering any reform of the existing law (Salend *et al.*, 1984) and advising caution with regard to the possibility that specific elder-focused laws might infantilise older people.

Reform or *status quo*?

The first annual conference of the organisation Action on Elder Abuse in 1994 took as its theme 'Elder Abuse and the Law'. A number of useful presentations were made concerning the need for reform of the existing law (Johnston, 1995; Williams, J., 1995); many of the delegates to the conference indicated in workshop sessions that reform was considered to be necessary. Stevenson (1995a) argues for a reform of the existing law on the following grounds, notwithstanding the views outlined:

- that reform would not increase the rights and freedoms of older people;
- that existing legal powers are underutilised;
- that current definitions are so imprecise as to be almost meaningless;
- that reform without adequate resources will be ineffective.

Stevenson suggests that such issues need to be fully and properly debated. Furthermore, she advocates that the fundamental question of protection versus autonomy (returned to in Chapter 6) should be more fully addressed. In addition, there is a further, somewhat contentious, issue of how far practitioners may wish or be prepared to use the law to protect vulnerable older people.

It is postulated that Phillipson's views do not necessarily lead to a conclusion that legal reform is not required, merely that the issues should be properly considered and adequately dealt with prior to any decision about reform being taken. It is Stevenson's contention that if there comes a point at which existing legal powers fail to be used, in particular if this is the result of a general perception that the law relating to older people is ineffective, reform may well be necessary in order to restore some sense of equilibrium (Stevenson, 1995a).

In January 1996 the Conservative government in England indicated that the proposals by the English Law Commission for the Mental Incapacity Act would not be enacted in their current form and stated that there was a need for further and wider public consultation concerning the issues involved. No statement was made at that time about the status of the comparable report from the Scottish Law Commission. It would seem, however, that the government was not entirely convinced of the need for reform in this area of the law, even if many practitioners were certain.

General legal principles

Hoggett (1989) has produced a framework that she considers should be utilised when legal reform is contemplated with regard to older people. It could also be employed, perhaps in particular when considering situations of the law relating to actual or suspected abuse. Although this framework predated the implementation of the community care reforms, it is still of relevance to current concerns. The procedures should be as follows:

- practical;
- especially tailored to the needs of older people (in particular individuals in need);
- a 'one-stop procedure' in which all needs and matters can be dealt with at the same time rather than in a piecemeal way;
- where mental capacity is affected, the principle of substituted judgment should be paramount (see Penhale, 1991, for a further exposition of this principle);
- interventions should be premised on the principle of the 'least restrictive alternative';
- services should allow for the retention of as much dignity and freedom as possible.

McDonald has considered the principles that ought to underpin any legal intervention in cases of actual or suspected abuse. She has established a framework including Hoggett's one-stop procedure, the principle of least restrictive intervention and the principle of substituted judgment for those whose mental capacity is impaired. Four further suggestions for the framework are then added by McDonald (1993):

- The principle of self-determination should be paramount.
- Rights to independent advocates (including legal advice) should exist for individual older people.
- Services should be based on entitlement through need and grounded firmly on principles of antidiscriminatory practice.
- Social Services Departments should have duties and rights to intervene when an elder is 'at risk'. It is argued that this could be achieved via an extension of Section 47(1) National Health Service and Community Care Act 1990.

It is possible to take issue with several of the above points, although a very detailed examination is precluded here. Whilst not denying that the views of individuals should always be sought and given some priority, careful consideration should be given within such complex situations to the absolute primacy of the right to self-determination. There may be situations where an incapacitated individual is so impaired cognitively, so much at risk (perhaps even in a life-threatening situation) or perhaps so intimidated that the right to protection may outweigh the right to autonomy. It is Stevenson's contention that there might be some situations where the need to protect and remove the vulnerable person may well override any need to maintain the *status quo* (Stevenson, 1995a). What is necessary is as much clarity as possible about such situations to guide and assist those charged with making such decisions. Practitioners and policy-makers need to be clear about such issues and receive adequate and appropriate guidance and support concerning these matters. Agencies involved in establishing multiagency guidelines and procedures concerning abuse should endeavour to make very clear statements for the benefit of individual practitioners and their clients.

The decision to remove a person against his or her will is never taken lightly and is generally the cause of much anxiety and concern for practitioners, but neither is it an issue that can be totally avoided. Knowledge and understanding about when to involve colleagues from other disciplines to assess the degree of incapacity and impairment of decision-making, for example, is clearly essential within this process. It is also necessary to acknowledge that there may be occasions arising when there is a need to take action to protect a vulnerable individual and that it might well be preferable to act sooner rather than later in doing this. The limits to intervention and self-determination and expectations of workers, together with the support that staff can expect from their respective organisations, should be as explicit as possible.

Although McDonald was writing prior to publication of the Law Commission's proposals concerning public law protection, and thus without the benefit of hindsight, it is difficult too to see how an amendment to the NHS and Community Care Act 1990 surrounding a duty to investigate would provide sufficient statutory basis for Social Services Departments within what are undoubtedly difficult, complex and sensitive situations. A duty to investigate, without any power in terms of a possible follow-through to intervention, would surely risk the creation of another 'toothless tiger' such as is already considered by practitioners to exist within the guardianship provisions of the Mental Health Act 1983.[1]

In addition, a right of access to an independent advocate may be fairly meaningless in the context of a very limited provision in this country of such schemes for older people. Equally, independent financial advice that is not prohibitively costly in terms of its provision may be virtually non-existent and thus restricted only to those with sufficient means to afford it. Individuals may otherwise be offered little but be forced to accept what is on offer on the terms on which that offer is based. The concept of rights for large numbers of older people, in particular older women, many of whom live in poverty (Arber and Ginn, 1992), may thus be redundant within such situations, little more than a lofty ideal or a pipedream. Action to establish such rights in terms of reality is surely preferable in this context. As Hoggett indicates, it may be preferable to consider such aspects in terms of more achievable aims such as dignity and privacy, rather than a notion of absolute freedom of choice, which is not attainable (Hoggett, 1989).

In a further consideration of the possible need for legal reform with particular regard to elder abuse, Slater attempts to widen the scope of the debate by reframing the issues in terms of fundamental principles of social policy (Slater, 1993). In a useful, if brief, article, he attempts to look at the appropriate boundaries between the duties of the state to protect the most vulnerable of its members and the rights and liberties of citizenship. Whilst it is arguable that older people are accorded full citizenship (and indeed there is much evidence to indicate that they are not; see Townsend, 1981, Walker, 1981 and Phillipson, 1982, for cogent examples), Slater suggests that to view elder abuse as a distinct and separate category and to pursue legislation specific to older people would be to risk the reinforcement of insidious and oppressive stereotypes of older people which already exist, particularly with regard to the use of 'age' in legislation (see also Scrutton, 1990). An approach to reform in terms of adults would, Slater argues, avoid such connotations and counteract any tendency to view vulnerability as a consequence purely of age.

Slater also notes the broadening of the definition of elder abuse in recent years to include at times a focus on the rights of older people and notions such as the violation of rights (Eastman, 1989). This has led, it is argued, to an extension of the scope for legal reform in a broad sense to be premised on a rather outmoded and paternalistic concern with the welfare of the individual. Again, comparisons with the provisions contained within the Mental Health Act 1983 (in particular those pertaining to guardianship), should warn against extending the law in this way for older people. In Slater's view, it would surely be preferable to concentrate on a narrower definition of abuse, such as is evident within the focus of the Children Act 1989, on 'significant harm', despite tendencies to equate comparisons between older people and children as indicative of the infantilisation of elders. Indeed, it is of interest to note that in the consultation documents produced by the Law Commission (especially Paper 130), the framework suggested is indeed that of vulnerable adults (albeit that one of the possible indicators of vulnerability was considered to be age), with an extension of the concept of 'significant harm' to adults. As noted earlier, however, there may be difficulties in applying this concept to adults since it is largely premised on notions of normal expectations of the physical development of children. The alternative view is that the notion could be adapted by a shift in focus to the consideration of development across the lifespan, and perhaps specifically in adulthood and later life.

Autonomy versus protection

The final parameter that Slater begins to explore concerns the issue already touched on above, that of the question of what constitutes the acceptable limits of intervention: the balance between autonomy and protection. Whilst it might be desirable to obtain access to an individual in order to adequately assess and offer appropriate assistance by a statutory power comparable to Section 115 of the Mental Health Act 1983, as advocated by Age Concern (1986) and BASW (1990), difficulties may well arise if the older person wishes to refuse that assistance and to continue to be exposed to actual or potential abuse or risk of abuse. A refusal to allow access under Section 115 (which does not allow for forcible entry) may create further difficulty; an application under Section 135 to a magistrate for a warrant to effect entry and removal of a person may not be necessary or desirable.

As stated above, there may be situations when, due to severe incapacity affecting decision-making coupled with grave or very serious risk, the need to protect may override the right to self-determination. In addition, there might be occasions on which an individual, although competent to take decisions, is so fearful or intimidated by the abusive situation that he or she cannot conceive of the situation being different or of life free from abuse and therefore state a wish for the position to remain unaltered. Allowing and assisting the individual to change such a decision over a period of a time may be necessary although at times difficult for practitioners to deal with. Such situations need to be clearly spelt out for practitioners and appropriate support and guidance provided for them to continue to be effective within such difficult areas of work.

Meanwhile it is necessary to state that the Law Commission's deliberations on this matter reached a point where there were clear statements that older people as adults had the right to refuse intervention if mentally capable of making an informed decision, and that an 'eccentric decision' that did not accord with the views of professionals could not be taken as evidence of incapacity (on the grounds of disagreement alone). Furthermore, access to an individual could only be legally effected if that individual could be assumed not to object to the access. If an individual was known to be likely to object to enforced access (and was not severely mentally impaired), even the right to access could not be legally effected. This is clearly an attempt to safeguard the rights of individuals but might be difficult to enforce: a power of entry to a premises (if necessary by force) to investigate a situation might be legitimately assumed to be objected to by the majority of the population, especially with regard to currently held notions about the right to privacy and lack of interference from the state! In such complicated situations, practitioners may need assistance to accept the limits to their interventions and the potential risks involved to individuals (and the rights of individuals to take those risks).

Such ethical and moral dimensions permeate much work with older people (indeed most vulnerable adults), particularly within the field of social care and community care (assisting people to remain living at home). The perception within social work of that work which is not connected to child and family care with its statutory basis as being stress-free and a soft option (Stevenson and Parsloe, 1978) clearly does not take account of the complex and at times difficult ethical considerations concerning the assessment and management of risk and abuse that arise in everyday situations. Stevenson and Parsloe (1993), in a recent work on empowerment and community care, usefully explore some of the exigencies of these philosophical minefields. These will be considered further in the chapter on interventions in situations of elder abuse (Chapter 6).

Summary and conclusions

This chapter has considered the legal dimensions of elder abuse and some of the associated issues concerning rights, autonomy and protection. An overview of the main legal provisions that currently exist and which might be used in situations of abuse has been provided, together with the case both for and against legal reform in this area and a summary of some of the specific recommendations for change produced by the English Law Commission. The general legal principles that many people consider should be adopted in work with older people have been outlined to give the reader an appreciation of the issues involved. It has been apparent through this chapter that there are difficulties in working in this area. These will be returned to in the following chapter on interventions, with its clear focus on what might be done about situations of abuse.

6

Dimensions of Interventions

Introduction

The last two chapters have developed a focus on differing aspects of the professional knowledge base that are useful for practitioners to be familiar with in their work in this area. The focus of this next chapter is to consider what is known about the differing strategies and techniques of intervention used within situations of abuse. Some of the difficulties associated with intervening in situations of elder abuse will be explored, including, where possible, remedies to these difficulties. Following a discussion concerning the comparative absence of strategies for intervention, there is a shift to examine the existence of different attitudinal sets towards interventions between professionals. Differing models of intervention will also be outlined for the reader.

A framework of the general and, perhaps of more relevance, the specific principles that should guide intervention, even at the level of initial assessment and investigation, will be suggested, as will the possible limits to intervention within abusive situations. The types of dilemma commonly faced by practitioners within these complex and difficult situations will be examined; suggestions for possible resolutions of these will be postulated. Possible future developments in terms of interventions will be suggested by way of conclusion.

Intervention problems

Protection or self-determination?

There may be difficulties surrounding intervention and treatment of elder abuse and neglect, including the appropriate treatment of those who abuse. One of the most crucial difficulties for professionals to deal with is that of achieving and maintaining a balance between the protection of the individual and the right to self-determination. Older people have the right in most cases to be autonomous. It is quite possible for professionals to work hard with individuals to determine both their needs and appropriate treatment options and for older people to then refuse such offers.

Older people can and do say no to offers of assistance. Generally, they have the right to do so, and they frequently exercise that right. This right to self-determination should remain one of the central tenets of practice: it should not be ignored. Fulmer and O'Malley (1987) found that older people preferred independence over safety and protection whenever possible. Risk-taking was seen very much as part of daily life, and the ability to take risks was seen as an essential and necessary part of growing older. It can be a critical and determining factor in the preservation of independence and autonomy for a significant number of individuals as they age.

Such findings should not be surprising, particularly when considering our own lives and wishes of how we should be allowed to age and how we may react when older. As Monk perceptively suggested, old age is the one stage of life which it is impossible to truly appreciate and be fully cognisant of since it is not possible to know how it feels to grow older ahead of time. For this reason, it may be difficult for practitioners to be truly empathetic in this field (Monk, 1986).

Additionally, there is some evidence that people are aware of the difficulties which social work practitioners in particular face in these areas. From discussions with a range of service users' and carers' organisations, it was apparent that people knew that social workers had to act to protect individuals on occasion and expected them to do so (Harding and Beresford, 1996). A view was expressed, however, that social workers were sometimes overprotective and did not allow for risk-taking, which was considered to be disempowering for the service user/client. The opposite view, that at times social workers did not act soon enough to protect children in particular and took too many risks, was also taken by certain groups (Harding and Beresford, 1996).

Practitioners have to learn to feel comfortable with such facts; they must be acknowledged and worked with as and when they occur. In particular, it is necessary to be mindful of our own likely needs, wishes and expectations on growing older. The maxim 'do as you would be done by' is clearly of central import in this regard; respect for the person is evidently a critical factor in such work. It is also necessary to retain the ability to empathise with individuals, irrespective of who or what they are, and to share the individual's pain and distress on occasion. If practitioners reach a point of being unable to feel another's pain, contain it appropriately and assist the person to deal with it, it is time critically to re-examine, with assistance, the nature of their own practice and its effect on those individuals whom they ostensibly are in business to work with and assist.

Protective responsibility

In addition, practitioners need to know when it is necessary for them to act in terms of 'protective responsibility' towards an older person or a carer (Stevenson and Parsloe, 1993). There are a number of distinct aspects to this concept: the practitioner must act, on occasion, in a way that is protective towards and of the older person, but this must be in a considered and responsible fashion that assists and empowers people rather than demeaning and disempowering them through the creation of unnecessary states of dependency on the part of the individual. Moreover, the concept confers on practitioners an imperative (if not an absolute duty in legal terms) to be protectively responsible towards their clientele. The fact that older people do refuse offers of help and express their rights to be self-determining should not mean, however, that offers of assistance are not made principally on the basis that they will be rejected by the older person anyway and are therefore not worth making. Practitioners need to be aware of the need to act protectively on occasion and may need guidance in recognising when such circumstances prevail. They must also approach such situations, once identified, in a wholly professional and responsible manner.

Whilst it is not uncommon for older people to refuse offers of assistance, unless individuals are mentally incompetent, in a legal sense, their decisions about such offers to intervene and assist should generally be taken as final at that particular time. The option of renewing the contact, should their decision be reversed (in the case of a refusal of assistance), should, however, be clearly established with the individual if at all possible. It can be very difficult, if not impossible, for an individual at the time of the initial contact with a health or welfare professional to be able to assimilate and take action on the advice and information given, especially if distressed. Therefore it is essential for people to be given a clear and unequivocal message that, even if unable to pursue actions at that particular time, they can return in future and gain appropriate levels of support and further assistance as necessary.

It is possible that older people may refuse offers of assistance and intervention initially but then return at some later point for further information and/or help. It is crucial therefore that sufficient ground-work is achieved during that first contact to enable the older person to come back in future (see also the section on education and prevention). Such work might include information about the following:

- abusive situations (in general terms);
- what systems for assistance and support might be available;
- identification of support networks for the person that might be utilised in future (safe people, safe houses and safety routes);
- how to summon help and assistance.

The amount of information given to the older person is likely to be dependent, of course, on the ability of an individual to assimilate a lot of information at one time. In such instances, caution needs to be exercised by the practitioner in terms of the amount of information that is given during the initial contact. One of the most crucial pieces of information, however, is likely to be how to renew contact with the practitioner in future when (if) this is considered by the older person to be necessary in order to obtain adequate assistance in resolving the position.

Within such situations, there is, of course, a strong educational component: it is very important for older people to have an under-standing that abusive situations rarely consist of single acts but that the abuse generally becomes more severe and more frequent over time (Breckman and Adelman, 1988). It is also clearly desirable for older people to appreciate that many other people (including what is likely to be a significant number of older people) experience abusive situa-tions and that the majority of them survive, some of them (although as yet an unknown proportion) managing to alter their situations so that they can live free from abuse or neglect. Additionally, the older person should gain enough knowledge and understanding of their particular situation to be able to obtain sufficient support and assistance if neces-sary in future.

A lack of intervention strategies

A further reason why there are particular difficulties in terms of techniques of intervention is that there are at present very few options in terms of proven and established intervention strategies within much of this area of work. For example, work with victims is as yet an underdeveloped area in this country and one which evidently requires quite urgent attention. It seems that, in general terms, intervention in the UK tends to revolve around the provision of practical services to support care-giving and reduce stress to alleviate situations (although as Homer and Gilleard, 1990, discovered, this may not resolve the problems). There is a need for coordinated effort concerning the provision of services, including perhaps most critically accommodation, for abusers, so that realistic options and alternatives do begin to develop. Work with those who abuse also requires attention in future, as indicated by Wolf (1993).

The provision of residential care for the abused person, thankfully, no longer seems to be the first choice of practitioners, as evidenced by the small-scale study of social workers in two London boroughs who claimed to be attempting primarily to maintain the abused older person at home wherever possible (DOH/SSI, 1992). This is in contrast to an earlier study by Eastman in which residential care was the favoured service option and outcome for the majority of his small sample (Eastman, 1984a). In particular, hospital social workers appeared to favour admission to residential care for their clients as a desired outcome: what is not clear from the survey, however, is whether hospital social workers saw the provision of residential care as distinctly preferable to the person remaining in hospital for lengthy periods of time. It is also possible that some of the situations with which hospital social workers deal will concern more severe instances of abuse and complexity, so the possibility of an older person returning home may be reduced. As yet, however, there is no research evidence concerning this aspect.

With the implementation of the NHS and Community Care Act, (DOH, 1990) in recent years, there has been a definite shift towards the maintenance of people in their own environments and communities for as long as possible. This can, of course, create its own set of difficulties, not least of which is the question of whether appropriate and satisfactory levels of care can be provided to people at home. As some more sceptical commentators have implied, community care could mean care *by* the community rather than care *in* the community (emphasis added). Additionally, given resource constraints on local authorities, it may be highly unlikely that people with severe impairments or the majority of elders with significant care needs will be enabled to remain at home as the costs of appropriate service provision will be too prohibitive.

The obverse situation to the older person remaining in his or her own home, however, is that in some situations it may be wholly desirable and indeed necessary to separate the individuals concerned, where the distinctions between abuser and abused may be too complex and where a splitting of the individuals concerned, whether this be by the victim or the abuser leaving the situation, although painful, may be what is required. It may be necessary that this separation should be effected relatively early in the process so that reparation work may begin as soon as possible, to the eventual benefit of all (Stevenson, O., personal communication, 1994). There is obviously a need to determine which of the parties should leave the situation. As we have seen in Chapter 3, removal of an older person to an institution is not necessarily a safeguard against further abuse taking place. Implementation of provisions of the (proposed) Family Law Act 1996, when enacted, to extend non-molestation orders to people other than spouses and cohabitees may well assist in this regard (see Chapter 5 for further detail).

Since the implementation of the community care reforms in April 1993, it is possible that preventative work is now considered (by virtue of sheer volumes of referrals, assessments and care plans that have to be processed) to be fairly low priority. From work in America, and additionally from what we have learned from child protection work, it seems unlikely that ideal, 'once and for all' solutions to elder abuse will in any case be found. It is also unlikely that adequate amounts of money will necessarily be forthcoming to improve or even develop techniques of intervention. Resources are finite and are unlikely to increase sufficiently to absolutely guarantee continual top-quality services.

Professional perceptions and attitudes

Yet a further area of potential difficulty with regard to intervention surrounds the fact that, due to the lack of strategies which have so far been proved to be effective, practitioners may feel inadequate to deal with abusive situations. They may then either avoid such situations or collude in them, possibly partly in order to protect themselves. Alternatively, they may set very low-level objectives for the outcomes of intervention. It is also possible that in their desire to do something (anything) to help, intervention which is not actually what is required to resolve the situation may be provided. The perceptions and attitudes of professionals are important in connection with this.

The practitioner may provide an inappropriate resource in order to feel absolved of any possible feelings of guilt about not being able to resolve the situation or to feel that they have at least provided a solution, even if this is not ideal. Indeed, the practitioner may feel in some respects satisfied with having dealt with the situation and resolved the immediate and most pressing difficulty. This seems particularly likely to occur in situations involving patterns of abuse within families which are of a longstanding nature, where change may be most difficult to achieve or where the resistance to change may be strongest.

Other practitioners, who may not feel capable of dealing with abuse and violence but who want to do something to assist, may offer intervention that is not in fact appropriate and perhaps not even related to the cause of the abuse. An example of this would be to focus on caregiving (and providing support with the tasks involved) when the actual reason for the abuse is not (or may not be) due to stress from caregiving (Bookin and Dunkle, 1985; Homer and Gilleard, 1990). The intervention offered should be clearly linked to the possible cause of the abuse in order to try to both alleviate the situation and prevent it from recurring.

It can be difficult too for professionals to work effectively with both victims and abusers; people may show particular aptitude with one or other group and should to be able to develop skills in such areas. Attitudes and perceptions about 'victims' and 'perpetrators' are likely to be important in connection with this. Professionals may find work in certain areas difficult, or impossible, due to their own feelings, attitudes and cultural biases. They may require assistance (through professional supervision) in recognising and dealing with such tendencies which could, if not resolved, hinder both the relationship with individuals and the work undertaken with them. It is possible, of course, that a practitioner might decide not to work with a particular client (or client group); this decision may require some examination, but individual practitioners should not be made to work in an area with which they are uncomfortable as this will not be productive for either the client or the practitioner.

It is important, too, that practitioners do not become either overprotective or too paternalistic towards the victims of abuse. Respecting the older person's right to autonomy can be difficult but is essential. Phillipson (1992) proposes that policies and strategies to address elder abuse should develop within the context of empowerment and advocacy for those people 'leading marginal lives'. For Phillipson, the emphasis must concentrate on enabling and empowering people to live free from abuse and mistreatment (and neglect, where this occurs). The promotion of abilities for self-care in later life is also a key element within this process (Phillipson, 1992).

Within the spectrum of research on elder abuse, a number of studies concerning professional attitudes have been conducted in recent years. Most of these are American in origin and focus on the awareness by different groups of professionals about the problem. Despite methodological difficulties concerning size of samples and so forth, a number of commonalities can be drawn from the findings. It would appear that the professional perspective is likely to affect a number of areas:

- the amount of knowledge about abuse (nurses, social workers and clergy were more aware than other professionals, such as doctors and lawyers; managers had less knowledge than did practitioners: Eastman, 1984b);
- perception of the prevalence of abuse (nurses and social workers viewed elder abuse as being as common as child abuse; police considered elder abuse to be less prevalent);
- perception of the type of abuse (psychological abuse, including neglect was perceived by social workers as occurring more often than physical abuse: Eastman, 1984b; police, lawyers and mental health workers perceived verbal abuse as more common than physical abuse; community psychiatric nurses reported more physical abuse whereas social services staff reported more financial abuse: Wilson, 1994; Marriott, 1995);
- which theory of causation was favoured (lawyers and social workers perceived stress and dependency as critical factors; nurses and the police favoured the life cycle of violence approach: Eastman, 1984a);
- approaches to intervention (social workers seek to change the situation or behaviour; police seek to detect and prevent crime; nurses attend to health needs: Quinn and Tomita, 1986).

Situational factors would also appear to be important in connection with this complex area of work. For example, the characteristics of the victim and the abuser, as perceived by the professional, are likely to affect the response of the professional. In one study by Phillips, which presented nurses with a series of vignettes, if the victim had a 'less desirable characteristic' or the abuser was perceived as frail or 'doing the best they could', the nurses were reluctant to recognise situations as abusive (Phillips, 1983b). Perceptions that the abuse was unintentional, that the victim was to blame for the abuse or that intervention would be difficult also had an effect in connection with this. In a follow-up study, the relationship between the professional and the abuser appeared to be of importance: if the relationship was described as 'good' and the abuser was considered to be cooperative, nurses were again reluctant to label a situation as abusive (Phillips and Rempusheski, 1986).

In situations in which the professional perceives the abuser as a 'victim' or concurs with a theory of causation postulating carer stress as largely instrumental in the aetiology of abuse, it is quite possible that situations will arise where the professional colludes with the abuser and the principal focus of the work will be with the abuser rather than the older person who has been abused. Whilst work with the abuser may be necessary, work with the abused individual is also essential to the process and attention must therefore be paid to the critical questions 'Who is the client?', 'Who represents whom?' and 'Is it possible for one worker to satisfactorily work with both parties?' A useful exploration of some of these factors has been produced by Biggs, using a series of triangles to denote the possible alliances that might occur between worker, victim and abuser within such situations (Biggs, 1994).

It is apparent that an increased awareness of elder abuse and factors concerned with its recognition increases the detection rate of abuse and abusive situations. An awareness of the existence of differing professional perspectives and attitudes about abuse is also needed, so that people do not operate on the assumption that their view will be shared by everyone else.

Additionally, an appreciation of the possible impact of such differences on working practices is needed, as is a recognition that particular situational factors will affect how different people will react within particular circumstances. Unresolved conflicts concerning roles and responsibilities between professionals have been suggested as one of the fundamental reasons for difficulties concerning identification of and intervention in situations of abuse (Phillips, 1989).

A shared awareness between different professionals of such differences and their potential impact is likely to reduce the amount of interprofessional conflict that may occur within situations. Such conflicts can, of course, arise within as well as between professions, especially when attitudes, perceptions and even definitions can vary on an individual basis (Bookin and Dunkle, 1989; Pritchard, 1992). Difficulties in inter- and intraprofessional communication, and the need to find ways to resolve these, are not new areas of work but are as pertinent in the protection of older people (and other vulnerable adults) as elsewhere. This is not an easy aspect of multiagency or joint working arrangements but is an essential part of the process of multidisciplinary work, and sufficient attention must therefore be paid to it. When working in complex, difficult and stressful situations, such as many concerned with elder abuse, it is crucial that these aspects are attended to on a regular basis.

A continuum of interventions

It is also necessary that professionals know what to do and what is expected of them when abuse is identified or suspected, and that such expectations are clearly set out and established for professionals.

Within some situations of abuse, it is possible that the degree of severity may not be fully appreciated by professionals for a number of reasons. Many professionals seem to consider their options for intervention as consisting of a continuum from least to most disruptive in terms of the effect on the parties involved (Phillips, 1989). Those strategies which are felt to cause the most disruption tend to be reserved for use very much as a last resort (DOH/SSI, 1992).

In any case, one of the principles which professionals seem to operate within situations is that the intervention used should be the 'least restrictive option' necessary, as is also employed within much work in the area of mental health. A reluctance to employ such strategies 'unless absolutely necessary' may mean that a situation that requires intensive intervention in order to protect the individual adequately might be inaccurately perceived by the professional involved. This could then result in a mismatch between the severity of the abusive situation and the methods employed to deal with it (Phillips, 1989).

Bennett and Kingston have identified interventions as ranging on a continuum from 'aggressive' to 'passive' (Bennett and Kingston, 1993). Those interventions which might be termed 'aggressive' include full use of the legal system, including the Mental Health Act 1983 and the provisions contained within that Act for use of the Court of Protection. Usage of the police and wider court processes would also form part of the remit of that end of the continuum. Those interventions which might be considered to be passive include such techniques as advocacy and empowerment.

A professional trained in therapy and treatment, rather than in the use of control (and the benign use of power in a beneficial sense), may prefer to use more passive approaches to intervention, thus possibly involving less risk and danger for the individuals concerned (including the professional!). It is quite conceivable, however, that the use of such passive techniques might in some respects miss the point and not actually deal with the principal difficulty, particularly if the focus required is from the more aggressive end of the spectrum.

What may be necessary is the establishment of some balance and equilibrium between the two approaches and some assistance for the practitioner in determining what intervention to use at which point. It is clearly necessary that the practitioner should be trained in assessing the risks contained within situations and, furthermore, what interventions may be required both to adequately manage and contain those risks and to provide effective solutions to the situations (please note that what is not being referred to here is any notion of 'cure' being possible for the majority of situations).

Professionals have to (or be assisted to) find ways of combatting tendencies to avoid or minimise difficult and painful situations, hard though this may be. The interventions used should if at all possible meet the needs of all the individuals involved in such situations. It would seem that for some individuals what may be required is an intervention that may otherwise be construed as maximally disruptive. For example, in some situations it may be necessary to separate the individuals involved, perhaps by admission to residential or nursing home care for the 'victim'.

Indeed, the 'staircase model', as proposed by Breckman and Adelman (1988), advocates that the goal of intervention is for the individual to attain an abuse-free existence, by separation from the abuser if this proves necessary. It may be highly preferable to effect this separation early in the intervention process in order that the pain of separation might be worked through and adjustments made to life apart as soon as possible (Stevenson, O., personal communication, 1994). Clearly, further work is necessary to assist practitioners to satisfactorily identify those situations where it would indeed be preferable to act and effect such changes sooner rather than later.

Care or control?

Generally speaking, health and social care professionals are trained in therapeutic rather than corrective methods. Most health and social care professionals are trained to 'cure' and not to punish, so that interventions that invoke the use of legal systems to provide redress or punish abusers tend not to be used unless it is pretty much unavoidable. In any case, it would appear likely that legal interventions will only really be considered by professionals if there is incontrovertible evidence that abuse has occurred, which is, of course, rarely the case (Phillips *et al.*, 1986, cited in Phillips, 1989).

There may be a reluctance to use what legal remedies exist due to connotations about punishment and blame. It is necessary to acknowledge that intervention may be a rather uneasy mixture of both legal and therapeutic strategies. Rosenfeld and Newberger (1977) have identified what they describe as two competing philosophies of care by which professionals operate, which link to Bennett and Kingston's continuum as described above. The two models described by Rosenfeld and Newberger are the compassion model and the correctional model.

The compassion model views abusive situations from a standpoint that is free from blame and does not seek punishment or any form of redress for the wrongs of abusers. Indeed, abusers may be viewed as victims who have been pushed to the extremes of acting abusively due to the intolerable circumstances in which they find themselves (for example extreme stress or other external factors such as unemployment or severe isolation). The clear danger in adopting such an approach *vis-à-vis* interventions is that the victim of the abuse may be left in a vulnerable and risky situation due to the failure of the practitioner to act in a manner that would serve adequately to protect the interests of the individual who is, or has been, the subject of the abuse.

Additionally, there is a danger of a degree of collusion (either overt or covert) by the professional with the abuser and a risk of absolving the perpetrator of their responsibility within the situation by a tendency to view the abuser wholly as a victim of circumstance. There are clearly situations in which the distinction between abuser and abused is finely drawn and in which abusers may be victims of the circumstances in which they find themselves and of structural concomitants (Phillipson and Biggs, 1995). However, it is equally important to acknowledge that abusers may not be innocent or injured parties in all circumstances. At times, it is clearly apparent that some abusers are motivated by factors such as greed, desire for revenge or even malevolence.

By contrast, the control model is premised on clearly defined notions of punishment, restitution and control generally by practitioners. Such an approach would see the legal process being used regularly and fully, and would additionally see the separation of abuser and abused as virtually inevitable. In this country, which does not have a strong framework of protective legislation regarding the protection of older people, such a scenario is perhaps a little unlikely at present. However, there remains a distinct danger that a failed use of the legal process would be the result of many situations that again might well result in increased levels of risk for the individual. The concomitant failure to use what might be considered to be 'softer' methods of intervention might well be detrimental to all involved in the face of inappropriate usage of other, less satisfactory interventions.

As previously noted, older people and their carers have the right to refuse intervention in most situations; it is rarely possible to force people to accept intervention. Use of the legal system may therefore appear to be a rather extreme option, particularly if the evidence about the abuse is inconclusive. Practitioners may not wish to risk making a situation worse for older people and their families, and, of course, there may be a real risk of doing just that quite unwittingly. An example of this could be where the separation of individuals deprives the older person of a crucial element of their support network, which is not then adequately replaced by the provision of a substitute form of care.

In the absence of clearly defined and effective interventions to assist those who abuse, it may well be the situation that the older person, and indeed the abuser too, may lose out through the destruction of the relationship, which may include positive as well as negative elements. There may be a danger, too, that the practitioner colludes with the abuser and allows the abusive situation to continue through overidentification with the abuser as victim, or fear (of violence from the abuser) or a failure to fully appreciate the nature of the situation and the risks involved for the individuals.

Such issues need to be addressed by professionals if they are to be successful in work in these difficult situations. Despite recent indications on the part of the Law Commission that reform of the law may be necessary (Law Commission, 1993a, 1995), any forthcoming legislative change is likely to take some years to place on the statute books. Practitioners should at present assist individuals to use the existing law properly (both wisely and well) in order to attain redress and some measure of protection.

Again, however, the emphasis is very much centred on enabling the individual and facilitating the use of such systems. This requires practitioners to be both knowledgeable about the law and the processes involved, and to be in a position where they can assist individuals to use the law as appropriate (and if they desire). Practitioners should also be comfortable with the concepts of empowerment and enabling of clients and of partnership with clients. The practitioner as enabler and facilitator is of critical importance in this area.

Principles of intervention

The principles outlined by Stevenson (1995a) as being essential within any consideration about possible intervention are as follows:

- Use of the law (especially concerning removal of the person) should be seen very much as a 'last resort'.
- Interprofessional working within such situations is crucial.
- Procedures should be developed carefully and sensitively (using knowledge learnt from the best and worst practice in child protection).
- Professional knowledge and skills should be fully utilised and based on a clear set of values.
- The position of carers requires diplomacy and sensitivity.
- Integration with all processes of assessment and care management is of paramount concern.

Additionally, the applicability of interventive strategies should be firmly based on a set of principles. Kingston and Phillipson (1994) have suggested that these should consist of the following:

- Practitioners should have an awareness of the possibility of abuse occurring (but in the context of no absolute criteria to aid recognition and no solutions that are likely to be acceptable to all).
- Shared decision-making is essential to provide adequate support for workers.
- Policies should encompass advocacy and the empowerment of elders.
- Ultimately, the goal of intervention is to assist elders to live free from mistreatment.

Whilst these are wholly laudable aims, it is easy to conflate issues arising between the first two principles, which seem to be anchored firmly in the needs of practitioners working in these difficult and sensitive areas and the more holistic needs of individual older people who are or who may be abused, which are reflected in the latter two principles. What is necessary is a separation of the two distinctive strands in the pursuit of clarity in this complex area.

A more productive approach in terms of trying to establish effective principles of intervention may be to view such principles as occurring on several different levels. An attempt should then be made to try to separate out the more global aims, objectives and principles that intervention should strive to attain from those secondary level principles designed, rather, to assist practitioners in the difficult tasks they undertake.

For example, one of the global aims is the general principle that strategies of intervention should seek to empower older people so that they do not, ultimately, require the support or assistance of social and health care agencies for protection and can live lives free from abuse and neglect. A further global aim can be derived from the work of Breckman and Adelman, with their clearly stated goal of not making the situation worse for the individuals involved (Breckman and Adelman, 1988). The general ethical principles that should underpin care work are autonomy, justice and beneficence (doing no harm; the promotion of welfare). Additionally, other principles, such as the preservation of freedom and safety for individuals, as far as possible, appear to be consistent with this more general framework. Practitioners are likely to need assistance, however, in applying these meaningfully and appropriately within their practice.

The global principles of intervention that Quinn and Tomita (1986) enunciated consist of the following aims: protection of adults should try to achieve (simultaneously but in the following order of importance) freedom, safety, least disruption of lifestyle and the least restrictive care alternative.

Intervention should be based, then, on those global principles that include a clear commitment to the ideal that whatever strategy is used should generally be the least restrictive of freedom and lifestyle for the individuals involved. Clough (1995) suggested that the two major principles in this type of work should be maximum autonomy and minimum intervention. There is also likely to be a need, however, for recognition that, in certain very serious situations, it may not be possible to totally uphold these principles. Practitioners are likely to need guidance on what might constitute such occasions. What will also be necessary in such situations are honesty, openness and integrity for all involved as to why this is the case.

An American lawyer, Regan, has suggested that the societal reaction to elder abuse appears to fluctuate between abandonment and indifference and protection. More crucially, perhaps, he stated:

> To what extent should an individual be free to live in whatever lifestyle suits him or her – to go to hell in a basket as the saying goes – so long as no harm is done to others? Or does a compassionate society have a duty to rescue its victims, those suffering from self-inflicted wounds or the cruelty of others, regardless of whether or not they want such help? (Regan, 1985, p. 5, cited in Collingridge, 1993).

Clearly, the tension here is that between societal paternalism and individual autonomy. There is a need to reach a point of equilibrium in order to resolve this tension. This requires a confrontation with the difficult and perhaps fundamental questions surrounding the legal and ethical bases on which intervention is based. Perhaps nowhere are these difficult questions more evident than with those people whom Collingridge has referred to as 'refusers and self-neglectors' (Collingridge, 1993).

There are differing, sometimes conflicting principles which operate within such complex areas:

- duty to care;
- informed consent;
- choice and autonomy (the right to refuse assistance);
- the least restrictive alternative to be used;
- individual right to privacy;
- self-determination.

Practitioners have to deal with many of these conflicting principles within their work, often on a daily basis and for many of their clients. There may be some internal conflict for the individual worker between a professional commitment to client self-determination and autonomy, including a right to privacy and to refuse assistance or protection, and a moral imperative, perhaps on a more personal basis, to protect individuals and to provide assistance for those who cannot provide such care for themselves.

For some practitioners, this latter aspect may extend to views concerning the provision of care and assistance to those people who choose not to care for themselves (self-neglectors). This is clearly a difficult area, perhaps the most difficult area ethically for practitioners to deal with. This may be, in particular, because there may often be no legal basis for the provision of assistance against an individual's expressed wishes. It is the role of the practitioner's supervisor or manager to help the practitioner to acknowledge and work through such conflicts and, above all, to support the practitioner facing such dilemmas as these.

Further principles suggested by Quinn and Tomita (1986) surround the area of conflicting principles. These would come within the framework of secondary level principles, those which assist practitioners in their work. Where there are competing or conflicting principles or interests between individuals, Quinn and Tomita suggest the following:

• Freedom is more important than safety.
• Adult clients should make all decisions unless they have either delegated this responsibility to another person voluntarily or a legal order exists which grants such responsibility to another.
• The practitioner should serve the adult client in situations where there may be conflict of interest between the client and the carer.

In the second statement, a legal order may be voluntarily effected, as in Powers of Attorney, or legally effected, as in the provisions that exist under the Mental Health Act 1983 concerning the Court of Protection.

Additionally, within the secondary tier of principles would come such frameworks as the following set of questions for practitioners to employ when considering intervention in general terms (Ogg, 1995):

• Where did the concerns originate from?
• What has triggered the concern now?
• What expectation does the referrer have of action?
• Is the older person/carer/vulnerable person aware of the concern and referral?
• Is an advocate needed or does the older person lack capacity?
• What is the likely outcome if help is refused?
• What safeguards (for example monitoring) might assist?

Such questions, with their clear focus on practice, may assist practitioners and their manager to consider some of the key issues involved at the initial planning stages of assessment and then later at the point of intervention and ongoing management, monitoring and review of the situation. Whilst not all the answers may be evident at this stage, such clarity may provide pointers for the practitioner to raise or test out in their future contacts with older people and their carers.

The values to which practitioners should adhere and which should inform practice would also fall within the remit of these second-level principles. These comprise dignity, privacy, choice, fulfilment, rights and independence (although originally developed elsewhere; DOH/SSI, 1989). To these can also be added the further subset of participation, autonomy, knowledge and equality as guiding the principles of work in this area (DOH/SSI, 1993).

The issue of shared decision-making is an interesting one as it impinges on both the professional and the personal arena for individuals and may thus appear at the more global primary level and also the secondary level. To expand in an attempt to elucidate: at the global level, it should be evident that in order to empower older people, decisions must be shared and individuals should (unless there are strong contraindications) be involved in determining their own outcomes, which clearly requires full participation of the individual in the whole process of assessment and intervention, including any strategy/network meetings or case conferences which are held concerning the person.

At the secondary level, however, shared decision-making refers specifically to the professional arena. From experiences gained in the child protection sphere, it is apparent that much-needed support for individual practitioners can be obtained by certain key decisions being taken jointly or within a forum designed specifically to assist in such situations. This then supports practitioners and helps them to feel that the responsibility for the work and decision-making in this situation is a shared one and does not rest solely with the individual. Additionally, as discussed elsewhere, it may lessen the tendency towards post-decisional regret occurring (see Penhale, 1993c, for a further exposition of this).

It may also reduce the possibility for practitioners to get caught up in collusive relationships with abusers in order to avoid any violence being directed at them. Such collusion may result from intimidation (of the practitioner by the abuser) on either an overt or a covert level. Fear of violence can also arise from the practitioner's own instinctive and basic needs for self-preservation (Stevenson, O., personal communication, 1996).

Furthermore, secondary principles of clear benefit to the practitioner require that intervention be firmly grounded in assessment, care planning, monitoring and evaluation (Manthorpe, 1993b; DOH/SSI, 1993). This needs to be within a well-defined framework developed by management, including the development of policies and procedures, support for practitioners, training, developing resources and commitment to interagency collaboration. As stated previously, elder abuse needs to be viewed as very much part of assessment and care management processes rather than as a separate entity; assessment should be needs led but clearly focused on abuse when necessary.

In addition, strategies for intervention need to be informed by and based on a clear understanding (from timely, adequate and appropriate assessment) of the characteristics of the situation, of the abuser and of the victim (including their status, both mental and physical) and also of the type of abuse which has occurred. The type of intervention chosen for particular situations should be determined by such considerations as these; what we do not have yet is adequate evidence on the comparative effectiveness of different strategies for certain situations (Penhale, 1992).

Adequate protection for the person who has been abused, to return to the notion of the proper exercise of the protective responsibility of professionals, may be a necessary and in some instances essential element of the process. It should, however, never be the sole aim: to assist individuals to find their own solutions, which they are comfortable with, and to reach a point at which, if desired, they can live without abuse should usually be the main goal. The principle of empowering the individual is critical in this type of work (Bennett and Kingston, 1993); individuals may require support and assistance, but they must also be empowered to find their own solutions to their problems.

Assessment processes

Prior to the implementation of any specific interventive strategy, there needs to be a full and comprehensive assessment of individuals and their circumstances. As suggested earlier, this should be needs led and holistic but abuse focused. The assessment process should, however, be adapted to the individual, and should avoid any stereotypical assumptions on the part of the assessor (Stevenson, 1989). Given the apparent reluctance of many older people to discuss abuse or abusive situations and the varied reasons for this (see Penhale, 1993c, for further examination of this), it may be necessary to spend time and care in establishing the assessment process, particularly in the initial stages. Engaging the individual who is reluctant may require much time, effort and skill on the part of the practitioner.

Assessment processes are likely to vary between practitioners and should in any case in ideal circumstances encompass a multidisciplinary approach (DOH/SSI, 1993). Ideally, as with child protection, skilled and qualified practitioners should undertake the most complex and difficult work. The assessment will need to focus on the following areas:

- the abuse (or abusive situation) including antecedents, consequences and likely future patterns;
- the individual's methods of dealing with the situation (including any ineffective coping strategies);
- degrees of disability, the nature of any dependency (of abuser and abused person) and risk factors, including stressors, both internal and external to the situation;
- family history, social context of the family and dynamics of family relationships within the situation, including information on the balance of power and of communication systems and interactions;
- the views, beliefs and attitudes of key players within the situation as to the nature of the situation and likely outcomes;
- consideration of the needs of all parties within the situation. It may not be appropriate or necessary to offer an abuser a separate assessment in every situation, but this aspect will require careful consideration; in any case an assessment of their distinctive needs will require integration into the overall assessment process.

A number of assessment protocols are now becoming available for use in this country, although these have largely been developed in the US (Quinn and Tomita, 1986; Breckman and Adelman, 1988). In addition, there is increasing information on how to ask difficult questions in a sensitive and appropriate manner (see for example Breckman and Adelman, 1988). Training courses for individuals are increasingly beginning to focus on such areas for practitioners to assist with the development of appropriate skills for assessment and intervention. These have developed from the first wave of education and training courses, which tended to focus on raising awareness of the nature of the problem.

Guidance from the SSI for England and Wales concerning the implementation of the community care reforms implored practitioners to adopt an approach of assessing the needs (in particular the social care needs) of individuals rather than assessing needs for service provision and for specific services (DOH/SSI, 1991a, b). The SSI document *No Longer Afraid,* referred to elsewhere, provides a clear statement that the protection of vulnerable older people should not be viewed or treated in isolation from the totality of the processes of assessment and care management (DOH/SSI, 1993, 1995a).

Assessment of the particular abusive situations in which individuals find themselves may need to be needs led but *abuse focused* (emphasis added). This seems to be a critical distinction for the proper assessment of abusive situations, risk and vulnerability. It is evident that there is likely to be a need for full and proper consideration of the abusive situation and how to effect lasting change, if possible, within that particular setting and environment. Any care plan that is developed as a result of the assessment process will of necessity reflect this and should include a focus on the needs of the individual for protection, if any exist, in addition to details of the plan to manage the situation appropriately.

Although some may see even the notion of protection as potentially paternalistic and disempowering, it is essential to note that there are some individuals who are vulnerable and in need of protective services and who are unable or unlikely to attain these without assistance. It is in connection with this type of situation that Stevenson and Parsloe's (1993) concept of 'protective responsibility', mentioned above, is crucial.

Additionally, there are other individuals who will require assistance to become empowered enough to find and enact their own solutions to their specific difficulties. A focus on the particular needs of the individual for protection within the assessment process and subsequent care planning stage should not preclude or prevent the empowerment of the individual. This would rather ensure that the focus is properly centred on the individuals, the abusive situation (or allegation) and the factors and circumstances that contribute to the situation. The totality of needs of those involved, including needs for protection and assistance, and how best to meet these would also form an essential part of the process. The care plan should also include details on the management of risk and vulnerability and how this is to be achieved to the benefit of all involved. What will also need to be considered adequately within such a framework is a full assessment and appropriate management of risk factors and risky situations.

As Homer and Gilleard found in their research sample, however, certain situations, in particular those involving longstanding relationship difficulties between the parties, appeared to be very resistant to change (Homer and Gilleard, 1990). In addition, such situations may not be affected by the mere provision of services and may not be conducive to the type of strategy designed to salvage the relationship. There may also be some inherent tensions arising from this slight shift in the emphasis of the focus to specific needs for protection by the individual as a principal part of an holistic assessment of need.

Intervention strategies

From the work that has been done in this field so far, it is becoming clear is that there is a need for a range of different techniques and strategies of intervention. Different types of intervention are likely to be necessary for different types of abuse; those who are abused and those who commit the abuse are likely to have differing needs and yet are perhaps equally in need of assistance (sometimes one more than another), from well-developed and coordinated practical services to more intensive therapeutic methods, from education and counselling about the intrinsic costs of caring to the provision of 'safe houses' (akin to refuges, but for older people) or alternative accommodation for those who abuse (see also Cabness, 1989, for a further exposition of this aspect). Access to services on an emergency basis may be required; strategies to provide assistance for abusers need to be developed (McCreadie, 1991; Riley, 1993, cited in DOH/SSI, 1993).

The development of specific forms of assistance and intervention for those who abuse may be necessary and is already underway in some areas (in particular within the field of domestic violence more generally), for example training in the use of stress reduction and anger management techniques and provision of assistance geared to those who abuse drugs and alcohol; training in care-giving might also be necessary for individuals who are caught in a cycle of abusive behaviour beyond the realms of their own self-control.

Empowerment of those who abuse might equally be a strategy to be adopted in certain situations to enable the individual to separate from a dominant, now elderly parent, for example, or to enable a partner to leave an abusive situation. Assistance via the provision of housing for the individual in their own right might be a critical part of this process. And, of course, the provision of some practical services may be of assistance to both the victim and the abuser in certain situations, even though practitioners need to be cautious of the tendency to provide services in order to feel that they are doing something to help the situation. It is also likely that careful and continuous monitoring of situations and services will be necessary in order to ensure that the needs of all the individuals involved are being met in the most appropriate ways (DOH/SSI, 1993).

Exchange theories of abuse, as promulgated by Gelles (1983), tend to suggest that interactions between individuals, even abusive interactions, are based on the social exchange value (and 'pay-off') that is derived from the situation. The aim of interventive strategies within such a framework is therefore to alter the values of the exchange system so that the interaction is no longer as profitable in terms of its intrinsic value to the key players and to provide other more valuable exchanges for individuals who perceive themselves to be at a disadvantage in terms of the social exchange involved. A perception by the individual of powerlessness and disadvantage *vis-à-vis* the situation, even if not wholly accurate and realistic from an objective standpoint, may need to be altered if the abuse is to cease; obviously, there may be a number of ways to achieve this aim. If the perception exists for individuals, it is this, the reality for them, which has to be acknowledged and worked with if successful outcomes are to be achieved.

The provision of practical services to alleviate stressful situations may assist in altering the dynamic of situations so that the exchange is no longer as 'profitable' to the abuser. Additionally, the introduction into the situation of other parties (for example those providing the services) will also alter the dynamic besides their value in terms of monitoring of the situation. However, the provision of more therapeutically oriented strategies, such as the provision of anger management skills or stress reduction techniques, might clearly also assist in achieving a shift in the balance of the interaction and of introducing a more positive interaction for the individuals involved in the situation.

Strategies for intervention need to encompass a wide range of different approaches; there may be differing but complementary strands involved. These are likely to include such aspects as advice, information, prevention, education, protection, support and empowerment. The difficulties of protecting yet empowering individuals should not be minimised. Additionally, specific interagency agreements may be necessary to secure the multiagency working that is seen as crucial in this area (DOH/SSI, 1993, 1995a).

The setting up of Adult Protection Committees (similar to Child Protection Committees) has already been advocated (ARC/NAPSAC, 1993). Whilst the guidance produced by the SSI in setting up policies and procedures provided a clear focus on elder abuse and neglect and the needs of vulnerable older people (DOH/SSI, 1993), a subsequent document produced as the outcome of two seminars for both Social Services and health participants acknowledged differing practices and indicated that the decision between a focus on older people and one on vulnerable adults was a local one that should rest on the particular needs and constraints of the agencies involved (DOH/SSI, 1995a). Where agencies had decided to focus more widely on the abuse of vulnerable adults, what was advocated was the development of specific procedures and guidance concerning the needs of particular service users. There are different groups of service users: older people and younger adults with learning difficulties, physical disabilities or mental health problems, all of whom might be subjected to abuse but be in need of radically different remedies and interventions (DOH/SSI, 1995a).

It is also necessary for careful and continuous monitoring of the number and type of cases reported, alongside monitoring of the service responses that take place (DOH/SSI, 1993). As well as training to provide much-needed knowledge about elder abuse in its many forms, there is a very real need for information about which strategies work. Training is also necessary concerning techniques of intervention, including guidance in how to ask difficult questions in a sensitive manner. Such knowledge and information needs to be disseminated as widely as possible. It is hoped that these further developments will take place speedily, alongside attention being paid to the wider goals of prevention of abusive situations and enabling and empowering individuals to live lives free from abuse and neglect. Empowerment of the individuals involved (both the abused person and in some respects the person who is abusive) may not be easily attained but is the essential objective.

Models of intervention

At present there are no well-tested UK models in terms of service delivery and responses to abuse. One of the challenges of the next few years is likely to be the development of alternative models of intervention and service delivery by the different agencies involved. The purpose of this section is to explore some of the possible responses that may develop and the possible advantages and disadvantages of pursuing particular models as opposed to others. What should be acknowledged from the outset is that some work is already beginning in this area, as will become apparent in due course. In addition to this, it will be necessary, once again, to examine evidence from America concerning developments in services there over the past decade.

Various commentators have begun to write about intervention in elder abuse from a UK perspective, although there is as yet very little information on what might constitute effective intervention in this context, let alone any research to substantiate the suggestions. This state was commented on by one of the present authors as long ago as 1992 (Penhale, 1992); unfortunately, we do not seem to be much further forward in this respect. Intervention strategies are still in the early stages of development in the UK, as are assessment techniques. As indicated earlier, intervention currently tends to focus on the provision of practical services to alleviate stressful situations. The main emphasis clearly surrounds maintaining people in the community wherever possible (DOH/SSI, 1992). What is becoming clear is that there is an urgent need for a range of different techniques and strategies in this field.

Some therapeutic interventions are already beginning to be employed by practitioners for situations involving relationship difficulties (see DOH/SSI, 1992, for a further exposition of this). There have also been suggestions that some family therapy techniques might be adapted and used with older people and their families and carers (Rathbone-McCuan *et al.*, 1983; Browne, 1989; Kingston and Reay, 1995) and these are beginning to be developed in the UK. This appears to be most evident within some multidisciplinary settings, where a focus on therapeutic involvement and the introduction of such techniques as stress reduction and anger management by psychologists is more apparent.

Much of the early writing merely seemed to list possible interventions in terms of lists of services that might be provided in order to alleviate abusive situations. For example, the guidance document produced by the SSI listed as potentially helpful the following types of intervention: flexible respite and home care services, carer groups, continence advice and laundry services, helplines, legal advice, financial advice, counselling services, refuges (for women) and residential care (DOH/SSI, 1993). Elsewhere in the same document is a suggestion that different types of abuse might merit differing responses in terms of service response, so, for example, abuse due to carer stress might warrant a different approach from abuse occurring within an 'abusive environment'. In the former, support and assistance would seem to be the order of the day, whilst in the latter, recourse to legal and police interventions, removal of the abuser or refuge placement for the older person are considered to be potentially of more use.

It would seem somewhat premature to the authors to totally categorise interventions in this way without a knowledge base informed by adequate and appropriate research and practice. At present, we just do not have sufficient evidence and knowledge on which firmly to base interventions with abused older people. In particular, it is not yet really possible to establish outcomes related to the perceptions of the particular individuals concerned (i.e. to ascertain what works for individuals within certain situations). Indeed, without additional research input, it will not be possible to be certain whether there are sufficient commonalities to enable firm statements to be made about usage of interventions. This would seem, however, to link to the notions derived from care management systems that care planning should be based on the needs of individuals (based on the appropriate assessment of need), and therefore individually tailored care arrangements should be arranged for people (DOH/SSI, 1991b).

The care plan encompassing the intervention strategy will need to be firmly anchored on the outcome of the assessment process and, as stated, should be tailored to the needs of the individual and where appropriate the family. The aim of the intervention, in both general and specific terms, for individuals needs to be established. For example, the overall general aim may be to enable and maintain change or to prevent further abuse within a situation; the specific case aim will be based on the particular situation and may, for instance, focus on the provision of resources such as day care to increase social contact for the individual and lessen the scope for abuse to occur.

Intervention strategies may be directed at the whole family, or individual members of the system (abuser or abused), either separately or together. Any action taken will depend on the views and wishes and needs of the individuals and should include where necessary consideration of the needs of those who are cognitively impaired, the degree of impairment and their decision-making capacity. There should also be as full a consideration of the risks involved and what might constitute adequate management of the risk(s) to the individual and others involved as necessary for the situation.

The US experience of intervention

Within the US, the main thrust of interventions appears to have focused on the development of Adult Protective Services Teams. These teams are mandated by legislation and have developed from the mandatory reporting requirement that exists in virtually every State of the US. These teams consist of specialist social workers, whose brief extends to cover all vulnerable adults but whose work generally consists of work with older people, in particular those who self-neglect. Indeed, somewhere around 50 per cent of the work of Adult Protective Services Teams consists of work with individuals (mainly older people) who self-neglect (Tatara, 1990).

More recently, the wider concept of human services teams has been developing in the US. These teams are multidisciplinary but do not necessarily exist as discrete entities. Rather, they are networks of individuals working in a particular geographical locality (State or County) who meet regularly to discuss issues and even cases of common concern. It is possible that the majority of situations of elder abuse require input from a number of different professionals; specialist teams that encompass a multidisciplinary focus would therefore be potentially beneficial in this regard. Service delivery stemming from intervention strategies range from education (about caring, illness, stress, etc.) to screening processes (for example the cost of caring for individuals; Kosberg and Cairl, 1986), to practical services to alleviate situations, to therapeutic interventions to try and resolve problematic relationships.

Model projects: the US experience

It is apparent that in America some attention has recently been paid to the development of so-called 'model projects' of service delivery to establish and promote best practice in elder abuse. This has been achieved through the establishment of research projects with evaluation of the outcomes. The dissemination of the findings of such projects is potentially instructive for the UK, particularly in terms of possible future developments. For example, four distinctive projects were established, monitored and evaluated in the early 1990s in different areas of the country (Wolf and Pillemer, 1993). These were:

- a multidisciplinary team (San Francisco) that met monthly to make assessments and review arrangements in multiagency, multiproblem elder abuse cases;
- a volunteer advocacy scheme (Wisconsin), which provided emotional support, linkage to direct services and advocacy in terms of both interpersonal and wider systems approaches;
- a victim support group (New York) for elders who had been abused by a member of their family;
- a specific training module for APS work developed at a school of social work (in Hawaii), including a specialised student training unit in an APS team.

All four projects were set up in large urban areas with an established base of clients and were well supported by local Adult Protective Services Teams and other local human services agencies dealing with elder abuse. Interagency cooperation was seen as vital and, although difficult, proved possible to maintain; all projects were located within a larger 'host' agency that allowed for some ready-made status and credibility for the projects as they were established.

All of the schemes were evaluated for their effectiveness. One of the aspects of note is that two of the projects were more directly involved with older people, whilst the other two concentrated on systems. The development of a student training unit as part of the APS team, and the establishment of a multidisciplinary team, appear in some respects more system and service oriented than client oriented (abused or abuser), and it is noticeable that the report of the project does not mention whether evaluation of the scheme by the clients formed part of the evaluation. The development of these projects appears to have been framed, to an extent, on the establishment and subsequent provision of the service and the value to the members of the team/unit rather than the client group served.

In contrast, both the victim support scheme and the volunteer advocacy scheme appear to be more firmly linked to the client group, that of abused older people. The evaluation of both these schemes appears to have incorporated the views of the older people who reported some benefits derived from the schemes in terms of emotional support and in some instances more practical forms of help. The victim support scheme in particular was reported by the members of the support group as having been more beneficial 'than any individual counselling they ever had' (Wolf, 1993, p. 16). Members of the group stated that they felt more in control of their situations and more aware of their options. It was also reported that even when the abusive situations had not ceased, the severity and frequency of the abuse had decreased.

All the projects were evaluated as being relatively cost effective and low cost to run, requiring only a part-time (but qualified) member of staff to coordinate the service, flexible and adaptable to different settings and organisations. Information and assistance on project development was also available and perceived as invaluable in the maintenace of the projects. Permanent funding for the projects to allow for full establishment and continuation of the programmes proved problematic, however, and the volunteer advocate scheme did not secure funding, thus ceasing to exist. It seems ironic that a scheme that appears to have been the most empowering for elders should be the scheme that did not continue. It is difficult to know, however, whether this related purely to financial and funding arrangement difficulties at that particular location.

Models of intervention: UK style

With regard to this country, a number of suggestions have been proffered concerning interventions within elder abuse. It is timely to consider a few of these, albeit briefly. It is necessary to acknowledge firstly, however, that an amount of work has been undertaken concerning the establishment of policies and procedures with regard to elder abuse (and, additionally, adult abuse that encompasses elder abuse).

Policies and procedures

One of the initial stages in terms of responding to elder abuse has been a focus on the formulation of policy responses to the problem and the development of associated operational procedures to guide practice. Indeed, the SSI in their guidance document made clear their expectations that Local Authority Social Services Departments would develop procedures concerning elder abuse and that these would be multiagency in remit and scope (DOH/SSI, 1993).There have in recent years been a number of surveys of both health and social care agencies to determine the levels of policy and procedural development (Kingston, 1990; Hildrew, 1991; Penhale, 1993a, b; Action on Elder Abuse, 1995b).

One of the difficulties is that all the surveys tend to have considered slightly different things, so that it is difficult to generalise from the work done. For example, the survey reported by Hildrew focused on determining which Social Services Departments in England and Wales had policies or procedures on elder abuse (Hildrew, 1991), whilst the survey by Kingston considered the policy and procedural responses of Health Authorities to elder abuse (Kingston, 1990). Penhale's survey was of all Social Services and Social Work Departments (and Health and Social Services Boards in Northern Ireland) in the UK in connection with elder abuse and abuse of vulnerable adults (Penhale, 1993a, b). The survey conducted by Action on Elder Abuse considered the policy responses of both Social Services Departments and Health Authorities/Commissions and relevant Health Trusts towards elder abuse and adult abuse, but only in in England and Wales (Action on Elder Abuse, 1995b).

The surveys have, however, highlighted a gradual increase in the number of policies and procedures that are being developed by agencies. There are more within Social Services agencies than within health, and substantially more health providers (i.e Trusts) have developed this type of response than have health purchasers (i.e. Authorities), who appear to see this as a responsibility of their provider units.

Many of the policies and procedures that have and are being developed are stated to be multiagency in approach, but there is some question over the reliability of such claims (Action on Elder Abuse, 1995b). Some policies and procedures do appear to be multiagency and have been jointly developed; others seem to have been developed by one agency (usually the Social Services Department) and adopted by several other agencies on a local basis (Action on Elder Abuse, 1995b). Yet other agencies have adopted common, jointly owned statements of policy and principles concerning work in this area and have then developed their respective procedures in connection with their own working practices and conditions.

What is rather more problematic is the perception of such developments: it is how these policies and procedures are operationalised, put into practice and disseminated to staff which is perhaps of critical importance in this regard. For instance, the most perfectly written procedure will be useless if staff do not know of its existence, how it applies to them and how it should be operationalised. Additionally, if there is a perception within the organisation that all that is needed is a policy statement or a procedure, this may well present difficulties for staff and for the organisation. As one of the present authors has noted:

> It is evident that procedures in themselves are not a solution to the problem and that agencies must be mindful of the resource implications and the possible need for service development when drawing up guidelines for practice. It is clearly useless to have guidelines and procedures if these are too restrictive or prescriptive for the staff who have to use them. If this occurs, then staff will not 'own' the guidelines, will not be comfortable with them, and will avoid using them. Guidelines should always be a tool to improved practice rather than an inhibiting factor (Penhale, 1993c, pp. 107–8).

Policies and procedures are clearly but the first step in the formulation of responses to the problem. It is not usual for procedures to contain the finer detail of what strategies of intervention should be employed in any given situation. The aim is rather to make clear the expectations and responsibilities of staff in terms of responses in the initial stages of receiving a referral; assessing a situation ('investigation') and the subsequent process in connection with the outcome of the assessment and formulation of the care plan.

Details of procedures concerning strategy meetings, case conferences, 'at-risk registers' and reviews are also likely to be found, together with statements concerning equal opportunities and support for staff. Guidance documents may be developed to accompany the procedures. These aim to clarify certain areas for staff, for example concerning identification of the different types of abuse and degrees of severity of situations and to provide additional information and assistance for those using the procedure.

Types of intervention

The following section considers the works of several UK authors in the field concerning the development of different types of intervention that might be applied in this country.

Kingston and Reay (1995) consider three specific types of intervention available to practitioners. These are:

- use of the 'staircase model', as developed by Breckman and Adelman (1988);
- use of family therapy techniques with abused older people, as developed by Edinberg (1986) using a systems theory approach;
- use of anger management techniques for carers, as developed by Novaco (1976).

Time precludes a detailed examination of these strategies here; all of them originated in America and are largely rooted in psychological traditions. Some aspects may well be of potential application in the UK, however, and, as stated earlier, development of these types of intervention is occurring here. This work of Reay, in the adaptation of anger management and stress reduction techniques for older carers who have been involved in abuse, is likely to be of particular value in future (Reay, 1997). The reader is advised to pursue source material for further detail of these specific techniques and interventions.

Garrod highlights the options in terms of models available in which to apply procedures and urges authorities to try to obtain a 'best fit' of procedure and model to the circumstances of the organisation (Garrod,

1997). Considerations of acceptability (is the model acceptable to 'key players'?), feasibility (resource consequences of model and viability) and suitability (does the model fit the identified situations?) are necessary in connection with this.

The sorts of models suggested by Garrod include the development of:

- APS teams;
- specialist 'flying squad' teams to deal with and resolve emergency situations (including such situations as closures of residential homes due to abuse);
- specialists/consultants within teams (perhaps comparable to Approved Social Workers within mental health work or senior practitioners);
- multidisciplinary teams based on specific function or geographical location;
- co-working systems between teams;
- specific external agencies to respond to referrals (for example the equivalent of NSPCC, only for adults).

At present, there are no well-developed and coordinated responses framed in the above way, although it is apparent that there may be within teams specialising in work with older people specialists or consultants developing their own remits, expertise and key-working systems. In addition, the concept of the Human Services Team referred to earlier is beginning to be actively considered in a number of Local Authorities as a potential development (with limited resource implications, which of course makes it an attractive option compared with such initiatives as the establishment of dedicated, specialist APS teams). The concept of a group of specialists from different disciplines coming together on a regular basis in a coalition or network to discuss issues of common concern and seek resolution of difficult situations (or at least support and sustenance) is a potentially valuable option.

Although it may be unlikely that the creation of APS-equivalent teams will occur in the UK (in part because their development in America was due to the legislative response to elder abuse in terms of mandatory reporting), the development of specialist multidisciplinary teams to assess and respond to referrals may be a possibility. For at least one of the authors, the logical place to site such a team would be in a hospital with some specialist units and emphasis on the care of older people (perhaps in a community unit setting rather than in an acute unit hospital).

The alternative model would be to view such a development as being most naturally located within a community locality setting, following the lead of Community Learning Disability and Community Mental Health Teams, especially those specialising in older people with dementia. The multidisciplinary team would then be located in the area from which its clientele was drawn. The size of localities would need careful attention, however, as it would be necessary to know beforehand that there would be sufficient numbers of referrals to the team from a particular area in order to sustain its work (without the process becoming professionally driven to the extent of professionals being involved in detection of cases at an early pre-referral stage). At this comparatively early stage of awareness and recognition of the problem, it is probably unlikely that a specialist team of this sort could be supported due to the resource implications of setting up and establishing such a team.

The final set of models to be examined are of a slightly different nature and do not refer directly to models of service delivery, which is what we have seen developed in the above section. In a recent text on elder abuse, what is developed is rather more of a conceptual framework for practitioners of the types of intervention strategy (in a broad sense) that are available to practitioners (Biggs *et al.*, 1995). This is constructive as it allows for a location and identification of practice within a general schematic framework. Five distinct but complementary models are offered by the authors. Time precludes any detailed examination of these, and in any case the reader is directed to the source material for further explanation, but in brief, the models are as follows:

- *The social network model:* this model examines the informal, non-institutional networks that are available to the majority of older people and proposes that particular social networks may affect both the risk of abuse occurring and the responses that develop in terms of intervention.
- *The advocacy and mediation model:* this model examines the potential role of advocacy and mediation in intervention in elder abuse in both community and institutional settings to promote the rights of individuals, particularly in relation to self-determination and empowerment.
- *The domestic violence model:* this model examines the extent to which response to situations of domestic violence for younger adults might be appropriate and adapted to situations of elder abuse in order to offer the older person immediate protection

from abuse (by use of emergency refuges, crisis intervention services, etc.).

- *The social work intervention model:* this model examines the possibilities that exist for social and health care professionals in adapting existing practices in assessment and care management processes and counselling to develop and provide responses to situations of elder abuse.
- *The legal intervention model:* this model examines the extent to which changes to the existing legal framework might be necessary for and beneficial to older people who experience abuse.

A set of guiding principles for intervention is then provided by the authors for practitioners by way of conclusion (Biggs *et al.*, 1995).

Conclusion

This chapter has reviewed for the reader some of the main areas of difficulty that exist in intervening in and providing appropriate responses to situations of elder abuse, wherever they occur. The available models of intervention, in terms of both broad strategy (conceptual frameworks) and service delivery, have been outlined, and suggestions have been made concerning the principles that should guide intervention in these difficult and complex areas, and possible future developments in this field.

It is apparent that there is a range of possibilities open to practitioners in terms of the way forward in work with victims and perpetrators of elder abuse. What is crucial in this respect is to engage older people themselves in the emerging debates about elder abuse and intervention stategies and techniques. In particular, this needs to be in connection with such issues as antidiscriminatory practice, human rights and empowerment within the social context of a reduction in welfare provision, inadequate resources, rationing and ageism. Despite this rather bleak scenario, there is some evidence of a groundswell of support and interest building concerning the issue generally, which should lead to cautious optimism regarding future developments to combat elder abuse in its many and varied forms.

The final chapter moves away from the UK focus to look more fully at developments from an international perspective and to consider research initiatives and the research agenda.

7

International Developments and the Research Agenda

Introduction

The main emphasis of the book until this point has been to concentrate on developments in the UK, with some reference, where appropriate, to what is happening elsewhere in the world. The focus of this final chapter is to consider the international perspective and developments occurring beyond the UK as this has manifestly increased in the past 5 years. This is followed by a consideration of the research agenda and some of the difficulties encountered in researching elder abuse.

An understanding of developments is useful for practitioners in order to both enrich the knowledge base and point to some potential areas of development in the UK in future, building on lessons learned from elsewhere.

Until comparatively recently, the published material available concerning elder abuse has been predominantly from the USA. The research base founded there in the late 1970s has served as a focus for much of the thinking around the subject internationally. Whilst invaluable, the need for cultural diversification was always there, and the international knowledge base began to expand in the late 1980s. The UK led the way and continues to be currently one of the most creative sources of material. Exciting new work is now appearing across many continents, with Australia becoming a source of some of the most innovative new work.

This chapter aims to provide the reader with a selection of material now available outside the US concerning developments and research. It has the deliberate aim of including a spectrum of reported research projects, some sophisticated in their approach, others less so. The small amount of reference to the US is deliberate on the part of the authors, who specifically wished to provide a much-needed focus on other areas of the world rather than detail the American experience, with which readers are possibly already familiar. The chapter therefore does not attempt to provide even a glimpse of the large amount of earlier published material concerning the US that is now available. This is best accessed via conventional sources including the *Journal of Elder Abuse and Neglect: An International Journal*, a prime source of material for interested individuals, including researchers.

Europe

There is a growing awareness of the importance of social policy in the development of the 'new' Europe. Within all the EC member states, there is, for example, a clearly identifiable trend towards community care and the resulting concerns that financial constraints should not jeopardise this policy (Eurolink Age, 1989). Following a conference held in 1987 under the auspices of the Council of Europe, a Study Group on family violence against older people was established, comprising individuals from a variety of disciplines throughout Europe. The Study Group produced a report with some striking findings (Council of Europe, 1991). It concluded that all European countries involved in the study have problems in recognising and dealing with elder abuse within the family setting.

This is clearly reflected in the legal domain, where existing national laws and regulations concerning crimes against the person are rarely used to deal with violence against older people in the family. In France, for example, there is no legal recognition whatsoever of neglect or financial abuse perpetrated by a son or daughter against a parent, suggesting that such an act is inconceivable. In the majority of European countries, including Britain, there is also the principle that the victim should initiate criminal proceedings. As in the majority of cases of domestic violence, few elderly victims of violence are able to report their concerns to the police or any other agency. Only in the case of Norway has legislation been amended in 1988 to make it a legal duty for the police to start an investigation in cases of family violence without the consent of the victim or any other witness.

The Study Group also found it difficult to measure the extent of elder abuse in Europe as, at the time of their research, there were no comprehensive prevalence studies. Shortly afterwards, the British survey of elder abuse estimated prevalence to be between 2 and 5 per cent, depending on the type of abuse (Ogg and Bennett, 1992).

The difficulties of intervening in situations of elder abuse appear to be present in all European countries. In the domestic setting, this seems to reflect a general uncertainty over the role of the family in providing care for an elderly relative. Civil laws in France, Germany, Iceland and Luxembourg impose a caring responsibility on adult children of older people for economic, health and social matters. However, legal proceedings against those adult children who fail to provide for their older parents are rare, suggesting that such moral obligations, enshrined in law, are not wholly practicable in modern society.

Initiatives in Europe for the protection of older people are patchy. As in Britain, most of the attempts to address elder abuse fall within the existing health and social care provisions of each country, such as services to assist carers, respite care (day care and residential or nursing home care) and primary health care. There are, however, some interesting developments:

- Finland, for example, has refuges for the victims of family violence for all ages and sexes, and approximately 7 per cent of residents are older people.
- Victim-aid associations in some European countries appear to offer help in cases of elder abuse in the family, in addition to their more traditional role of counselling following crime by a stranger.
- Telephone helplines developed in the independent sector, such as victim support groups, have recently been promoted in France to provide a point of referral to those older people who are concerned about real or potential abuse or mistreatment.
- The creation of a government-funded Resource and Research Centre on family violence in Norway in 1995 has provided a possible focal point for European research on elder abuse.

The European Study Group made recommendations for the prevention of elder abuse to be tackled on three levels. Primary prevention of elder abuse entails the continuing struggle for the demarginalisation of older people and their empowerment. From this perspective, the abuse and mistreatment of older people is in part a consequence of their lack of rights. Secondary and tertiary prevention includes the recognition of elder abuse by social and health care workers as a social problem and includes the promotion of flexible services such as telephone helplines and the development of victim support organisations. There is also the possible development beyond counselling to advocacy schemes and greater interagency collaboration in tackling abusive situations.

The recognition of elder abuse in Europe is therefore taking place at a time when the shape of social and health care for vulnerable older people is uncertain. As to future coordinated responses at a primary level between European countries, much depends upon the evolution of the Social Charter (to which Britain is currently not a signatory) and the future of an integrated Europe as a whole.

UK

At present, the UK continues to expand in the range and depth of research and developments in elder abuse. The period up until 1992 is quite comprehensively covered elsewhere (see Bennett and Kingston, 1993, which contains a chapter detailing the difficulties of the research process and outlining key papers up until publication). In 1993, one edition of the US *Journal of Elder Abuse and Neglect* was devoted to UK work. It contains a critique of UK writing on the subject from 1975 to 1992 (McCreadie, 1994). This article includes reviews of what until that point were the most significant research papers published on elder abuse in the UK, including papers by Levin *et al.* (1989), Wilson (1991), Homer and Gilleard (1990) and Ogg and Bennett (1992).

The same UK edition contains an article by Pritchard introducing the concept of gang abuse, using findings and case studies from research carried out in Sheffield (Pritchard, 1993). This is followed by a preliminary article on research work into sexual abuse of older people in Britain (Holt, 1993). Other research-based articles include a short paper investigating the financial affairs of 25 older people with dementia living in the community (Rowe *et al.*, 1993). The same year also saw the publication of a book of selected readings on elder abuse (Decalmer and Glendenning, 1993, updated in 1997).

In June 1994 the UKCC launched its report *Professional Conduct – Occasional Report on Standards of Nursing in Nursing Homes* (UKCC, 1994), as mentioned in Chapter 1. This report highlighted the rising numbers of cases against nurses brought before its Professional Conduct Committee for abuse in nursing homes. The report called for government legislation to ensure that standards could be legally enforced and to ensure an effective Nursing Homes Inspectorate. The report attracted substantial political comment and media coverage.

Research into a group of carers using an inpatient respite care facility in South London did not show any particular increase in need or benefit amongst abusive couples compared with non-abusive carers and their dependants (Homer and Gilleard, 1994). Seventy-seven carers and the older people they cared for were interviewed separately. There was no observable improvement in the carers' emotional well-being as a whole, although the functional ability and social behaviour of some of the patients improved. Within this group of 77 carers, 35 admitted to verbal abuse, 11 to physical abuse and 8 to neglect of the person for whom they cared.

Both carers and patients were asked whether they would like more respite care or a different sort of respite care. Compared with the control group of carers who did not admit to abuse, there was no significant increase in the demand for respite care, nor was it seen as more valuable by the carers or patients who were in abusive relationships. This also held true for the patients who abused their carers.

Significant texts were also published in 1994, including books on the law and older people (Ashton, 1994) and the second edition of Mervyn Eastman's seminal text (Eastman, 1994).

Action on Elder Abuse, the UK organisation launched in 1993, continues to raise awareness about the topic and promote the key research areas. 1995 saw progress in many important areas. All health and Social Service Departments in the UK were surveyed to ascertain the policies and procedures in place (Action on Elder Abuse, 1995b). The organisation also undertook a consultation exercise to formulate a new definition of elder abuse (Action on Elder Abuse, 1995a). National conferences concerning elder abuse are now held on an annual basis.

The UK government (Department of Health) funded a 1-year pilot project to evaluate the use of telephone helpline services for victims, perpetrators and others concerned about elder abuse. Four pilot sites were chosen (inner city, urban and rural) and different local advertising techniques used. Telephone calls were routed to a central London number where trained volunteers received them. Callers requiring further input were directed to appropriate local Social Services and health service departments. The official launch occurred in September 1995.

Major publications in 1995 included a book of readings on family violence edited by Kingston and Penhale (1995b) and new editions of established UK elder abuse texts. Further exciting developments included the expansion of the US *Journal of Elder Abuse and Neglect* to international status, with an expanded editorial board including UK members. The volume of UK research work and other European projects indicated the need for a dedicated international journal. Channelling this work via an established reputable journal benefited all parties. The European work has a vehicle for publication whilst the US journal expands, diversifies and achieves greater prominence.

1996 saw the publication of *Elder Abuse: Update and Research* (McCreadie, 1996), the completely updated second edition of this groundbreaking publication and a must for all researchers in the field.

France

In common with most of Europe, the issue of elder abuse in France is a slowly emerging one. Regional work (for example Dr Huguenot in Grenoble) is gaining recognition, with local conferences being held and services set up. A research project based on a questionnaire format assessed the abuse of older people living at home (Jarde *et al.*, 1992). Fifty-five cases of elder abuse using the definition of elder mistreatment proposed in the *Journal of the American Medical Association* (1987) were reported via questionnaire format from two hospitals (n = 22) and the home nursing services of the Lille region (n = 33) in northern France.[1]

There were 43 male victims and 12 female victims with the same average age (80 years). The older people concerned had physical and mental disabilities with only three people living independently. Of the older people, 19 lived with their children whilst 36 lived in their own home with the adult children or another relative present. The average length of this arrangement was 1 year, most of the cases of maltreatment occurring after 10 months of living together. The overwhelming reason given for such joint living arrangements was financial. Residential needs (i.e. housing needs) were also given as reasons. A combination of both financial and housing needs was mentioned by some respondents.

In an analysis of the precipitating factors in the mistreatment, alcohol-related problems were cited in 19 cases. Perceptions by a carer of a behavioural problem of the elderly person was indicated in 23 cases. Financial difficulties resulted in abuse in 18 cases, the remainder of cases containing factors described as being 'interactional and temperamental'. Adult children were the aggressors in 31 cases; other relatives involved included grandchildren (n = 19), nephew or niece (n = 5) and children-in-law (n = 2). Twenty-six aggressors were themselves aged between 50 and 60 years. All forms of mistreatment were found to be present. Physical abuse, mental cruelty and 'neglect' appeared most frequently. Three older people who had been admitted to hospital because of their injuries requested legal action, but none pursued it.

In the discussion, the authors indicated that it has in France been a social and political expedient to maintain older people at home in recent years, but there has been a failure to anticipate the demographic factors and increasing levels of dependency of some older people. The authors also considered that the physical and mental impairment of the victims was a precipitating factor in the most severe forms of abuse which occurred. Adult children were considered to be least accepting of the caring role and as having the lowest threshold of tolerance compared with other family members.

The legal system in France has no specific laws relating to older people, provision being made via the Civil and Penal Codes. Two articles of the Civil Code impose an obligation on children to feed their parents and parents-in-law. One article in the Penal Code pertains to the assault of an older person (no relationship specified). The role for doctors appears to be somewhat uncertain, with strong imperatives to keep professional confidentiality and not to become involved in 'family affairs'. A plea is made by the authors that the French legal system should be changed to provide specific legislation for the protection of older people.

Greece

The phenomenon of elder abuse was first reported in Greece in 1991 (Spinellis and Pitsiou-Darrough, 1991). A more recent paper appeared in 1995 in the *Journal of Abuse and Neglect* (Pitsiou-Darrough and Spinellis, 1995). One of the most significant findings was the multiple forms of abuse suffered by older people in the research sample. In this study, more women were abused than men, and victims tended to be in the younger age range (under 70 years). Just over half the sample were abused by a relative. The most frequent form of abuse was psychological, specifically verbal abuse. The authors highlighted the need for further research to determine the social and economic costs of elder abuse.

Poland

A study reported in the *Journal of Abuse and Neglect* was carried out in the city of Bialystok in 1989 (Halicka, 1995). Six cohorts, elderly men and women aged 60, 70 and 80 years, were included in a survey by questionnaire. The majority of older people claimed that manners towards older people had deteriorated, and the younger cohort was concerned about being assaulted on leaving home. Physical aggression featured as the most frequent form of abuse experienced (for all forms of abuse in all settings), although rates of psychological abuse were higher within abusive families. Alcohol problems were present in the sample of elderly people (3.3 per cent admitting to alcohol addiction). As in other research in this field, alcohol abuse within the family also featured highly (5–14 per cent of perpetrators being reported as having alcohol addiction problems). Conflict within families was found more frequently than neglect (present in 16–35 per cent of cases as opposed to 5–13 per cent for neglect) but was reported as sporadic rather than frequent in occurrence. Material abuse was also found to be present (this was defined as being free use of property, robbery and inappropriate use of money) in 12 per cent of cases (Halicka, 1995).

Republic of Ireland

In 1990 O'Neill detailed three examples of abuse against elderly women admitted within a short period to a Dublin hospital and O'Loughlin wrote a social work article on the abuse of older people in the domestic setting, which provoked much media interest (O'Loughlin, 1990; O'Neill *et al.*, 1990). O'Loughlin has continued her research interest in this subject and as part of a post-qualifying course she compiled a report entitled *Awaiting Advocacy – Elder Abuse and Neglect in Ireland.* (O'Loughlin, 1991). Her latest research work has been completed as part of her MA thesis; this consisted of a detailed study of 14 cases of abuse. A detailed case recording tool, based on the evidence concerning risk factors, was devised as part of the research (O'Loughlin, 1995).[2] An overview report concerning Ireland published in 1995 concluded:

> it would be an exaggeration to state the problem of elder abuse has received official recognition in Ireland (Horkan, 1995, p. 135).

The report considered that elder abuse in Ireland was likely to achieve further recognition within the development of the Women's Movement and recognition of domestic violence in that country (Horkan, 1995).

Spain

In common with other European countries, awareness of the problem of elder abuse occurred in Spain following a survey published in 1990 (Marin *et al.*, 1990). This was followed by a Nursing Convention on Elder Abuse in Toledo in 1993. The National Ombudsman reported on elder abuse in 1994, and in the same year the Generalitat de Catalunya requested research into elder mistreatment, abuse and discrimination against older people (Dept de Benestar Social).

A symposium on elder abuse was held in Spain in May 1995 (Peralta and Riera, 1995). The conference confirmed that the work of earlier Spanish researchers (Marin *et al.*, 1990) was in line with results from the rest of Europe (8.6 per cent of people over 65 entering a tertiary centre[3] are considered to be the victims of elder abuse). The study by Peralta and Riera revealed cases of elder abuse in the family context as well as in nursing homes and hospitals (Peralta and Riera, 1995). The awareness of elder abuse as a phenomenon is, however, at a very rudimentary stage in Spain, with no specific information programmes or training for professionals. In addition, there are no specific judicial regulations relating to elder abuse. There are, however, penal codes (one on family abandonment and another concerning violence inside the family) that can be applied in certain situations. The second code relates to an 'incapacitated' older person, and the definition appears to be in some doubt.

Scandinavia

The research work being undertaken in the Scandinavian countries, in particular Norway and Sweden, together with the creation of the government-funded Resource and Research Centre on Family Violence in Norway, makes those countries one of the most influential areas within Europe working on elder abuse. The countries will be considered in turn.

Finland

The earliest reports of elder abuse in Finland date back to the mid-1980s following the experience of shelters to assist younger women who had been subject to domestic violence being contacted by older women in need of similar assistance (Heinanen, 1986). A more recent study to determine prevalence indicated a prevalence rate of 5 per cent of 1,086 older people experiencing elder abuse among people aged 65 years and over living in private dwellings in a semi-industrialised town in Finland (Kivelä *et al.*, 1992). The same research identified abuse related to poor health, depression, loneliness and a low level of life satisfaction amongst the victims. The perpetrators were mostly spouses, adult children or other close relatives with poor family relationships relating to the abuse.

Sweden

The Swedish context of elder abuse has been excellently summarised by Saveman (1994). Her report is based on data obtained between 1985 and 1991. Sweden is experiencing an ageing phenomenon on a par with other countries in Europe, with 18 per cent of the population aged over 65 years and an increase in the proportion of the population who are very old (80+ years). Although there are no legal responsibilities for children to take care of their parents, informal caring by the family remains the most common option should older people require assistance with their care.

The fundamental principle of the Swedish welfare system is that social services and health care for older people are a public responsibility. These systems provide a sophisticated matrix of care. Information on elder abuse is extensive. From an historical perspective, there are Swedish criminal statistics from the 17th century confirming that violence against a parent could be a capital offence – from 1750 to 1850 more than half of all cases of violence recorded concerned violence against parents. With the abolition of capital punishment and a cessation of recording of the abuse of parents, elder abuse became invisible. In 1985 research indicated that there were no modern Swedish criminal statistics available on parental abuse (Norberg and Axelsson, 1985).

More recent research has identified awareness of elder abuse and knowledge of actual cases (Tornstam, 1989). The abuse of older people with dementia by informal carers has also been recognised through research (Grafstrom *et al.*, 1992).

In one study aimed at determining patterns of abuse of older people living in their own homes in a county in Sweden, 12 per cent of district nurses reported 30 cases (Saveman *et al.*, 1993). Half of the victims had a disturbed mental state; the abuser was most commonly a relative. The most frequent form reported was psychological abuse. A further study described cases of elder abuse reported by home care service personnel across Sweden (Saveman and Norberg, 1993). The article also included information on the type of intervention offered and opinions on additional intervention strategies. Overall, 97 cases of abuse were reported (the majority of victims being female). Many of those abused were physically or psychologically disabled; the perpetrator was most commonly either the spouse or an adult child. Psychological abuse and financial exploitation were the most common forms of abuse encountered. In 75 per cent of cases, intervention was offered to assist the situation.

Norway
The research focus in Norway has concentrated on family conflict and has been led by an anthropologist Sigurd Johns and his research colleague Ida Hydle (Johns *et al.*, 1991). The prevalence figure that they obtained from a pilot project in a community of Oslo is 2.5 per cent (Johns, 1993). Johns considered that the insecurity and lack of knowledge and training among professionals was a major problem. In addition, the fact that elder abuse is a complex issue appeared to result in repeated consultations to agencies, frequently resulting in onward referral to another service. Victims and their family experience this as being turned away, with several using the expression, 'I met the wall' (Hydle and Johns, 1992). The Ministry of Social Affairs has provided firm support for the issue and some government funds for initiatives. Recent developments include the establishment of a National Resource Centre for Information and Studies on Violence.

The Netherlands

A report from one particular centre in the Netherlands[4] details cases of elder abuse in two Dutch centres (van Weeghel and Faber, 1995). 'Rivierenland' and 'Zuid-Kennermerland' were set up for a 2-year period in 1991 to raise awareness and increase insight into the phenomenon of elder abuse and to become centres for reporting cases.

The local situations are described within the report, and the authors detail how both centres were placed within existing care organisations (a district home nursing service in Rivierenland and a Victim Support Centre in Haarlem, Zuid-Kennermerland). This was seen as important to allow for maximum liaison and appropriate care input. In addition, two separate models of intervention utilised in the different centres were assessed. These models were to provide extra care (at the Rivierenland centre) or increased use of the police and judiciary (at Zuid-Kennermerland) .

Over the 2-year period of the study, the centres received 193 reports involving 197 suspected victims of abuse. An analysis of those cases revealed that 70 per cent of reporting came directly to the centre and 30 per cent were referred by care or service organisations. Of 51 older people who presented personally, only 1 met the centres' definition of elder abuse. Family members made 19 per cent of reports; GPs reported only 2 cases. Care providers (including district nurses, social workers and psychiatric nurses) were the most frequent reporters in Rivierenland (where the centre was based in the district home nursing service). By contrast, in Zuid-Kennermerland, 9 cases were reported via the police, victim support centres and telephone help services (the project was housed in a victim support centre).

A large majority of reports failed to comply with the researchers' criteria for the following reasons:

- failure to meet the definition;
- living outside the agreed areas of the study;
- living in an institution.

Of the remaining 54 reports, 67 per cent of victims experienced some form of psychological abuse, 44 per cent experienced some physical abuse, financial exploitation was experienced in 41 per cent of cases and neglect in 22 per cent of cases. Violation of civil rights (such as confinement) occurred in 9 per cent of cases. There were no reports of sexual abuse made to either project centre.

The majority of victims were older people over 75 years, the majority of whom were women (79 per cent). The victims lived with a partner in 22 per cent of cases, and in 39 per cent of cases the victim lived with a family member. The majority of abusers were men (in 80 per cent of cases). These were usually close relatives: a partner (in 19 per cent of cases), son, brother or cousin in 65 per cent of cases. The researchers also analysed the characteristics of the victims, the abusers and the living situations. Victim characteristics were reported as vulnerability due to illness, disability or age. Abuser characteristics included addiction, criminality and abnormal psychological states as well as financial or economic difficulties. The living situation encompassed emotional dependence (the nature of the relationship and loyalty), the social network (observability and significant others) and cultural values, including conceptualisation of older people and ageism.

The report also details how the centres publicised their work, the identified lack of support from GPs, the differences between the centres and how cases were handled, as well as making specific recommendations.[5]

Hong Kong

Older people are the fastest growing sector of the world's population and in one key area, the Far East, these trends have major policy implications. It has been estimated that by the year 2025 there will be more than one billion people in the world over the age of 60, and 70 per cent of these will be living in the developing countries (Anstee, 1989).

It is recognised that traditional Chinese culture reveres older people, emphasising an old age epitomised by respect and dignity (Koo, 1984). As long as there were children, becoming older was seen as a good period of life, with a secure status, formal deference and respect from others due to a perceived state of greater experience, wisdom and power within the family (Queen *et al.*, 1985). The basis for this tradition has been outlined by Baker, who reviewed the two major philosophical traditions that revere longevity, Confucianism and Taoism (Baker, 1979). Traditional Confucian teaching, according to Baker, specified that there are five human relationship pairs: ruler and master, father and son, elder brother and younger brother, husband and wife, elder and younger person. The relationships are arranged in order of priority, with the situation that when the relationships are harmonious the health of the entire social group is maintained – filial piety being the root of all virtue. In this way, Confucian doctrines taught young people that they were obligated to respect, care for and obey their elders (Cowgill, 1986). Failure to carry out these obligations resulted in criticism or being ostracised from society (Dawson, 1915). This backing from society, including the judicial system, helped to reinforce the concept of filial respect. Currently, however, there are rapid changes in both demographic structure and socioeconomic circumstances, placing increasing pressure on the traditional values, family life cycle and structure, as well as older people facing changes in the kinship roles and status (Chan, 1988).

With the above synopsis as a framework, Kwan has reported on two local studies concerning elder abuse (Kwan, 1991a). Hong Kong is described as a highly urbanised city of nearly six million people.

Approximately 12.8 per cent of the population are aged over 60, and this is projected to rise by 2001 to 14.1 per cent. The life expectancy is higher than in Europe, and Kwan predicted that a rising population of older people will result in a corresponding increase in demand for services of quality and variety for older people. The industrialisation and urbanisation of the society have had far-reaching repercussions for older people from a traditional culture who have experienced the transitions of marked social change.

Older people report more interpersonal problems within their families (Leung, 1991). Care-givers are reported as feeling obliged to look after older relatives because there are no alternatives (Leung, 1991). The most negative effect of these aspects appears to have been a rapid increase in suicide among older people (Kwan, 1988). Elder abuse is placed in context in Hong Kong as a possible outcome of the tension resulting from the traditional family structures being threatened by new family laws (Starak, 1988). One manifestation of this new culture is that in 5 years 205,000 Hong Kong residents have migrated to other countries, leaving behind some 30,000 older people with unfulfilled social service needs (Wu, 1991).

In the first study on elder abuse in the domestic setting in Hong Kong, 93 cases were identified by social and health service agency staff after agreeing specific indicators of four categories of abuse (physical abuse, abuse in daily living, financial abuse and psychological abuse). Factors associated with being a victim included being aged 70 years or older, female or widowed, having low educational attainment, financial dependency, poor self-care and poor health, and living in a larger household with poor family relationships (Chan, 1985). Within the same study, a territory-wide household opinion survey involving 637 households with older people was carried out. This survey estimated, using the abuse indicators selected for the survey, that a total of 136,000 older people (22.6 per cent of the older population) were at risk of being abused.

The second study interviewed 150 care-givers. The findings indicated that care-givers tended to be widowed, without formal education and in poor health. It also attempted to assess potentially abusive behaviours; within this schema, psychological abuse predominated over physical abuse. This potential behaviour appeared to be significantly and positively related to the stress level of informal support systems and the level of physical assistance provided by other care-givers (Leung, 1989). Despite some differences in definitions of elder abuse in Hong Kong and the US, the similarities were considered to be of more relevance, with the most vulnerable, impaired, dependent and isolated older people being subject to abuse (Kosberg and Kwan, 1989).

Since the emergence of reports of elder abuse in Hong Kong as an acknowledged problem, Kwan indicates that a number of intervention programs and services have been recommended (Chan, 1985; Leung, 1988; Kwan, 1991a). Current social welfare policy in Hong Kong appears to emphasise the importance of the family, particularly the role of adult sons and daughters (Social Welfare Department, 1991). Kwan suggests strongly that day centre provision, a greater range of social services generally and education and counselling services to support the efforts of the family would all assist in resolving and possibly preventing abuse from occurring (Kwan, 1991a).

Australasia

The research work being undertaken in the Australasian countries, together with the creation of the government-funded initiatives, makes those countries one of the most influential newer areas within the world working on elder abuse. The countries will be considered in turn.

Australia

In Australia, the recognition of the phenomenon of elder abuse has resulted in a number of published studies from New South Wales (Kurrle *et al.*, 1991, 1992), Victoria (Barron *et al.*, 1990) and South Australia (McCallum, 1990). In New South Wales (NSW), a Task Force on Abuse of Older People was established and released an influential report (Office on Ageing, 1993). Following this, the NSW Minister for Community Services appointed an Advisory Committee to implement the recommendations of the report, including the development of protocols and procedures for cases of abuse, education and research into the problem and the provision of flexible accommodation and community services. In April 1993 the Federal Minister for Community Services authorised the formation of a Working Party on the Protection of Older People as a means of the Commonwealth addressing the issue.

In a descriptive article containing case reports, Kurrle *et al.* state:

In Australia today, the medical profession has played a minor role in the detection and treatment of elder abuse (Kurrle *et al.*, 1992, p. 676).

The annual rate of referrals including elder abuse to a NSW Geriatric and Rehabilitation Service was 4.6 per cent (Kurrle *et al.*, 1992). It was concluded that increasing the levels of awareness and knowledge about the problem amongst medical practitioners was a priority to be dealt with.

In Adelaide, a small-scale study attempted to define the range of the problem as experienced by service workers in an urban setting (McCallum *et al.*, 1990). If the 4.6 per cent rate given above is adjusted for the population and those older people in institutions, this results in an overall occurrence rate of about 3 cases per 1,000 population (McCallum, 1993). In the same article, McCallum cites McDermott who proposed that the term 'elder abuse' be abandoned and that instead policies be formulated to deal with a range of typical situations, including neglect, domestic violence, conflict and financial exploitation. The stated objective was to have the different services responding to different situations (McDermott, 1993).

McCallum also introduced the terms 'maximisers' and 'minimisers' (McCallum, 1993). Maximisers are held to believe that the problem is larger than quoted prevalence rates because of the existence of hidden cases: the 'tip of the iceberg' phenomenon. Victims are ashamed and guilty and unable to disclose abuse perpetrated by family members. The victims may be fearful of retaliation or be unable to communicate (for example chronic confusion or stroke). There may also be fear of loss of independence or removal from their homes. Minimisers, whilst accepting that abuse exists, are considered to resist the 'social construction' of abuse. Instead the issue is viewed by minimisers as much exaggerated by the media.

Intervention strategies that have been developed in Australia include local models (Barron *et al.*, 1990) and a major input from the Carers Association. They have produced a Carer Support Kit that includes information and aids such as a stress reduction audiotape. The governments of individual states have also been developing policies and protocols for intervention. In NSW, the Commonwealth Government has established a Working Party on Protection of Older People, with a focus on human rights rather than prosecution or retribution.

Legal interventions in Australia appear to depend very much on the severity of the crime. The Crimes Act deals with the most severe cases, whilst the Family Law and other Acts can be utilised in less severe cases. In NSW (under the Crimes Act), an Apprehended Violence Order can be used to restrict or prohibit violent acts in order to ensure the safety of an individual.

A review article concerning developments in recognition of a response to the need for protection of older people in Australia indicated variations in the nature and progress of responses between the States and Territories (Kurrle, 1993b). This was thought to reflect the differing natures and structures of relevant services. The paper presents an overview of the ways in which the issues have been dealt with at research, community and government levels. It presents a standard report for each State and Territory summarising recent developments, approaches and outcomes (for NSW, Victoria, Queensland, South Australia, Western Australia, Tasmania, Northern Territory and the Australian Capital Territory). The article also shows how the Commonwealth Office for the Aged has drawn together some of the themes that are common across the country to produce a view of the national situation as it has been developing. The Working Party on Protection of Frail Older People in the Community set up by the Commonwealth should also consider measures that can be used to help protect the rights of older people resident in nursing homes and hostels.

Part 1 of this paper reported on clinical cases and interventions (Kurrle, 1993a). The interventions used and outcomes achieved were reviewed in a follow-up study of 54 cases of abuse identified in a 1-year study of a population using 'aged care services'. The article indicated that the provision of community services, counselling and respite care as intervention strategies was initially successful. In a few cases, the situation was resolved and the client remained at home. There were some cases of continuing abuse where the client chose to stay in the abusive situation and relationship. In the majority of cases, however, the long-term outcome was institutionalisation. This was reported as indicative of the need to separate victim and abuser to resolve the situation completely and also because of the high levels of disability and dependency in the population studied.

The results of this study allowed the author to construct two comparative charts. Table 7.1 indicates how different types of abuse arise for different reasons. Table 7.2 attempts to correlate interventions with the major causative factor in each case of abuse. This was held to suggest that knowledge of the major causative factors in a situation can assist in the decision surrounding the most appropriate and effective intervention strategies to use within the situation.

Table 7.1 Typology and causative factors

TYPES OF ABUSE BY CAUSE OF ABUSE

Type of abuse	Cause of abuse				
	Dependency of victim	Psycho-pathology of abuser	Family violence	Carer stress	Reverse abuse
Physical	Yes	Yes	Yes	Yes	Yes
Psychological	Yes	Yes	Yes	Maybe	Maybe
Financial	Yes	Maybe			
Neglect	Yes	Maybe	Maybe	Maybe	

Source: Kurrle, 1993. Reproduced by permission.

Table 7.2 Interventions and causative factors

USEFUL INTERVENTIONS BY CAUSE OF ABUSE

Intervention	Cause of abuse				
	Dependency of victim	Psycho-pathology of abuser	Family violence	Carer stress	Reverse abuse
Crisis care	Maybe	Yes	Maybe	Maybe	Maybe
Community care	Yes	Maybe		Yes	Maybe
Respite care	Yes	Maybe		Yes	Maybe
Counselling	Maybe	Yes	Yes	Yes	Maybe
Alternative accommodation	Yes	Yes	Maybe	Yes	Yes
Guardianship	Yes	Maybe			
Domestic violence legislation		Yes	Yes		Maybe

Source: Kurrle, 1993. Reproduced by permission.

The paper concludes with an outline of suggested principles that should guide intervention in cases of abuse (Farr, 1992):

1. Give full information to the victims of abuse and their representatives about services they can use and the various options available to them.
2. Allow full involvement of the victims of abuse in decisions about their care. Unless they are suffering from dementia or other psychiatric illness, individuals are able to make decisions for themselves. Many older people

value autonomy above personal safety and comfort, and they may prefer to live at home in an abusive situation rather than in an institution. This right to self-determination must be respected even though we may disagree with their decision.
3. Minimise disruption to the life circumstances, well-being and dignity of the victim.
4. Take a non-judgemental approach to the abusive situation as it is often a 'victim-victim' situation. In many cases, little is to be gained by identifying a guilty party and punishing them. Instead, the unmet needs of both victim and abuser need to be addressed if at all possible.

New Zealand

In 1989 a national workshop was held concerning elder abuse. This recommended the establishment of a sound research base and the development of a resource kit. Age Concern (New Zealand Inc.) developed the resource kit with funding from many sources, including the Lottery Aged Committee. A series of 24 seminars to launch the kit throughout the country were arranged by Age Concern nationally, and in each area a working group was formed. The kit was developed via a consultative approach involving over 100 agencies, groups and individuals to ensure that a multidisciplinary and multiagency perspective was obtained concerning the problem and possible solutions.

Pilot schemes have been established in Whangarei, Wellington, Christchurch and Invercargill, with a part-time paid coordinator appointed in each area. A National Elder Abuse and Neglect Advisory Group has been established whose remit is to provide a national perspective on the development of strategies for the care and protection of older people. This National Group also monitors the pilot schemes, lobbies for improved services, holds an overview concerning research in progress and monitors and reviews the Elder Abuse and Resource Kit (Age Concern, NZ Inc. *Elder Abuse Newsletter*, 1993).

Information is available on the prevalence of family violence in New Zealand (Good, 1992), although specific reference to elder abuse is omitted.

The resource kit is a manual made up of a series of modules (Age Concern New Zealand, 1992) including:

- Rights and Responsibilities of Older People and Carers;
- The Nature and Extent of Elder Abuse and Neglect;
- Cultural Differences;
- Caring and Stress;

- Signs of Elder Abuse and Neglect;
- Preventing Elder Abuse and Neglect (at home and in institutions);
- Developing Policies and Practice Procedures.

Each module uses a clear, referenced approach, incorporating the findings from international research work where necessary. A summary and action planning section end each module and are followed by references. Case studies are used to illustrate certain areas, including cultural differences. Sections for carers include identifying stress symptoms and how to reduce stress (including suggested further reading specifically for carers). Signs and symptoms of elder abuse and neglect are comprehensively covered, although caution is urged in order to avoid any tendency to jump to conclusions. Appendices include care policies and practice checklists, including an elder abuse and neglect assessment record. Guidance on possible responses to an initial request for assistance is also given. The document is clear and instructive and should serve as the template of an information and communication resource around the world.

Japan and Japanese-American elders

This section considers elders from Japan and the Japanese-American community within the US. Studies of elder mistreatment within the Japanese community in the US (first-generation elders) and in Japan itself has been extensively reviewed (Tomita, 1994). It is indicated that the first-generation Japanese immigrants to the US (the *Issei*) brought with them the cultural context of Japan's Meijo Era (1868–1912) of a patriarchal system committed to community but also to the success of the next (*Nisei*) generation. It is the third generation of Japanese Americans (the *Sansei*) who are currently in the care-giving role. These individuals are reported as completely integrated into US culture compared with the older relative they care for or visit, yet some distinctive and influential cultural values are thought to have been retained. As Tomita stated, 'some Asian Americans are viewed as having a two-layered personality, a deeper core personality associated with the traditional culture that is sometimes not obvious to others, and an outer layer, associated with the acculturation to American and Western influences' (Tomita, 1994, p. 40).

Japanese cultural values are extremely complex. Conflict within family situations can be generated over the breaking of very precise rules concerning perceived favour or indulgence. Competition for receipt of favour leads to either a feeling of being indulged and dependent (*amae*) or being useless and in the way (*jama*).

Relationships within a Japanese household develop dynamics around an inner circle (usually husband, wife and any in-laws). A façade of good relationships despite inner turmoil is expected to be upheld. This façade is seen as projecting an overt absence of any conflict. The results of this tendency is that 'the victim mentality seems to be an extremely common everyday underlying component of the Japanese mentality' (Doi, 1973, p. 130).

Japanese people are judged to have a strong sense of the collective, with a general feeling of mutual and interdependent obligations (Kondo, 1990). Such obligations are classified as social obligations (*giri*), personal indebtedness (*on*) and natural feelings or desires (*ninjo*) (Befu, 1971; Bachnik, 1992). Not unexpectedly, Japanese people living in America can experience difficulties reconciling these different feelings. On occasions, it would appear necessary for individuals to choose between obligations towards parents and obligations towards children.

There is a well-known Confucian practice of respect of elders which is commonly ascribed to the Japanese (and other Eastern cultures). Less well known is the tradition of *obasute* ('discarding of grandmother'), in which older people, predominantly female, were taken to the mountains and left to die (Donow, 1990). This is rationalised as preserving resources and hence ensuring the survival of the younger, fitter generations. The concept of contemporary situations akin to *obasute* such as the failure to provide the basic necessities of life, for example food and clothing, failure to obtain medical help for an older person when necessary, and failure to provide adequate warmth has been introduced by Tomita (1994).

The victim mentality mentioned earlier seems to include a sense of fatalism amongst older Japanese people. A term conveys this '*shikata ga nai*' (literally, 'it cannot be helped'). Tomita found that this term was used by elderly victims of abuse (Tomita, 1994). A somewhat unique aspect of the study of elder abuse amongst Japanese people concerns non-verbal communication (which appears to be culturally unique). Cultural and societal norms demand that verbal expressions of anger do not occur, and that conflict and loss of face must be avoided. Hence there is great emphasis on non-verbal communication or use of silence (Johnson, 1993). This is exemplified by an account of bullying by daughters-in-law of their mothers-in-law (*ijime*) in Japan (Kaneko and Yamada, 1990). The most commonly found forms of abuse were either that of no conversation followed by the making of rude remarks or that of ignoring the person. To older Japanese people, this treatment is perceived as a major form of abuse (Tomita, 1994). This type of situation has been interpreted as aggressive (Foner, 1984) and even as a form of death-hastening behaviour (Glascock and Feinman, 1981).

Disclosure of abuse is an emotionally fraught situation and is likely to be extremely difficult for older people in Western societies using conventional verbal communication processes. It is suggested that an elderly victim in Japan may never admit to abuse if verbal verification contravenes tradition (Tomita, 1994). This situation imposes difficult dilemmas for health and social care professionals involved in the management of cases of abuse and neglect. A high level of suspicion coupled with an expectation of a non-supportive family is encouraged on the part of professionals in order to counteract such difficulties (Tomita, 1994).

Use of a direct, client-centred approach may need to be replaced with group or family therapy. Such cultural differences have implications for the research goals and research process. As Tomita indicated:

> the diverse interpretation of silence makes it one of the greatest sources of misunderstanding, one of the most elusive of all communicative behaviours to measure, and most inaccessible to traditional forms of inquiry (Tomita, 1994, p. 49).

A research proposal focusing on the comfort and frequency of silence between family members has been outlined (Tomita, 1994). Measurement tools such as the Conflicts Tactics Scale (Straus, 1979), which measure physical and verbal aggression, would need to be modified to reflect such cultural differences and to consider the role of silence as mistreatment. It is noted that:

> the major task for researchers is to carefully review culturally-specific behaviours related to elders, and to decide whether and how to redefine some usually acceptable behaviours, when manifested in extreme forms, as elder mistreatment (Tomita, 1994, p. 50).

Israel

Elder abuse has recently been acknowledged as a social problem in Israel. However, definitions of elder abuse have proved difficult to establish in a country composed of a wide variety of cultures, each with its own customs, norms and values. Israeli researchers have indicated that definitional problems become critical when related to law (Neikrug and Ronen, 1993). Israeli Law (Penal Code, Amendment 26, 1989) does not incorporate operational definitions. This means that it is not easily possible to differentiate clearly between abuse and unpleasant but non-abusive family situations.

Research has attempted to discover how the Israeli general public views violence against older people (Neikrug and Ronen, 1993). Cluster samples covered a wide range of employment groupings with the sampling guaranteeing a range of ages, varied educational levels and social status. A total of 452 subjects were interviewed using a specially constructed questionnaire incorporating short vignettes.

Findings indicated a high level of awareness of elder abuse as a social phenomenon. Abuse and neglect of older people within institutions was rated as the most severe form of abuse; abuse occurring within a family setting was rated as less severe. Physical abuse was rated by the respondents as a more severe form of abuse than psychological abuse, neglect or abuse of rights or property. Analysis of the demographic variables showed that women and younger adults viewed elder abuse as more serious than did men and older subjects. It is of note that the neglect of an older person by a family member was rated as more severe than other forms of abuse. It was concluded that the results indicated that the public had a relative tolerance and acceptance of acts of violence within the family if they occurred within the context of the caring relationship (Neikrug and Ronen, 1993).

India

Reports on the abuse of older people in India appeared in the International Edition of the *Journal of Elder Abuse and Neglect*. Researchers Shah *et al.* give case accounts concerning most of the commonly accepted forms of elder abuse (Shah *et al.*, 1995). Of particular note was the indication that financial and psychological abuse appeared to be more prevalent in India than physical abuse. The reason for this was postulated by the authors to be due to some retention of the veneration of older people within Indian culture generally. Contemporary Indian society is, however, changing, and factors that have been identified elsewhere seem to lead to an increased vulnerability for many older Indian people. It would appear that there are as yet no specific policies, programmes or services in this area within India. The issue has, however, begun to receive attention, in particular from sections of the media.

South Africa

The first reports on the abuse of older people in South Africa to reach
Western countries also appeared in the International Edition of the
Journal of Elder Abuse and Neglect. The authors, Eckley and Vilakazi,
provided an overview of the situation in South Africa. The report indicated that the phenomenon of abuse in that country appeared little
different from elsewhere (Eckley and Vilakazi, 1995). It was postulated
by the authors of the report that it was the particular sociopolitical
perspective – that of apartheid – that was extraordinary in South Africa.
Some of the reported major effects of apartheid were the apparent
disintegration of family and community life and the development of
endemic violence.

The issue of institutional abuse in South Africa received some attention and was reported on in 1992 (Conradie and Charlton, 1992). Eckley
and Vilakazi noted that the South African Council for the Aged launched
the first declaration on the rights of the older person in 1993 and also
negotiated for the establishment of a government ombudsman for senior
citizens (Eckley and Vilakazi, 1995). Profiles of both victims and
abusers, the effects of abuse and the development of new prevention and
intervention strategies were reported (Eckley and Vilakazi, 1995).

Included within such strategies were the provision of guidelines to
families surrounding such issues as decision-making, social interaction,
independence, relationship-building and support, care-giver support
programmes and the development of preventative initiatives in order to
combat elder abuse in institutions. Within the community setting, the
creation of people empowerment programmes by community workers
was advocated as providing 'curative intervention' for individuals and
their families (Eckley and Vilakazi, 1995).

US

It is almost a cliché to acknowledge the debt to American researchers
for their pioneering work in the early years of the modern emergence of
elder abuse (see for example Block and Sinnott, 1979; Lau and
Kosberg, 1979; O'Malley *et al.*, 1979). To present the myriad of American research findings adequately is not possible here. The following is
therefore a brief résumé of the social construction of elder abuse as a
problem within the US, following the taxonomy devised by Blumer
(1971; see Chapter 1).

Legitimation of the issue appears to have occurred with the publication of a report to the United States House Select Committee on Aging in 1980 (US Congress House Select Committee, 1980). This was reinforced by the results of a Harris poll in November 1981, which indicated that 79 per cent of the general public believed elder abuse and neglect to be a serious problem and that 72 per cent believed it to be the responsibility of government to resolve (Harris, 1981). Mobilisation of action occurred with continued research into elder abuse and neglect, considering both the quantitative dimensions (the size of the problem) and qualitative dimensions (causes and intervention strategies). Agencies concerned with ageing also began to become involved in the debates at this time.

The formulation of an official plan was characterised by changes in the law and continued research into the social problem of elder abuse and neglect (Bennett and Kingston, 1993). By 1988, all 50 States had enacted legislation addressing elder abuse and neglect. Forty-three States were then operating State-wide reporting systems, while the remaining States administered non-mandatory reporting systems or those which were not State-wide in scope (APWA/NAUSA, 1986). Thus by the late 1980s the US had implemented an official plan of action throughout the country concerning elder abuse and neglect. It is of note, however, that despite consistent and committed work over the past 20 years, the problem of elder abuse remains rife within American society.

Research

In his review of the research field, Ogg states:

> Elder abuse in Britain is emerging as a social problem not on the basis of empirical research but on account of action within the social and health care professions based on the anecdotal evidence of many forms of elder abuse in several diverse settings (Ogg, 1993, p. 37).

He and many others find this lack of firm knowledge about the subject worrying when a large number of health and social agencies are currently devising strategies or guidelines around identification, intervention and prevention. Two broad areas within the research process can be analysed further to give an insight into the difficulties encountered around this whole topic of research. They are:

- methodological difficulties in developing indicators of abuse, and
- ethical issues around self-disclosure/victimisation.

Methodological difficulties

Despite more than a decade of research work in the US there is still marked controversy around such issues as definitions of elder abuse, indicators of abuse and the role of neglect in the spectrum of abusive behaviour. There is also intense debate concerning the continuum of violence and such questions as 'At what stage does (or should) marital violence become delineated as elder abuse?' This can result in a state of affairs where there is a question mark over the usefulness of further research work: the validity of each completed piece of research may be disputed in that different research projects tend to look at slightly different aspects of the problem. Comparing data may then become almost impossible. This can virtually make the concept of the abuse of older people meaningless for researchers, and is perhaps one short step from making it confusing and meaningless for the wider general public.

Research into other forms of family violence has incurred similar problems (Chelucci and Coyle, 1992). For some years now, the abuse of children and the abuse of women in domestic situations have been established as social problems. Research difficulties do not, therefore, appear to have influenced the development of social concern in the same way as with abuse of older people. However, even these fields are not without difficulty in research terms; for example, in a review of the field, Weiss commented on the substantial discrepancies amongst estimates of the prevalence, incidence and correlates of family violence, which tends to compromise the utility of the research results (Weiss, 1988), and Taylor has questioned the reliability of estimates of child abuse (1989).

The first aim of the researcher is to develop the questions that need to be answered and to formulate a hypothesis. This is comparatively easy when dealing with concrete forms but much more difficult with abstract issues, such as abuse, that involve comparative behaviour patterns as well as the influence of attitudes, societal norms and structural concomitants such as ageism. Ogg (1993) has set out research principles that relate specifically to the study of elder abuse and can be summarised thus:

- Older people have the legal and moral right to self-determination.

- They have the right of protection from harm or exploitation.
- There is no consensus on the respective roles of the state and family in the care of dependent older people.
- Domestic violence often continues into old age.

Ogg's first three points highlight the differences that are present between one group in society and another. Children are seen as a vulnerable group in need of extensive protection. The statutory and legal framework promoted in the Children Act 1989 has protective functions towards children who, as minors, have limited decision-making or choice-making capacity in legal terms.

Mentally competent older people often choose to remain in abusive circumstances. This may be in the face of strong pressure from health and Social Services workers to do the contrary. The reasons for staying in such situations are undoubtedly complex but will include, in some cases, the desperate lack of options – the alternatives being stay and be abused or be placed in an institution. There are very limited legal powers to overrule such a decision by a competent older person, although the perpetrator is not necessarily immune from prosecution.

The most difficult area for professionals in such situations has been where there is doubt over the older person's mental competence and decision-making capacity. This dilemma, having been ignored for many years, has recently been expertly addressed by a series of papers from the Law Commission (Law Commission, 1991, 1993a, b, c, 1995), although its remit was to consider the issues concerning decision-making and mentally incapacitated adults, rather than exclusively older people. One of the recommendations made within the proposals is for an emergency assessment order to investigate difficult circumstances (Law Commission, 1993c). The maintenance of personal autonomy is stressed throughout the reports, however, leaving as much decision-making with the older person as possible. If mental competence is not at issue, the full right to self-determination prevails (see Chapter 5 for further detail on these proposals).

The concept of duty to care forms a stark contrast when children and dependent older people are compared. There is no doubt within society that parents have an obligation to care for their children, and any form of abuse is seen therefore as a failure to carry out that caring task and provide protection. There is no similar social analogy to the care of either physically or mentally dependent adults and older people by their family. Although there is no actual duty to care, there may be the perception by individuals of a societal pressure and moral obligation to do so. The concept of responsibility stops short of the same total care expected for children but, if a person assumes the caring role of an adult, then the concept of duty of care will apply from that point onwards. There is, however, an assumption that the state has a key role in the provision of care for this sector of the population. Abuse by a carer is now beginning to be recognised, even though their total caring role may not be. It is somewhat ironic that, if the state does have a major role in provision of care, there may also be 'societal abuse' by the state with the presence of patchy service provision from Social Services and an underfunded health service.

Ogg points out that there is a further problem in developing indicators of elder abuse in the situation of domestic violence continuing into old age. He considers that it is possible to distinguish between situations where abuse is linked to issues of gender and power in interpersonal relationships from those where the abuse results from dependency and vulnerability due to disability (Ogg, 1993). Additionally, Ogg highlights the need for further research in this area because, in the past, this distinction has been somewhat unclear and situations may arise where a combination of the two types of abusive situations occur.

There is at present no research in the UK that identifies the current knowledge base of either GPs or hospital doctors concerning elder abuse. This lack of information makes the planning of curricula to meet specific educational needs within the profession extremely difficult. Although, as stated in Chapter 4, there is a well-established continuing medical education format within general practice, it is only in its infancy for hospital doctors. This new educational requirement could coincide with the realisation that hospital doctors especially are inadequately trained in the recognition and management of elder abuse cases.

There is some justification for assuming that most doctors in the UK are aware of the issue of child abuse and that certainly most doctors working in Accident and Emergency Departments and those specialising in child health would have some degree of expertise in the topic. This knowledge base would include some insight into the law, the need for special and accurate data gathering, the role of other professional groups, especially social work, and the existence of specific guidelines on how to deal with suspected cases. There is easy access to specialist expertise and legal help, and myriad articles, chapters and books on every aspect of the issue.

There is no justification at all in assuming that most doctors have even heard of the phenomenon of elder abuse. This lack of awareness probably extends to Accident and Emergency Departments, although specialist physicians who deal with older people are increasingly becoming aware of some aspects of elder abuse, especially physical violence.

There has been some general consensus over five types of abuse in the research literature, these are physical violence, psychological abuse, sexual abuse, financial abuse and neglect. They have been defined more closely for the purpose of research:

- *Physical abuse:* the non-accidental infliction of physical force that results in bodily injury, pain or impairment.
- *Psychological abuse:* the infliction by threat, humiliation, bullying or by non-verbal abusive behaviour of mental or emotional distress, which could be manifested in physical symptoms.
- *Sexual abuse:* sexual contact without consent.
- *Financial abuse:* the unauthorised and improper use of funds, property or any resources of an older person.
- *Neglect:* failure by the care-giver to fulfil his or her care-taking obligations or duties that result in harmful effects to the older person.

Doctors may be considered key personnel in the primary identification of abuse:

a) in its more severe manifestations the effects of abuse may be the direct reason for referral to a medical practitioner;
b) doctors are often the only professional in contact with an older person;
c) through their ability to examine patients, they are in the best position to identify certain types of abuse;
d) a doctor may be the person to whom an older person is willing to talk about abuse.

Doctors face a number of difficulties, however, in identifying and responding to abuse. Abuse is a highly sensitive issue, with many older people often denying the existence of maltreatment. Many people may indeed have their own strategies for dealing with it. It is suspected therefore that an unknown number of cases remain hidden from view. Doctors, however, may be dealing with the effects of abuse presenting in some other guise, and they may fail to recognise it. The prevalence of elder abuse remains a difficult issue. Current prevalence estimates are low and research into this area is highly problematic. Accepting low prevalence for the foreseeable future still means a large random element of exposure of some doctors to cases (providing, of course, that they are recognised as abuse cases).

Funding for all forms of research is becoming increasingly difficult. Research grants in the field of sociomedical research are notoriously hard to obtain, reflecting the difficulties of the research process involved. The methodological constraints are immense and have been well summarised by Ogg (1993).

In her concluding remarks concerning the prevention of elder abuse, McCreadie quotes Rosalie Wolf: 'the challenge is to make sure that efforts on behalf of mistreated older persons do more good than harm and do not lead to the neglect of other societal needs' (Wolf, 1992, cited in McCreadie, 1996, p.111). Her updated book on research in the UK indicates that research and training are the basic building blocks of policy and that policy itself needs to distinguish between:

- settings;
- client groups;
- types of abuse; and
- protection and other kinds of need for help.

Research is the fundamental process by which we continue to develop the knowledge base and, as McCreadie (1996) states, 'training is the means by which this knowledge is communicated and applied'.

McCreadie (1996, p. 104) ends her publication with an invaluable indication of:

Twelve Ideas for Elder Abuse Research
- factors distinguishing abused from non-abused people, by type of abuse;
- comparisons of abuse in different client groups;
- abuse in specific ethnic groups;
- prevalence of financial abuse involving property;
- abuse in different income groups;
- abuse in day care;
- abuse in residential and nursing home care;
- marital relationships in old age and the place of caring in abuse;
- comparing policies and procedures;
- examining records of elder abuse cases;
- awareness in different professional groups;
- comparing availability of services, by type of abuse, in different areas.

Ethical issues

There are important ethical issues surrounding research into elder abuse encompassing such areas as disclosure and confidentiality. One particularly problematic area has been the issue of the Ethics Committee. All research involving human subjects must have the approval of a properly constituted Ethics Committee. Its job is to study critically every aspect of the research process in order to satisfy all concerned that the research is not only ethically sound but worthwhile. At the same time, the Committee has to satisfy itself that important areas within the research process are adhered to. The first main principle is that of informed consent. This means that the nature of the research has to be explained in straightforward language and all the risks (if any) outlined. The explanation has to include an outline of any procedure to be used and/or any questions to be asked, indicating whether these may touch on sensitive or embarrassing subjects. In this way, a person has the right to refuse any form of research in any setting if they feel that their physical or mental well-being could be compromised. This also means that only mentally competent individuals can give consent (usually verbally and in writing) for any particular research. This therefore excludes mentally frail people, whom many believe are one of the groups vulnerable to abuse. This is seen as a major methodological weakness in the self-disclosure survey research and victimisation surveys. Many researchers have also found that, by indicating the type of questions to follow in a questionnaire, the covering letter may discourage people from participating in the research process.

The second major principle is that of confidentiality. This is inherent in all research work but is especially important when dealing with a sensitive topic such as abuse. There is a major dilemma that has been identified, however. What is the correct course of action if, during a research interview, the client discloses severe and possibly life-threatening abuse and does not allow the researcher to break confidentiality? Is it correct for the researcher to allow a serious crime to be on-going or committed even to the point of murder? If it is not correct, to whom is the researcher to disclose and break confidentiality? These difficult areas are as yet formally unresolved and each research project has to arrive at a local agreement between its researchers and the Ethics Committee.

Research design is therefore influenced by organisational, ethical and social constraints which arise because of the nature of the research itself. Ogg feels that the methodological and ethical issues which arise from the unique nature of elder abuse research should also be made more explicit when findings are reported, since these issues shape research projects, thereby influencing the way they are presented (Ogg, 1993). He considers that our understanding of the problem of elder abuse is in part determined by the types of questions which research projects pose and the methodological and ethical constraints within which these projects are undertaken.

Self-disclosure and victimisation surveys still need to be performed but future research will also need to move beyond the more descriptive accounts and start to analyse, by qualitative interviews, the questions around the process of abuse. Ogg identifies that this will need both 'victim' and 'perpetrator' interviews, but in situations where the conflict has been resolved (Ogg, 1993). There is no doubt that the researchers will themselves need de-briefing, counselling and support networks when dealing in great detail with potentially extremely harrowing and distressing incidents.

Conclusion

The national responses devised by different countries to the phenomenon of elder abuse are as diverse and complex as the issue itself. Despite civil laws available in many European countries that impose a caring responsibility on adult children for various aspects of their parents' lives, this approach has not gained wholesale favour. In the UK, the government decided in early 1996 not to implement recommendations from the English Law Commission without a period of review and further public consultation (see Chapter 5 for further detail on the recommendations made by the Commission). It would appear that elder abuse as a social problem has insufficient public groundswell in the UK in the late 1990s to result in change of this potential magnitude and that change will not be imminent.

It is interesting to note the duplication of studies concerned with prevalence, as if these provide a legitimation for further research. This is despite the acknowledged difficulties of research in this area, the consistently low prevalence rates obtained from such research and the disenfranchised client groups concerned.

Many of the reports give the reader an insight into the particular cultures involved, providing a context in which the research results must be viewed. Some authors also touch upon religious themes that colour their work, again providing a national context. The coordinated pieces of work that have appeared from Australia could act as a template for many countries, particularly as they are concerned with the inclusion of intervention strategies that are much needed in this area of work. The New Zealand resource manual is an excellent example of a modular document and has useful case histories. Similar manuals developed in each country, perhaps pump-primed by government resources, would be an invaluable information and education tool in the struggle to both prevent and resolve elder abuse wherever it occurs.

Perhaps most noticeable is the relative lack of legislative intent around the world compared with the US. Most countries that have identified elder abuse and neglect have opted for health and welfare interventions based on existing service provision. The advantages of this type of approach have been noted by various commentators (Crystal, 1986; Callahan, 1988). There may also be disadvantages, as stated by Biggs and Kingston:

> Whilst both policy makers and contributors from a number of countries point out that elder abuse can be responded to by using existing services, the meaning of this relationship is ambiguous. It might, for example, mask an unwillingness to fund appropriate services or to rely on experience from established areas such as child protection, which may not be appropriate (Biggs and Kingston, 1995, p. 1).

The issue that challenges the imagination from the work described in this chapter is the importance of sharing knowledge and developments in this field and how best to do this. Clearly, because developments in individual countries are slow, sharing the wider developments cross-culturally, as attempted here, may offer the possibility of insights that could take years for individual countries to discover and develop. The development of cross-cultural networks for information exchange and comparative research would be a very valuable avenue to pursue in future years. The commitment to do so is evident with recent developments in this respect in Europe. What is required is sufficient time and resources to develop appropriate and lasting links, together with an absolute willingness to share rather than compete in the mutual endeavour of combatting and ultimately preventing elder abuse.

Conclusion

Elder abuse looks set to become one of the phenomena of interpersonal violence that will create needs for social policies well into the next millennium. At a macro-political level, we need to consider the concept of 'institutionalised ageism' and providing solutions (Jack, 1992). A more radical perspective is offered to us all by Phillipson and Walker:

> in social policy terms, the task... is to break the link between growing old and becoming dependent. This will involve action on both political and economic fronts; but this will also involve... a challenge to our work as carers – in both formal and informal settings. Crucially it will demand that old people become centrally involved in the planning and administration of services; in the running... of *their* welfare state (Phillipson and Walker, 1986, p. 290).

This book has introduced the concept of abuse throughout the life course. The wide-ranging nature and different forms of abuse have been considered alongside the emergence of concern about elder abuse in the middle of this last decade of the 20th century. The dimensions of abuse have been explored at the macro (political), mezzo (community) and micro (individual) levels. The difficult area of definitions has been critically analysed, together with the knowledge surrounding the size of the problem, the prevalence of elder abuse.

The authors have placed the phenomenon of elder abuse within the total context of family violence. Elder abuse is both similar to and yet different from other forms of familial abuse and should thus be considered distinctly but within a more generic family violence framework. Our current knowledge and understanding of elder abuse strongly indicates that, despite the evident differences, the phenomenon should be considered as part of a wider continuum of family violence rather than an entirely separate entity; it is important to acknowledge, however, that there are aspects of the phenomenon, such as much institutional abuse, that do not fit within the spectrum of familial violence.

Indeed, significant amounts of abuse are found in different settings, and it is for this reason that the third chapter serves as a juxtaposition, with its focus on those forms of abuse that occur outside family violence. Institutional abuse is an area of major prominence within the spectrum of the continuum of interpersonal violence, in part due to the expansion and social acceptance of residential and nursing home care as the likely panacea to the needs of older people. The principal concern is the regular monotony with which scandals and enquiries occur and the apparently total absence of any political will to rectify the situation. The research base on which our knowledge is constructed is largely anecdotal and enquiry led, whilst empirical data are noticeable by their absence save for the work in North America. The chapter on institutional abuse has considered the role of legislation and the concept and practicality of whistleblowing. A series of recommendations that will hopefully move the debate forward have been made.

The medical and health perspective on elder abuse is an undeniably powerful one. The demographic changes occurring worldwide are quite without parallel in human history, resulting in the global phenomenon of an increased percentage of the total population now living to be old. This change will prove challenging to most health and social service provision. At the same time, the clinical knowledge base concerning both ageing and the medical aspects of elder abuse is growing. The medical components of the knowledge base have been set out in detail for the reader in order both to inform and to provide an understanding of the medical and health perspectives for non-health personnel. The clinical presentation of actual cases of elder abuse is likely to guide the professional through this difficult area. Formal elder abuse protocols may be the tool of the future, and the example given has provided an outline of the use of such assessment protocols. The clinical basis of diagnosis is one of the most rapidly developing areas within the knowledge base of elder abuse, and as new information becomes verified it should become incorporated into the education and training curricula of all professional staff. Education in this subject is an important area of change that could result in improved awareness and attitudes amongst practitioners; this is likely to be at all levels: undergraduate, postgraduate and indeed non-professional training.

An important aspect that the book has covered concerns the legal dimensions of elder abuse and the associated issues concerning rights, autonomy and protection. This is valuable for anyone who has not been legally trained in order to provide information and knowledge on the issues concerning elder abuse from a legal perspective. An overview of the main legal provisions that currently exist and which might be used in situations of abuse has been provided, together with the case both for and against legal reform in this area, including some of the specific recommendations for change produced by the English Law Commission. The general legal principles that should be adopted in work with older people have been outlined; some of the difficulties of work in this area have been raised. This is also complemented by sections in the chapter on interventions.

The chapter on interventions has reviewed for the reader some of the main areas of difficulty that exist in intervening in situations of elder abuse, wherever they occur. The available models of interventions, in terms of both broad strategy (conceptual frameworks) and service delivery, have been outlined, and suggestions have been made concerning the principles that should guide intervention in these difficult and complex areas. Some of the possible future developments in this field have also been described.

The international dimensions of the problem have taken the reader beyond the knowledge base already developed in the US and UK and form the focus of the final chapter. There are important European initiatives currently taking place, including the creation of a government-funded Resource and Research Centre of Family Violence (including elder abuse) in Norway. This makes Scandinavia (along with the UK) one of the most influential areas in Europe working on elder abuse. Some of the most innovative and productive work appears to be emanating from Australasia. In Australia, intervention strategies include local models with a major role from the Carers Association. In New Zealand, a national workshop has resulted in the formation of a research base and the development of a resource kit (developed by Age Concern NZ Inc.). This resource manual is a template to be emulated and developed around the world, providing an invaluable information and education tool.

Progress in the field of interpersonal violence, and indeed of many social problems, is very much based on research. The position at present is aptly described by Ogg:

> elder abuse... is emerging as a social problem not on the basis of empirical research but on account of action within the social and health care professions based on the anecdotal evidence of many forms of elder abuse in several diverse settings (Ogg, 1993, p. 37).

The remedy to this situation is not, however, at all straightforward, and there are significant methodological difficulties that may be encountered in this type of research. These have been explored with the reader, as has a discussion of the possible future research agenda.

The authors have provided readers with the current knowledge base concerning this important social topic. The book encompasses the dimensions of this pernicious problem and, as may be expected, many additional questions have been posed, as well as recommendations for change in various areas being set out.

Interpersonal violence is a social phenomenon that is being increasingly reported and acknowledged as a problem. Within this context, elder abuse, in all its many and varied forms, must achieve a greater public and professional awareness. This is the route to increased knowledge and information, research activity and social and government concern. From this, legitimation of the problem and action taken to resolve it will hopefully result. The overall aim must be to understand the problem in all its dimensions, to provide solutions and resolutions, where possible, and ultimately to act preventatively, to stop as much harm as possible from occurring, and to prevent the conditions that initiate, perpetuate and exacerbate abuse and violence. We hope that the information contained in the book is a contribution towards this task.

Notes

Chapter 1

1   The Panopticon was a circular prison, proposed by Bentham in 1791, in which prison staff could maintain total surveillance over prisoners but prisoners had only limited vision.

2   Diogenes of Sinope was a Greek philosopher of the 4th century BC, who was known as an advocate of self-sufficiency, freedom from social restraints and rejection of all luxury. He lived as he preached, sleeping rough in public buildings, some believe in a barrel, and begging for food.

3   Reports from the American Welfare Association suggest that, in 1990, a total of 211,000 reports were received from 46 states. Of these, 51.4 per cent concerned self-neglect. If the reports concerning self-neglect are omitted from the total, 45.2 per cent of cases are related to neglect, with physical abuse accounting for 19.1 per cent, financial abuse 17.1 per cent and emotional abuse 13.8 per cent of the overall totals (Tatara, 1990). This clearly indicates that, in the US, the majority of the work of such teams is focused on issues concerned with neglect of one form or another.

Chapter 4

1   This study found a prevalence rate of verbal abuse amongst older people (visited at home as part of a general survey) of 5 per cent (i.e. older people stating that they had been verbally abused). Of the sample, 2 per cent indicated that they were the recipients of physical violence or misappropriation of goods. The same survey interviewed adults having close contact with older people and revealed that whilst only 1 per cent admitted physical violence, 10 per cent had verbally abused an older person 'sufficient to frighten them'. These findings are broadly in line with the large-scale surveys that have been carried out in the US and Canada (Pillemer and Finkelhor, 1988; Podnieks, 1992; see also Chapter 1).

2   This term refers to the elasticity of the skin. The clinician should particularly look for evidence of decreased elasticity, which may indicate dehydration.

3   This term refers to a specific form of bruising in old age which may be spontaneous and is quite commonly found.

4   This term refers to loss of hair, or baldness.

5   This term refers to fractures that have not been previously detected.

Chapter 5

1   One of the criticisms of the guardianship provisions of the Mental Health Act 1983 has been that it does not allow practitioners sufficient authority to implement it fully. For example, although Section 7 of the Act allows for a stipulation on where the person (subject to guardianship) should reside, there is no power to convey the person to that place.

Chapter 7

1   The definition of elder mistreatment which was used was that proposed by the US Council on Scientific Affairs in a report concerning elder abuse and neglect which was reported on in the *Journal of the American Medical Association* (Council on Scientific Affairs, 1987).

2   This appears to be the largest series of cases reviewed in Ireland to date. In a consideration of causal/risk factors in respect of the cases, the following findings were apparent:
   * There was little evidence to support intergenerational transmission of violence.
   * The data did not show high levels of dependency of victims; in contrast, dependency of the abusers (for finance and housing) was strongly apparent.
   * Psychopathology of abusers was confirmed, especially with regard to alcohol abuse.
   * Care-giver stress, whilst apparent, did not appear as significant as the previous two factors. Life stress for abusers, in particular regarding unemployment, appeared in over 50 per cent of the cases.
   * In all of the cases, the victim lived with the abuser.
   * Social isolation was evident in over 50 per cent of the cases examined.

3   The term 'tertiary centre' is used to denote a specialist medical centre (for example a hospital specialising in particular disorders).

4   Centrum Geestelijke volksgezondheid (NcGv).

5   Report: Melding van Ouderenmishandeling (Reporting elderly abuse) by Jaap van Weegtel and Ed Faber, Nederlands centrum Geestelijke volksgezandheid, PO Box 5103, 3502 J.C.Utrecht, The Netherlands.

References

Aber, J.L. and Zigler, E. (1981) Developmental considerations in the defi-
nition of child maltreatment, *New Directions for Child Development*,
11:1–29.
Action on Elder Abuse (1993) *Report on Proceedings of the 1st International Symposium on Elder Abuse.* Working Paper No. 1. London,
Action on Elder Abuse.
Action on Elder Abuse (1995a) Action on Elder Abuse's definition of elder
abuse. *Action on Elder Abuse Bulletin*, May/June.
Action on Elder Abuse (1995b) *Everybody's Business: Taking Action on
Elder Abuse.* London, Action on Elder Abuse.
Adelman, R., Michele, G.G., Churon, R. and Friedman, E. (1990) Issues in
the physician–geriatric patient relationship, in Giles, H., Coupland, N.
and Wieman, J.N. (eds) *Communication, Health and the Elderly.*
Manchester, Manchester University Press.
(ADSS) Association of Directors of Social Services (1995) *The Mistreat-
ment of Older People: A discussion document.* Northallerton, ADSS.
Age Concern (1986) *The Law and Vulnerable Elderly People.* London,
Age Concern.
Age Concern (1990) *The Law and Vulnerable Elderly People*, 2nd edn.
London, Age Concern.
Age Concern New Zealand (1992) *Promoting the Rights and Well-being of
Older People and Those who Care for Them: A resource kit about elder
abuse and neglect.* Wellington, New Zealand, Age Concern NZ.
Allen, I., Hogg, D. and Peace, S. (1992) *Elderly People: Choice, partici-
pation and satisfaction.* London, Policy Studies Institute.
Alzheimer's Disease Society (1993) *A Response from the Alzheimer's
Disease Society.* London, Alzheimer's Disease Society.
Anderson, J., Martin, J.M., Mullen, P., Romay, S. and Herbison, P. (1993)
Prevalence of childhood sexual abuse experiences in a community
sample of women, *Journal of the American Academy of Child and
Adolescent Psychiatrists*, **32**(5):911–19.
Anetzberger, G., Korbin, J.E. and Austin, C. (1994) Alcoholism and elder
abuse, *Journal of Interpersonal Violence*, **9**(2):184–93.
Anstee, M.J. (1989) Impact of the aging world, *Hong Kong Journal of
Gerontology*, **3**(1):3–5.
APWA (American Public Welfare Association)/NASUA (1986) *A Compre-
hensive Analysis of State Policy and Practice Related to Elder Abuse: A
focus on role activities of state level agencies, interagency co-ordination*

efforts, public education/information campaigns. Washington DC, APWA/NASUA.

Arber, S. and Ginn, J. (1992) *Gender and Later Life.* London, Sage.

ARC/NAPSAC (1993) *It Could Never Happen Here.* Nottingham, ARC/NAPSAC.

Armstrong, D. (1983) *Political Anatomy of the Body: Medical knowledge in Britain in the twentieth century.* Cambridge, Cambridge University Press.

Ashton, G.R. (1994) *The Elderly Client Handbook: The Law Society's guide to acting for elderly people.* London, Law Society.

Ashton, G.R. (1995) *Elderly People and the Law.* London, Butterworths.

Backnik, J.M. (1992) Kejime: Defining a shifting self in multiple organisational modes, in Rosenberger, N. (ed.) *Japanese Sense of Self.* Cambridge, Cambridge University Press.

Baker, A.A. (1975) Granny battering, *Modern Geriatrics*, (8):20–4.

Baker, H.D.R. (1979) *Chinese Family and Kinship.* New York, Columbia University Press.

Barron, J. (1990) *Not Worth the Paper...? The Effectiveness of Legal Protection for Women and Children Experiencing Domestic Violence.* Bristol, Women's Aid Federation.

Barron, B., Cran, A., Flitcroft, J., McDermott, J. and Montague, M. (1990) *No Innocent Bystanders: A study of abuse of older people in our community.* Melbourne, Office of Public Advocate.

Basaglia, F. (1989) Italian reform as a reflection of society, in Ramon, S. and Gianichedda, M.-G. (eds) *Psychiatry in Transition.* London, Macmillan.

BASW (British Association of Social Workers) (1990) *Parliamentary Briefing: Proposed legislation for vulnerable adults.* Birmingham, BASW.

BASW (British Association of Social Workers) (1992) *Residential Care for Older People: A policy document.* Birmingham, BASW.

BASW/RCN (British Association of Social Workers/Royal College of Nursing) (1994) *Joint Amendment to the Deregulation Bill.* London, BASW/RCN.

Baumann, E. (1989) Research rhetoric and the social construction of elder abuse, in Best, J. (ed.) *Images of Issues: Typifying contemporary problems.* New York, Aldine de Gruyter.

Beachler, M.A. (1979) Mistreatment of Elderly Persons in the Domestic Setting. Unpublished manuscript, Brasoria County, Texas, USA.

Befu, H. (1971) *Japan: An anthropological introduction.* San Francisco, Chandler.

Belsky, J. (1978) Three theoretical models of child abuse: a critical review, *Child Abuse and Neglect*, 2(1):37–49.

Bennett, G.C.J. (1990) Assessing abuse in the elderly, *Geriatric Medicine*, (July):49–51.

Bennett, G.C.J. and Ebrahim, S. (1995) *Essentials of Health Care of Old Age,* 2nd edn. London, Edward Arnold.
Bennett, G.C.J. and Kingston, P. (1993) *Elder Abuse: Concepts, theories and interventions.* London, Chapman & Hall.
Biggs, S. (1993) *Understanding Ageing.* Buckingham, Open University Press.
Biggs, S. (1994) Failed individualism in community care: an example from elder abuse, *Journal of Social Work Practice,* **8**(2):137–49.
Biggs, S. and Kingston, P. (1995) (eds) Elder abuse in Europe, *Social Work in Europe,* **2**(3):1–2.
Biggs, S., Phillipson, C. and Kingston, P. (1995) *Elder Abuse in Perspective.* Buckingham, Open University Press.
Binstock, R.H. and Post, S.G. (1991) *Too Old for Health Care: Controversies in medicine, law, economics and ethics.* Baltimore, Johns Hopkins Press.
Birchall, E. (1989) The frequency of child abuse, in Stevenson, O. (ed.) *Child Abuse: Public policy and professional concern.* London, Harvester Wheatsheaf.
Blakely, B.E and Dolon, R. (1991) The relative contribution of occupation groups in the discovery and treatment of elder abuse and neglect, *Journal of Gerontological Social Work,* **17**:183–99.
Block, M.R. and Sinnott, J.D. (1979) *The Battered Elder Syndrome: An exploratory study.* College Park, University of Maryland Centre on Aging.
Blumer, H. (1969) *Symbolic Interactionism.* Englewood Cliffs, NJ, Prentice Hall.
Blumer, H. (1971) Social problems as collective behaviour, *Social Problems,* **18**(3):298–306.
Bokunewicz, B. and Copel, L.C. (1992) Attitudes of emergency nurses before and after a 60-minute educational presentation on partner abuse, *Journal of Emergency Nursing,* **18**(1):24–7.
Bond, J. and Coleman, P. (1990) *Ageing and Society: An introduction to social gerontology.* London, Sage.
Bookin, D. and Dunkle, R.E. (1985) Elder abuse: issues for the practitioner, *Social Casework,* **66**(1):3–12.
Bookin, D. and Dunkle, R.E. (1989) Assessment problems in cases of elder abuse, in Filinson, R. and Ingman, S.R. (eds) *Elder Abuse: Practice and policy.* New York, Human Sciences Press.
Borsay, A. (1989) First child care, second mental health, third the elderly, *Research, Policy and Practice,* **7**(2):27–30.
Brammer, A. (1994) The Registered Homes Act 1984: safeguarding the elderly, *Journal of Social Welfare and Family Law,* **4**:423–37.
Breckman, R.S. and Adelman, R.D. (1988) *Strategies for Helping Victims of Elder Mistreatment.* Newbury Park, CA, Sage.
Bristowe, E. and Collins, J. (1989) Family mediated abuse of non-institutionalised frail elderly men and women in British Colombia, *Journal of Elder Abuse and Neglect,* **1**:45–64.

Brocklehurst, J.C., Tallis, R.C. and Fillit, H.M. (1997) (eds) *Textbook of Geriatric Medicine and Gerontology*, 5th edn. Edinburgh, Churchill Livingstone (in press).

Brown, H. and Craft, A. (1989) *Thinking the Unthinkable: Papers on sexual abuse and people with learning difficulties*. London, FPA Education Unit.

Browne, K. (1988) The nature of child abuse and neglect: an overview, in Browne, K., Davies, C. and Stratton, P. (eds) *Early Prediction and Prevention of Child Abuse*. Chichester, John Wiley & Sons.

Browne, K. (1989) Family violence: elder and spouse abuse, in Howells, K. and Hollin, C.R. (eds) *Clinical Approaches to Violence*. Chichester, John Wiley & Sons.

Brungardt, G.S. (1994) Patient restraints: new guidelines for a less restrictive approach, *Geriatrics*, **49**(6):43–50.

Burston, G. (1977) Do your elderly relatives live in fear of being battered?, *Modern Geriatrics*, **7**(5):54–5.

Cabness, J. (1989) The emergency shelter: a model for building the self-esteem of abused elders, *Journal of Elder Abuse and Neglect*, **1**(2):71–82.

Callahan, D. (1987) *Setting Limits: Medical goals in an aging society*. New York, Touchstone.

Callahan, J.J. (1986) Guest editor's perspective, *Pride Institute Journal of Long-term Care*, **5**:2–3.

Callahan, J.J. (1988) Elder abuse: some questions for the policymakers, *Gerontologist*, **28**(4):453–8.

Carson, D. (1988) Breaking the barrier of silence, *Health Service Journal*, 25 February, 245.

Carson, D. (1993) Disabling progress: the Law Commission's proposals on mentally incapacitated adults' decision making, *Journal of Social Welfare and Family Law*, **3**:304–20.

Carter, G. (1995) Matching care to client need, *Nursing Times*, **91**(32):58–9.

Case, S.M. and Swanson, D.B. (1992) *Item Writing Guide*. Washington, National Board of Medical Examiners.

Chan, H.T. (1985) *Report of Elderly Abuse at Home in Hong Kong*. Hong Kong, Hong Kong Council of Social Services.

Chan, Y.K. (1988) Modern society and aged population, *Hong Kong Journal of Gerontology*, **2**(1):37–9.

Chelucci, K. and Coyle, J. (1992) *Elder Abuse Acute Care Resource Manual*. Toledo, OH, Elder Abuse Specialists.

Chez, N. (1994) Helping the victim of domestic violence, *American Journal of Nursing*, **94**(7):32–8.

Clark, A.N.G., Manaker, G.O. and Gray, I. (1975) Diogenes syndrome: a clinical study of gross neglect in old age, *Lancet* **1**:366–8.

Clark-Daniels, C.I., Daniels, R. and Baumhover, L. (1990) Abuse and neglect of the elderly: are emergency department personnel aware of mandatory reporting laws?, *Annals of Emergency Medicine,* **19**(9):970–7.

Cloke, C. (1983) *Old Age Abuse in the Domestic Setting: A review.* Mitcham, Age Concern.

Clough, R. (1987) Unpublished report to the Wagner Committee on Residential Care.

Clough, R. (1995) Foreword – Elder Abuse and the Law: Paper from the 1st Annual Conference of Action on Elder Abuse, Lancaster University, March 1994. London, Action on Elder Abuse.

Cohler, B. (1993) Aging, morale, and meaning: the nexus of narrative, in Cole, T.R., Achenbaum, W.A., Jacobi, P.L. and Kastenbaum, R. (eds) Voices and Visions of Aging. New York, Springer.

Cole, A.J. and Gillett, T.P. (1992) A case of senile self neglect in a married couple: Diogenes à deux, *International Journal of Geriatric Psychiatry,* **7**:839–41.

Collingridge, M. (1993) Protection of the elderly: some legal and ethical issues, *Australian Journal on Ageing,* **12**(4):32–7.

Conradie, G. and Charlton, K. (1992) *Malpractices and Mistreatment of Residents of Homes for the Aged.* Cape Town, HSRC/UCT Centre for Gerontology, University of Cape Town.

Cornell, C.P. and Gelles, R.J. (1982) Adolescent to parent violence, *Urban Social Change Review,* **15**:8–14.

Council of Europe (1991) *Violence Against Elderly People.* Strasbourg, Council of Europe.

Council on Scientific Affairs (1987) Elder abuse and neglect: Council report, *Journal of American Medical Association,* **257**:966–71.

Counsel and Care (1991) *Not Such Private Places: A study of privacy and the lack of privacy for residents in private and voluntary residential and nursing homes in Greater London.* London, Counsel and Care.

Counsel and Care (1992) *What if They Hurt Themselves: A discussion document on the uses and abuses of restraint in residential care and nursing homes for older people.* London, Counsel and Care.

Counsel and Care (1993) *The Right to Take Risks.* London, Counsel and Care.

Counsel and Care (1995) *Care Betrayed.* London, Counsel and Care.

Cowgill, D. (1986) *Aging Around the World.* Belmont, CA, Wordsworth.

Creighton, S. (1992) *Child Abuse Trends in England and Wales, 1988–1990.* London, NSPCC.

Crystal, P. (1987) Elder abuse: the latest crisis, *Public Interest,* **88**:55–66.

Crystal, S. (1986) Social policy and elder abuse, in Pillemer, K.A. and Wolf, R.S. (eds) *Elder Abuse: Conflict in the family.* Dover, MA, Auburn House.

Curtis, Z. (1993) On being a woman in the pensioners' movement, in Johnson, J. and Slater, R. (eds) *Ageing and Later Life.* London, Sage.

Dawson, M.M. (1915) *The Ethics of Confucius.* New York, Putnam.

Decalmer, P. and Glendenning, F. (1993) (eds) *The Mistreatment of Elderly People.* London, Sage.

Department de Benestar Social (1994) *Maltractamento, abusos i disanminations a la gent gran, a Catalunya.* Department de Benestar Social, Generalitat de Catalunya (In Catalan).

Dissenbacher, H. (1989) Neglect, abuse and the taking of life in old people's homes, *Ageing and Society,* **9**(1):61–72.

Dobash, R.E. and Dobash, R. (1979) *Violence Against Wives.* New York, Free Press.

Dobash, R.E. and Dobash, R. (1992) *Women, Violence and Social Change.* London, Routledge.

DOH (Department of Health) (1989a) *Caring for People: Community care in the next decade and beyond.* Cmnd 849. London, HMSO.

DOH (Department of Health) (1989b) *Working for Patients.* London, HMSO.

DOH (Department of Health) (1990) *National Health Service and Community Care Act.* London, HMSO.

DOH (Department of Health) (1992) *Report of the Committee of Inquiry into Complaints about Ashworth Hospital,* vol. I, Cmnd 2028-I. London, HMSO.

DOH (Department of Health) (1996) *A New Partnership for Care in Old Age.* Cmnd 3242. London, HMSO.

DOH/SSI (Department of Health/Social Services Inspectorate) (1989) *Homes Are For Living In.* London, HMSO.

DOH/SSI (Department of Health/Social Services Inspectorate) (1991a) *Care Management and Assessment: Manager's guide.* Milton Keynes, HMSO.

DOH/SSI (Department of Health/Social Services Inspectorate) (1991b) *Care Management and Assessment: Practitioner's guide.* Milton Keynes, HMSO.

DOH/SSI (Department of Health/Social Services Inspectorate) (1992) *Confronting Elder Abuse.* London, HMSO.

DOH/SSI (Department of Health/Social Services Inspectorate) (1993) *No Longer Afraid: The safeguard of older people in the domestic setting.* London, HMSO.

DOH/SSI (Department of Health/Social Services Inspectorate) (1995a) *Abuse of Older People in Domestic Settings: A report on two SSI seminars.* London, HMSO.

DOH/SSI (Department of Health/Social Services Inspectorate) (1995b) *Responding to Residents: Messages for staff from inspections of local authority residential care homes.* London, HMSO.

DOH/SSI (Department of Health/Social Services Inspectorate) (1996) *Domestic Violence and Social Care.* London, HMSO.

Doi, T. (1973) *The Anatomy of Dependence* (trans. John Bester). Tokyo, Kodansha International.

Doll, R. (1971) The age distribution of cancer: implications for models of carcinogenesis, *Journal of the Royal Statistical Society*, **134**(A):133–55.

Donow, H. (1990) Two approaches to the care of the elder parent, *Gerontologist*, **30**(4):486–90.

Douglass, R.L. (1991) Reaching 30 million people to prevent abuse and neglect of the elderly: AARP's Strategy for Public Education, *Journal of Elder Abuse and Neglect*, **3**(4):73–85.

Douglass, R.L., Hickey, T. and Noel, C. (1980) *A Study of Maltreatment of the Elderly and Other Vulnerable Adults*. Ann Arbor, University of Michigan Institute of Gerontology.

Dowd, J.J. (1975) Aging as social exchange: a preface to theory, *Journal of Gerontology*, **31**:584–95.

Dunning, A. (1995) *Citizen Advocacy with Older People: A code of good practice*. London, Centre for Policy on Ageing.

Duquette, A., Kerouac, S., Sandhu, B.K., Ducharme, F. and Saulinier, P. (1995) Psychosocial determinants of burnout in geriatric nursing, *International Journal of Nursing Studies*, **32**(5):443–56.

Eastman, M. (1982) Granny battering: a hidden problem, *Community Care*, 27 May, 12–13.

Eastman, M. (1984a) At worst just picking up the pieces, *Community Care*, 2 Feb, 20–2.

Eastman, M. (1984b) Honour thy father and thy mother, *Community Care*, 26 Jan, 17–20.

Eastman, M. (1984c) *Old Age Abuse*. London, Age Concern.

Eastman, M. (1988) Granny abuse, *Community Outlook*, (Oct):15–16.

Eastman, M. (1989) Studying old age abuse, in Archer, J. and Browne, K. (eds) *Human Aggression: Naturalistic approaches*. London, Routledge.

Eastman, M. (ed.) (1994) *Old Age Abuse: A new perspective*, 2nd edn. London, Age Concern/Chapman & Hall.

Eastman, M. and Sutton, M. (1982) Granny battering, *Geriatric Medicine*, (Nov):11–15.

Eckley, S.C.A. and Vilakazi, P.A.C. (1995) Elder abuse in South Africa, *Journal of Abuse and Neglect*, **6**(3/4):171–82.

Edinberg, M.A. (1986) Developing and integrating family orientated approaches in the care of the elderly, in Pillemer, K. and Wolf, R.S. (eds) *Elder Abuse: Conflict in the family*. Dover, MA, Auburn House.

Emerson, R.M. and Messinger, S.L. (1977) The micro-politics of trouble, *Social Problems*, **25**(2):121–34.

Estes, C. (1979) *The Aging Enterprise*. London, Jossey Bass.

Estes, C.L., Swan, J. and Gerard, L. (1982) Dominant and competing paradigms in gerontology: towards a political economy of ageing, *Ageing and Society*, **2**(2):151–64.

Eurolink Age (1989) *Alternatives to Traditional Forms of Socio-medical Care for Older People within the European Community.* London, Age Concern.

Evans, J. Grimley (1992) Challenge of ageing, *British Medical Journal,* **303**:408–9.

Evans, J. Grimley and Caird, F.I. (1982) Epidemiology of neurological disorders in old age, in Caird, F.I. (ed.) *Neurological Disorders in the Elderly.* Bristol, John Wright.

Farr, M. (1992) Developing Policy and Procedural Responses to the Abuse and Neglect of Older Persons. Paper presented to Conference of the Task Force on the Prevention of Intimidation and Abuse of the Elderly, Brisbane, 1991.

Fear, J.D., Hatton, D. and Renvoize, E.B. (1988) Section 47 of the National Assistance Act: a time for change?, *British Medical Journal,* **296**:860c.

Fennell, P. (1989) The Beverly Lewis case: was the law to blame?, *New Law Journal,* (139):1557.

Ferree, M.M. (1990) Beyond separate spheres: feminism and family research, *Journal of Marriage and the Family,* **52**:866–84.

Filinson, R. (1989) Introduction, in Filinson, R. and Ingman S.R. (eds) *Elder Abuse: Practice and policy.* New York, Human Sciences Press.

Filinson, R. and Ingman S.R. (eds) (1989) *Elder Abuse: Practice and policy.* New York, Human Sciences Press.

Finkelhor, D. (1984) *Child Sexual Abuse: New theory and research.* New York, Free Press.

Finkelhor, D. (1991) The scope of the problem, in Murray, K. and Gough, D. (eds) *Intervening in Child Sexual Abuse.* Aberdeen, Scottish Academic Press.

Finkelhor, D. and Pillemer, K.A. (1988) Elder abuse: its relationship to other forms of domestic violence, in Hotaling, G.T., Finkelhor, D., Kirkpatrick, J.T. and Straus, M.A. (eds) *Family Abuse and its Consequences.* Newbury Park, CA, Sage.

Finkelhor, D., Gelles, R.J., Hotaling, G. and Straus, M.A. (eds) (1983) *The Dark Side of Families: Current family violence research,* Beverly Hills, CA, Sage.

Folstein, M.F., Folstein, S.E. and McHugh, P.R. (1975) The mini-mental state: a practical method for grading the cognitive state of patients for the clinician, *Journal of Psychiatric Research,* (12):289–98.

Foner, N. (1984) *Ages in Conflict: A cross-cultural perspective on inequality between old and young.* New York, Columbia University Press.

Foner, N. (1994) Nursing home aides: saints or monsters?, *Gerontologist,* **34**(2):245–50.

Foucault, M. (1976) *The Birth of the Clinic.* London, Tavistock.

Foucault, M. (1979) *Discipline and Punishment.* London, Tavistock.

Francis, J. (1992) The power to choose, *Community Care,* (5 Nov):20.

Freeman, M.D.A. (1987) *Dealing with Domestic Violence.* Bicester, CCH Editions.

Friedan, B. (1993) *The Fountain of Age.* London, Simon & Schuster.

Froggatt, A. (1990) *Family Work with Elderly People.* London, BASW/ Macmillan.

Frost, M. and Stein, M. (1989) *The Politics of Child Welfare.* Hemel Hempstead, Harvester Wheatsheaf.

Fulmer, T. and O'Malley, T. (1987) *Inadequate Care of the Elderly: A health care perspective on abuse and neglect.* New York, Springer.

Garbarino, J. (1977) The human ecology of child maltreatment, *Journal of Marriage and the Family,* **39**(Nov):721–35.

Garrod, G. (1997) Modelling procedures for mistreatment, *Community Care* (in press).

Gelles, R.J. (1980) Violence in the family: a review of the research in the seventies, *Journal of Marriage and the Family,* **42**(Nov):873–85.

Gelles, R.J. (1983) An exchange/social control theory of intra-family violence, in Finkelhor, D., Gelles, R.J., Hotaling, G. and Straus, M.A. (eds) *The Dark Side of Families: Current family violence research.* Beverly Hills, CA, Sage.

Gelles, R.J. (1987) *Family Violence,* 2nd edn. Sage Library of Social Research, No. 84. Beverly Hills, CA, Sage.

Gelles, R.J. (1989) Child abuse and violence in single parent families: parent absence and economic deprivation, *American Journal of Orthopsychiatry,* **59**(Oct):492–501.

Gelles, R.J. and Cornell, C.P. (1985) *Intimate Violence in Families.* Beverly Hills, CA, Sage.

Gelles, R.J. and Loseke, D.R. (eds) (1993) *Current Controversies on Family Violence.* London, Sage.

Gelles, R.J. and Straus, M.A. (1979a) Determinants of violence in the family: towards theoretical integration, in Burr, W., Hill, R., Nye, F.I. and Reiss, I. (eds) *Contemporary Theories about the Family.* New York, Free Press.

Gelles, R.J. and Straus, M.A. (1979b) Violence in the American family, *Journal of Social Issues,* **35**(2):15–39.

Gil, D. (1970) *Violence Against Children: Physical child abuse in the United States.* Cambridge, MA, Harvard University Press.

Gil, D. (1981) The United States versus child abuse, in Pelton, L. (ed.) *The Social Context of Child Abuse and Neglect.* New York, Human Services Press.

Gilleard, C. (1994) Physical abuse in homes and hospitals, in Eastman, M. (ed.) *Old Age Abuse: A new perspective.* London, Chapman & Hall.

Glascock, A.P. (1990) By any other name, it is still killing: a comparison of the treatment of the elderly in America and other societies, in Sokolovsky,

J. *The Cultural Context of Aging: World wide perspectives.* New York, Bergin and Garvey.

Glascock, A. and Feinman, S. (1981) Social asset or social burden: treatment of the aged in non-industrial societies, in Fry, C. (ed.) *Dimensions: Aging, culture and health.* New York, Praeger.

Glendenning, F. (1993) What is elder abuse and neglect?, in Decalmer, P. and Glendenning, F. (eds) *The Mistreatment of Elderly People.* London, Sage.

Goffman, E. (1961) *Asylums: Essays on the social situation of mental patients and other inmates.* Reading, Penguin.

Goffman, E. (1963) *Stigma: Note on the Management of Spoiled Identity.* Englewood Cliffs, NJ, Spectrum/Prentice-Hall.

Good, R. (1992) *Family Violence Prevention Co-ordinating Committee Quality Control Group: Discussion paper.* Wellington, New Zealand, Department of Social Welfare.

Goode, W.J. (1971) Force and violence in the family, *Journal of Marriage and the Family,* **33**(Nov):624–36.

Grafstrom, M., Norberg, A. and Wimblad, B. (1992) Abuse is in the eye of the beholder. Reports by family members about abuse of demented persons in home care. A total population-based study, *Scandinavian Journal of Social Medicine,* **21**(4):247–55.

Gray, J.A. Muir (1980) Section 47, *Age and Ageing,* **9**:205–9.

Greene, M., Adelman, R., Charan, C. and Hoffman, S. (1986) Ageism in the medical encounter: an exploratory study of the doctor–elderly patient relationship, *Language and Communication,* **6**:113–24.

Grief, L.C. and Elliot, R. (1994) Emergency nurses' moral evaluation of patients, *Journal of Emergency Nursing,* **20**(4):275–9.

Griffiths, A., Grimes, R. and Roberts, G. (1990) *The Law and Elderly People.* London, Routledge.

Griffiths, A., Roberts, G. and Williams, J. (1993) Elder abuse and the law, in Decalmer, P. and Glendenning, F. (eds) *The Mistreatment of Elderly People.* London, Sage.

Grundy, E. (1992) The epidemiology of ageing, in Brocklehurst, J.C., Tallis, R.C. and Fillit, H.M. (eds) *Textbook of Geriatric Medicine and Gerontology,* 4th edn. Edinburgh, Churchill Livingstone.

Grunfeld, A.F., Ritmiller, S., Mackay, K., Cowan, L. and Hatch, D. (1994) Detecting domestic violence against women in the emergency department: a nursing triage model, *Journal of Emergency Nursing,* **20**(4):271–4.

Gunn, M. (1994) The law's contribution to protecting people with learning disabilities from physical and sexual abuse, in Harris, J. and Craft, A. (eds) *People with Learning Disabilities at Risk of Physical or Sexual Abuse.* British Institute of Learning Disabilities Seminar, Paper No. 4. Kidderminster, Cookley Press.

Hague, G. and Malos, E. (1993) *Domestic Violence: Action for change.* Cheltenham, New Clarion Press.

Halamandaris, V.J. (1983) Fraud and abuse in nursing homes, in Kosberg, J. (ed.) *Abuse and Maltreatment of the Elderly: Causes and interventions.* Bristol, John Wright.

Halicka, M. (1995) Elder abuse and neglect in Poland, *Journal of Elder Abuse and Neglect,* **6**(3/4):157–69.

Hallett, C. (1995) Child abuse: an academic overview, in Kingston, P. and Penhale, B. (eds) *Family Violence and the Caring Professions.* Basingstoke, Macmillan.

Harden, R.McG., Stevenson, M., Downie, W.W. and Wilson, G.M. (1975) Assessment of clinical competence using objective standard examination, *British Medical Journal,* **2**:447–51.

Harding, T. and Beresford, P. (1996) *The Standards We Expect.* London, National Institute of Social Work.

Harris, L. (1981) Americans believe government should take major responsibility in coping with the abuse problem. News release. Washington, The Harris Survey.

Heinanen, A. (1986) (ed.) The Elderly and Family Violence. Report No. 8 of Federation of Mother-Child Homes and Shelters. Helsinki.

Heine, C.A. (1986) Burnout among nursing home personnel, *Journal of Gerontological Nursing,* **12**:14–18.

Hildrew, M. (1991) New age problem, *Social Work Today,* **22**(49):15–17.

Hocking, E.D. (1988) Miscare: a form of abuse in the elderly, *Update,* (15 May):2411–19.

Hoggett, B. (1989) The elderly mentally ill: procedures for civil commitment and guardianship, in Eekelaar, J. and Pearl, D. (eds) *An Aging World.* Oxford, Clarendon Press.

Holt, M.G. (1993) Elder sexual abuse in Britain: preliminary findings, *Journal of Elder Abuse and Neglect,* **5**(2):63–71.

Homer, A. and Gilleard, C. (1990) Abuse of elderly people by their carers, *British Medical Journal,* **301**:1359–62.

Homer, A. and Gilleard, C. (1994) The effect of inpatient respite care on elderly patients and their carers, *Age and Ageing,* **23**:274–6.

Homer, P. and Holstein, M. (1990) *A Good Old Age: The paradox of setting limits.* New York, Touchstone.

Homer, A. and Kingston, P. (1991) Screening by nurse practitioners could prevent elder abuse, *Care of the Elderly,* (May).

Horkan, E.M. (1995) Elder abuse in the Republic of Ireland, *Journal of Elder Abuse and Neglect,* **6**(3/4):119–37.

Horrocks, P. (1989) Conference Paper at the British Society of Gerontology Conference. Cited in Tomlin, S. *Abuse of Elderly People: An unnecessary and preventable problem.* London, British Geriatrics Society.

House of Commons (1992) *The Report of the Inquiry into the Removal of Children from Orkney in February 1991.* London, HMSO.

House of Representatives (1981) *Report of the Hearing of the Select Committee on Aging.* Washington, DC, House of Representatives.

Hudson, M. (1994) Elder abuse: its meaning to middle-aged and older adults. Part ii: Pilot results, *Journal of Elder Abuse and Neglect*, 6(1):55–82.

Hughes, B. (1995) *Older People and Community Care: Critical theory and practice.* Buckingham, Open University Press.

Hughes, B. and Wilkin, D. (1989) Physical care and quality of life in residential homes, *Ageing and Society*, 7(4):399–425.

Hugman, R. (1994a) *Ageing and the Care of Older People in Europe.* Basingstoke, Macmillan.

Hugman, R. (1994b) Social work and case management in the UK: models of professionalism and elderly people, *Ageing and Society*, 14(2):237–55.

Hunt, G. (1995) *Whistleblowing in the Health Service: Accountability, law and professional practice.* London, Edward Arnold.

Hydle, I. and Johns, S. (1992) *Closed Doors and Clenched Fists: When elderly people are abused in their homes.* Oslo, Kommuneforlaget.

Ingram, R. (1994) Taking a pro-active approach: communicating with women experiencing violence from a known man in the emergency department, *Accident and Emergency Nursing*, 2:143–8.

Isaacs, B., Livingstone, M. and Neville, Y. (1972) *Survival of the Unfittest: A study of geriatric patients in Glasgow.* London, Routledge & Kegan Paul.

Ivers, V. (1994) *Citizen Advocacy in Action: Working with older people.* Stoke-on-Trent, Beth Johnson Foundation.

Jack, R. (1992) Institutionalised elder abuse, social work and social services departments, *Baseline*, (50):24–7.

Jarde, O., Marc, B., Dwyer, J., Fournier, P., Carlier-Pasquier, H. and Lenoir, L. (1992) Mistreatment of the aged in the home environment in northern France: a year survey in 1990, *Médicine et Loi*, 11:641–8.

Jezierski, M. (1992) Guidance for intervention by ED nurses in cases of domestic violence, *Journal of Emergency Nursing*, 18(1):28A–30A.

Johns, S. (1993) Family Life and Solidarity across the Generations. Paper delivered at the annual conference of the British Society of Gerontology, University of East Anglia, September 1993.

Johns, S. and Juklestad, O. (1994) Research and Action on Elder Abuse in Norway. Paper presented to the 2nd International Symposium on Elder Abuse, Stoke-on-Trent, 7 September 1994.

Johns, S., Hydle, I. and Aschjem, O. (1991) The act of abuse: a two-headed monster of injury and offence, *Journal of Elder Abuse and Neglect*, 3(1):53–64.

Johnson, F. (1993) _Dependency and Japanese Socialisation: Psychoanalytic and anthropological investigations into amae._ New York, New York University Press.

Johnson, M.P. (1995) Patriarchal terrorism and common couple violence: two forms of violence against women, _Journal of Marriage and the Family_, **57**(May):283–94.

Johnson, N. (1995) Domestic violence: an overview, in Kingston, P. and Penhale, B. (eds) _Family Violence and the Caring Professions._ Basingstoke, Macmillan.

Johnson, T. (1991) _Elder Mistreatment: Deciding who is at risk._ Westport, CT, Greenwood Press.

Johnston, C. (1995) Proposals for changing the law: are they needed?, in Action on Elder Abuse Working Paper No. 2. _Elder Abuse and the Law._ London, Action on Elder Abuse.

Jones, A. and Schechter, S. (1992) _When Love Goes Wrong._ New York, HarperCollins.

Jones, J.S. (1990) Geriatric abuse and neglect, in Bosker G., Schwarz, G.R., Jones, J.S. and Sequeira, M. (eds) _Geriatric Emergency Medicine._ St. Louis, MO, Mosby.

Jones, J.S. (1994) Elder abuse and neglect: responding to a national problem, _Annals of Emergency Medicine_, **23**(4):845–8.

Kaneko, Y. and Yamanda, Y. (1990) Wives and mothers-in-law: potential of family conflict in post-war Japan, _Journal of Elder Abuse and Neglect_, **2**(1/2):87–99.

Kaufman, J. and Zigler, E. (1987) Do abused children become abusive parents?, _American Journal of Orthopsychiatry_, **57**(2):186–92.

Kaye, C. and MacManus, T. (1990) Understanding complaints, _Health Service Journal_, 23 Aug, 1254–5.

Keele University (1996) MA in Adult Protection: Law and practice course flyer. Keele, Keele University.

Kempe, C.H., Silverman, F.N., Steele, B.F., Droegmuller, W. and Silver, H.K. (1962) The battered-child syndrome, _Journal of the American Medical Association_, **181**:17–24.

Kenny, T. (1990) Erosion of individuality in care of elderly people in hospital: an alternative approach, _Journal of Advanced Nursing_, **15**:571–6.

Kingston, P. (1990) Elder Abuse. Unpublished MA dissertation, University of Keele.

Kingston, P. and Brammer, A. (eds) (1997) _Caring in Trouble._ Basingstoke, Macmillan.

Kingston, P. and Hopwood, A. (1994) The elderly person in the Accident and Emergency Department, in Sbaih, L. (ed.) _Issues in Accident and Emergency Nursing._ London, Chapman & Hall.

Kingston, P. and Penhale, B. (1995a) *Family Violence and the Caring Professions*. Basingstoke, Macmillan.

Kingston, P. and Penhale, B. (1995b) Elder abuse and neglect: issues in the Accident and Emergency Department, *Accident and Emergency Nursing: An International Journal*, **3**:122–8.

Kingston, P. and Penhale, B. (1997) Elder Abuse and Neglect, *Practice Nurse* (in press).

Kingston, P. and Phillipson, C. (1994) Elder abuse and neglect, *British Journal of Nursing*, **3**(22):1171–90.

Kingston, P. and Reay, A. (1995) Elder abuse and neglect, in Woods, B. (ed.) *The Handbook of the Clinical Psychology of Ageing*. London, John Wiley & Sons.

Kingston, P., Penhale, B. and Bennett, G. (1995) Is elder abuse on the curriculum?: the relative contribution of child abuse, domestic violence and elder abuse in social work, nursing and medicine qualifying curricula, *Health and Social Care in the Community*, **3**(6):353–62.

Kitzinger, J. and Hunt, K. (1993) *Evaluation of Edinburgh District Council's Zero Tolerance Campaign*. Edinburgh, Edinburgh District Council Women's Committee.

Kivelä, S.L., Kongas-Saviaro, P., Kesti, E., Pahkala, K. and Ijas, M. (1992) Abuse in old age-epidemiological data from Finland, *Journal of Elder Abuse and Neglect*, **4**(3):1–18.

Kondo, D.K. (1990) *Crafting Selves: Power, gender and discourses of identity in a Japanese workplace*. Chicago, University of Chicago Press.

Koo, L.C. (1984) Traditional Chinese concepts towards the elderly, in Mental Health Association of Hong Kong, *Mental Health and Old Age*. Hong Kong, MHA of Hong Kong.

Korbin, J.E., Anetzberger, G.J. and Austin, C. (1995) The intergenerational cycle of violence in child and elder abuse, *Journal of Elder Abuse and Neglect*, **7**(1):1–17.

Korbin, J.E., Anetzberger, G.J. and Eckert, J.K. (1989) Elder abuse and child abuse: a consideration of similarities and differences in intergenerational family violence, *Journal of Elder Abuse and Neglect*, **1**(4):1–14.

Kosberg, J.I. and Cairl, R. (1986) The cost of care index: a case management tool for screening informal care providers, *Gerontologist*, **26**(3):273–8.

Kosberg, J.I. and Kwan, Y.H. (1989) Elder Abuse in Hong Kong and the United States: A comparative analysis with international implications. Paper presented at the symposium on cross-cultural perspectives on elder abuse, International Congress of Gerontology, Acapulco, Mexico, June 1989.

Koss, M.P. and Cook, S.L. (1993) Facing the facts: date and acquaintance rape are significant problems for women, in Gelles, R.J. and Loseke, D.R. (eds) *Current Controversies on Family Violence*. London, Sage.

Kurrle, S.E. (1993) Elder abuse: a hidden problem, *Modern Medicine of Australia*, 58–71.

Kurrle, S.E. (1993a) Cases and interventions, *Australian Journal on Ageing*, Part I, **12**(4):5–9.

Kurrle, S.E. (1993b) A review of developments, *Australian Journal on Ageing*, Part II, **12**(4):24–31.

Kurrle, S.E., Sadler, P.M. and Cameron, I.D. (1991) Elder abuse – an Australian case series, *Medical Journal of Australia*, (155):150–3.

Kurrle, S.E., Sadler, P.M. and Cameron, I.D. (1992) Patterns of elder abuse, *Medical Journal of Australia,* (157):673–6.

Kwan, Y.H. (1988) Suicide among the elderly: Hong Kong, *Journal of Applied Gerontology*, **7**(2):248–59.

Kwan, Y.H. (1991a) Elder abuse in Hong Kong; a new problem for the Old East? Paper presented at the conference on Adult Protective Services, San Antonio, USA, November 1991.

Kwan, Y.H. (1991b) *A Study of the Coping Behaviour of Caregivers in Hong Kong*. Hong Kong, Writers' and Publishers' Co-operative.

Lachs, M. and Pillemer, K. (1995) Abuse and neglect of elderly persons, *New England Medical Journal*, **332**(7):437–43.

Laing, R.D. (1964) *The Divided Self*. Harmondsworth, Penguin.

Langan, J. and Means, R. (1995) *Personal Finances, Elderly People with Dementia and the 'New' Community Care*. London, Anchor Housing Association.

Lau, E. and Kosberg J.I. (1979) Abuse of the elderly by informal caregivers, *Aging*, **229**:10–15.

Law Commission (1991) *Mentally Incapacitated Adults and Decision Making: An overview*. Consultation Paper No. 119. London, HMSO.

Law Commission (1992) *Family Law, Domestic Violence and Occupation of the Family Home*. Report No. 207. London, HMSO.

Law Commission (1993a) *Mentally Incapacitated Adults: A new jurisdiction*. Consultation Paper No. 128. London, HMSO.

Law Commission (1993b) *Mentally Incapacitated Adults: Medical treatment and research*. Consultation Paper No. 129. London, HMSO.

Law Commission (1993c) *Mentally Incapacitated and Other Vulnerable Adults: Public law protection*. Consultation Paper No 130. London, HMSO.

Law Commission (1995) *Mental Incapacity*. Report No. 231. London HMSO.

Law Society (1989) *Decision Making and Mental Incapacity: A discussion document*. London, Law Society.

Leeder, E. (1994) *Treating Abuse in Families: A feminist and community approach*. New York, Springer.

Leung, W.H. (1988) Social services for the abused elderly, in Hong Kong Society for the Aged, *Proceedings of Seminar on Services for the Elderly*. Hong Kong, Hong Kong Society for the Aged.

Leung, W.H. (1989) Elderly abuse in Tuen Mun public housing estates, *Hong Kong Journal of Gerontology*, **3**(1):6–9.

Leung, W.H. (1991) The family relationship of older persons, *Social Welfare Quarterly*, (116):11–15.

Levin, E., Sinclair, I. and Gorbach, P. (1989) *Families, Services and Confusion in Old Age*. Aldershot, Gower.

Liukkonen, A. and Laitinen, P. (1994) Reasons for uses of physical restraint and alternatives to them in geriatric nursing: a questionnaire study among nursing staff, *Journal of Advanced Nursing*, **19**:1082–7.

Lloyd, S. (1995) Social work and domestic violence, in Kingston, P. and Penhale, B. (eds) *Family Violence and the Caring Professions*. London, Macmillan.

Lunn, J.E. (1995) Whistle-blowing: a legal perspective, *British Journal of Nursing*, **4**(17):1032–4.

McCall, G.J. and Simmons, J.L. (1966) *Identities and Interactions*. New York, Free Press.

McCallum, J. (1993) Elder abuse: the 'new' social problem?, *Modern Medicine of Australia*, (Sept):74–83.

McCallum, J., Matiasz, S. and Graycar, A. (1990) *Abuse of the Elderly at Home: The range of the problem*. Adelaide, Office of the Commissioner of Ageing.

McCleer, S.V. and Anwar, R. (1989) A study of battered women presenting in an emergency department, *American Journal of Public Health*, **79**:65–6.

McCreadie, C. (1991) *Elder Abuse: An exploratory study*. London, Age Concern Institute of Gerontology.

McCreadie, C. (1994) From granny battering to elder abuse: a critique of UK writing, 1972–1992, *Journal of Elder Abuse and Neglect*, **5**(2):7–25.

McCreadie, C. (1996) *Elder Abuse: Update on research*. London, Age Concern Institute of Gerontology.

McDermott, J. (1993) Elder Abuse, in Eight Scenarios in Search of a Construct. Paper presented at the Crime and Older People Conference, Adelaide, 1992.

McDonald, A. (1993) Elder abuse and neglect: the legal framework, *Journal of Elder Abuse and Neglect*, **5**(2):81–96.

McDonald, A. and Taylor, M. (1993) *Elders and the Law*. Birmingham, Pepar.

McDonald, P.L., Hornick, J.P., Robertson, G.B. and Wallace, J.E. (1991) *Elder Abuse and Neglect in Canada*. Toronto, Butterworth.

McDonnell, A.A. (1996) The physical restraint minefield: a professional's guide, *British Journal of Therapy and Rehabilitation*, **3**(1):45–8.

Manthorpe, J. (1993a) Elder abuse and key areas in social work, in Decalmer, P. and Glendenning, F. (eds) *The Mistreatment of Elderly People*. London, Sage.

Manthorpe, J. (1993b) Major publications reviewed: elder abuse: concepts, theories and interventions, *Action on Elder Abuse Bulletin*. London, Age Concern.

Mapp, S. (1994) Breaking bounds, *Community Care*, 7–13 Jul, 24.

Margolin, L. (1992) Beyond maternal blame: physical child abuse as a phenomenon of gender, *Journal of Family Issues*, **13**(Sept):410–23.

Marin, N. *et al.* (1990) Sindrom del maltrato y abuso en el anciano, *Revista Española de Geriatría y Gerontología*, **25**(1):66.

Marin, R.S. and Morycz, R.K. (1990) Victims of elder abuse, in Ammerman, R.T. and Hersen, M. (eds) *Treatment of Family Violence: A sourcebook*. New York, John Wiley & Sons.

Marks, W. (1992) Physical restraints in the practice of medicine, *Archives of Internal Medicine*, **152**:2204–6.

Marriott, A. (1995) Elder abuse: staff attitudes and beliefs, *PSIGE Newsletter*, **55**(Dec 1995/Jan 1996):14–17.

Martin, N. (1984) *Hospitals in Trouble*. Oxford, Basil Blackwell.

Maxwell, R.J., Silverman, P. and Maxwell, E.K. (1982) The motive for gerontocide, *Studies in Third World Societies*, **22**:67–84.

Meddaugh, D.I. (1993) Covert elder abuse in the nursing home, *Journal of Elder Abuse and Neglect*, **5**(3):21–37.

Millar, J. (1993) Fifth of Britons now in poverty, *Times Higher Educational Supplement*, 3 Sept, 5.

Miller, R.B. and Dodder, R.A. (1989) The abused–abuser dyad: elder abuse in the state of Florida, in Filinson, R. and Ingman, S.R. (eds) *Elder Abuse: Practice and Policy*. New York, Human Sciences Press.

Millard, P. and Roberts, A. (1991) Old and forgotten, *Nursing Times*, **87**(22):24–8.

Minois, G. (1989) *History of Old Age: From antiquity to the renaissance*. Cambridge, Polity Press.

Monk, A. (1986) Social work with the aged: principles of practice, in Mayer, C. (ed.) *Social Work with the Ageing*, 2nd edn. Maryland, NASW.

Mount Sinai Victim Services Agency Elder Abuse Project (1988) *Elder Mistreatment Guidelines for the Health Care Professional*. New York, Mount Sinai Victim Services Agency Elder Abuse Project.

Murphy, J.E. (1988) Date abuse and forced intercourse, in Hotaling, G.T., Finkelhor, D., Kirkpatrick, J.T. and Straus, M.A. (eds) *Family Abuse and its Consequences: New directions in research*. London, Sage.

National Audit Office, Report by the Controller and Auditor General (1994) *Looking After the Financial Affairs of People with Mental Incapacity*. London, HMSO.

Nazarko, L. (1995) Upholding the standards, *Nursing Times*, **91**(32):55–7.

Neikrug, S.M. and Ronen, M. (1993) Elder abuse in Israel, *Journal of Elder Abuse and Neglect*, 5(3):1–19.

New South Wales Task Force on Abuse of Older People (1993) *Final Report and Recommendations*. Sydney, Office on Ageing.

Nichol, J. (1993) *Working with Elderly Survivors of Sexual Abuse*. Social Work Monographs. Norwich, University of East Anglia.

Nolan, M. (1994) Deregulation of nursing homes: a disaster waiting to happen?, *British Journal of Nursing*, 3(12):595.

Norberg, A. and Axelsson, K. (1985) Mistreatment (neglect and abuse) of elderly in their homes in Sweden, *Sjuksköterskan*, (Nov):23–5.

Novaco, R.W. (1976) Treatment of chronic anger through cognitive and relaxation controls, *Journal of Consulting and Clinical Psychology*, 44(4):681.

Office on Ageing (1993) *Abuse of Older People in Their Homes: Final report and recommendations*. Sydney, Office on Ageing.

Ogg, J. (1993) Researching elder abuse in Britain, *Journal of Elder Abuse and Neglect*, 5(2):37–54.

Ogg, J. (1995) Choosing to intervene, in Department of Health/Social Services Inspectorate, *Abuse of Older People in Domestic Settings: A report on two SSI seminars*. London, HMSO.

Ogg, J. and Bennett G.C.J. (1992) Elder abuse in Britain, *British Medical Journal*, 305:998–9.

Ogg, J. and Dickens, J. (1995) Social perspectives on child abuse, in Kingston, P. and Penhale, B. (eds) *Family Violence and the Caring Professions*. Basingstoke, Macmillan.

O'Leary, K.D. (1988) Physical aggression between spouses: a social learning perspective, in van Hasselt, V.B., Morrison, R.L., Bellack, A.S. and Hersen, M. (eds) *Handbook of Family Violence*. New York, Plenum Press.

O'Loughlin, A. (1990) Old age abuse in a domestic setting, *Irish Social Worker*, 9(2):4–7.

O'Loughlin, A. (1991) *Awaiting Advocacy – Elder Abuse and Neglect in Ireland*. Dublin, Irish Association of Social Workers.

O'Loughlin, A. (1995) Elder Abuse: A new reality about old age in Ireland? Unpublished thesis, Dublin, University College, Dublin.

Olshansky, S.J., Bruce, A., Cassel, C. and Cassel, C.K. (1993) The aging of the human species, *Scientific American*, (Apr):18–24.

O'Malley H., Segars, H. and Perez, R. (1979) *Elder Abuse in Massachussets: A survey of Professionals and Paraprofessionals*. Boston, MA, Legal Research and Services for the Elderly.

O' Neill, D., McCormack, P., Walsh, J.B. and Coakley, D. (1990) Elder abuse, *Irish Journal of Medical Science*, 159(2):48–9.

Opportunities for Women (1990) *Carers at Work*. London, Opportunities for Women.

Pahl, J. (1995) Health professionals and violence against women, in Kingston, P. and Penhale, B. (eds) *Family Violence and the Caring Professions*. Basingstoke, Macmillan.

Parke, R.D. and Collmer, C. (1975) *Child Abuse: An interdisciplinary analysis, review of child development research*, Vol. 5. Chicago, University of Chicago Press.

Parkin, A. (1995) The care and control of elderly incapacitated adults, *Journal of Social Welfare and Family Law*, **17**(4):431–44.

Pathy, M.S.J. (1997) (ed.) *The Principles and Practice of Geriatric Medicine*, 3rd edn. London, John Wiley & Sons (in press).

Pelton, L. (1981) Child abuse and neglect: The myth of classlessness, in Pelton, L. (ed.) *The Social Context of Child Abuse and Neglect*. New York, Human Sciences Press.

Penhale, B. (1991) Decision making and mental incapacity: practice issues for professionals, *Practice*, **5**(3):186–95.

Penhale, B. (1992) Elder abuse: an overview, in *Elders*, **1**(3):36–48.

Penhale, B. (1993a) Local authority guidelines and procedures, in *Ageing Update: Conference proceedings, elder abuse: new findings and policy guidelines*. London, Age Concern Institute of Gerontology.

Penhale, B. (1993b) Abuse on the map, *Community Care*, 10 Jun, 20–1.

Penhale, B. (1993c) The abuse of elderly people: considerations for practice, *British Journal of Social Work*, **23**(2):95–112.

Penhale, B. and Kingston, P. (1995a) Elder abuse: an overview of recent and current developments, *Health and Social Care in the Community*, **3**(5):311–20.

Penhale, B. and Kingston, P. (1995b) Social perspectives on elder abuse, in Kingston, P. and Penhale, B. (eds) *Family Violence and the Caring Professions*. Basingstoke, Macmillan.

Peralta, A. and Riera, C. (1995) Dimensio i Caracteristiques dels abusos que pateix la gent gran a Catalunya. Unpublished manuscript.

Phillips, J. (1992) *Private Residential Care: The admission process and reactions of the public sector*. Aldershot, Avebury.

Phillips, L.R. (1983a) Abuse and neglect of the frail elderly at home: an exploration of theoretical relationships, *Journal of Advanced Nursing*, **8**:379–92.

Phillips, L.R. (1983b) Elder abuse – what is it? Who says so?, *Geriatric Nursing* (May/Jun):167–70.

Phillips, L.R. (1986) Theoretical explanations of elder abuse: competing hypotheses and unresolved issues, in Pillemer, K.A. and Wolf, R.S. (eds) *Elder Abuse: Conflict in the family*. Dover, MA, Auburn House.

Phillips, L.R. (1989) Issues involved in identifying and intervening in elder abuse, in Filinson, R. and Ingman, S.R. *Elder abuse: Practice and policy*. New York, Human Sciences Press.

Phillips, L.R. and Rempusheski, V.F. (1986) Making decisions about elder abuse, *Social Casework*, **67**(3):131–40.

Phillipson, C. (1982) *Capitalism and the Construction of Old Age*. London, Macmillan.

Phillipson, C. (1992) Confronting elder abuse: fact and fiction, *Generations Review*, **2**(3):2–3.

Phillipson, C. (1993) Abuse of older people: sociological perspectives, in Decalmer, P. and Glendenning, F. (eds) *The Mistreatment of Elderly People*. London, Sage.

Phillipson, C. and Biggs, S. (1992) *Understanding Elder Abuse: A training manual for helping professions*. London, Longman.

Phillipson, C. and Biggs, S. (1995) Elder abuse: a critical overview, in Kingston, P. and Penhale, B. (eds) *Family Violence and the Caring Professions*. Basingstoke, Macmillan.

Phillipson, C. and Walker, A. (1986) (eds) *Ageing and Social Policy: A critical assessment*. Aldershot, Gower.

Pillemer, K.A. (1986) Risk factors in elder abuse: results from a case control study, in Pillemer, K.A and Wolf, R.S. (eds) *Elder Abuse: Conflict in the family*. Dover, MA, Auburn House.

Pillemer, K.A. (1993) The abused offspring are dependent: abuse is caused by the deviance and dependence of abusive caregivers, in Gelles, R.J. and Loseke, D.R. (eds) *Current Controversies on Family Violence*, London, Sage.

Pillemer, K.A. (1997) *Intergenerational Ambivalence and Later Life Relationships* (in press)

Pillemer, K.A. and Bachman-Prehn, R. (1991) Helping and hurting: predictors of maltreatment of patients in nursing homes, *Research on Aging*, **13**(1):74–95.

Pillemer, K.A. and Finkelhor, D. (1988) The prevalence of elder abuse: a random sample survey, *Gerontologist*, **28**(1):51–7.

Pillemer, K.A. and Moore, D.W. (1989) Abuse of patients in nursing homes: findings from a survey of staff, *Gerontologist*, **29**(3):314–20.

Pillemer, K.A. and Suitor, J. (1988) Elder abuse, in van Hasselt, V., Morrison, R., Belack, A. and Hensen, M. (eds) *Handbook of Family Violence*. New York, Plenum Press.

Pillemer, K.A. and Wolf, R.S. (1986) (eds) *Elder Abuse: Conflict in the family*. New York, Auburn House.

Pink, G. (1994) The price of truth, *British Medical Journal*, **309**:1700–5.

Pitkeathley, J. (1994) *Carers, Abuse and the Law*. Action on Elder Abuse Working Paper No. 2. Elder Abuse and the Law: Papers from the 1st Annual Conference of Action on Elder Abuse, 1993. London, Age Concern.

Pitkeathley, J. (1995) Elder abuse: carers' perspectives, *Nursing Times*, **91**(42):30–1.

Pitsiou-Darrough, E.N. and Spinellis, C.D. (1995) Mistreatment of the elderly in Greece, *Journal of Elder Abuse and Neglect,* **6**(3/4):45–65.

Pleck, E. (1987) *Domestic Tyranny: The making of social policy against family violence from colonial times to the present.* New York, Oxford University Press.

Podnieks, E. (1989) *National Survey on the Abuse of the Elderly in Canada.* Ottawa, Ryerson Polytechnical Institute.

Podnieks, E. (1992) National survey on the abuse of the elderly in Canada, *Journal of Elder Abuse and Neglect,* (4):5–58.

Pritchard, J. (1992) *The Abuse of Elderly People: A handbook for professionals.* London, Jessica Kingsley.

Pritchard, J. (1993) Dispelling some myths, *Journal of Elder Abuse and Neglect,* **5**(2):27–36.

Ptacek, J. (1988) Why do men batter their wives?, in Yllö, K. and Bograd, M. (eds) *Feminist Perspectives on Wife Abuse.* Newbury Park, CA, Sage.

Queen, S.A., Haberstein, R.W. and Quadagno, J.S. (1985) *The Family in Various Cultures,* 5th edn. New York, Harper and Row.

Quinn, M. and Tomita, S. (1986) *Elder Abuse and Neglect: Causes, diagnosis and intervention strategies.* New York, Springer.

Ramsey-Klawsnik, H. (1993) Interviewing elders for suspected sexual abuse: guidelines and techniques, *Journal of Elder Abuse and Neglect,* **5**(1):5–19.

Rathbone-McCuan, E., Travis, A. and Voyles, B. (1983) Family intervention: the task-centred approach, in Kosberg, J.I. (ed.) *Abuse and Maltreatment of the Elderly: causes and interventions.* Boston, MA, J. Wright.

RCN (Royal College of Nursing) (1993) *A Scandal Waiting to Happen.* London, RCN.

RCN (Royal College of Nursing) (1994) *The Privacy of Clients: Electronic tagging and closed circuit television.* Issues in Nursing and Health Series. London, RCN.

RCN (Royal College of Nursing) (1995) *The Hidden Abuse.* Nursing Update Series. London, RCN.

Reay, A. (1997) *The Use of Anger Management and Education as Intervention within Elder Abuse and Neglect* (in press).

Reder, P., Duncan, S. and Gray, M. (1993) *Beyond Blame: Child abuse tragedies revisited.* London, Routledge.

Rees, J.L. (1982) Secular changes in the incidence of proximal femoral fracture in Oxfordshire: a preliminary report, *Community Medicine,* (4):100–3.

Riley, P. (1993) Differences between child abuse and adult abuse, in DOH/SSI *No Longer Afraid: The safeguard of older people in the domestic setting.* London, HMSO.

Robb, B. (1967) *Sans Everything: A case to answer.* London, Nelson.

Robertson, A. (1991) The politics of Alzheimer's disease: a case study in apocalyptic demography, in Minkler, M. and Estes, C. (eds) *Critical Perspectives on Aging: The political and moral economy of growing old.* New York, Baywood.

Rose, A.M. (ed.) (1962) *Human Behaviour and Social Processes: An interactionist approach.* London, Routledge & Kegan Paul.

Rosenfeld, A. and Newberger, E.H. (1977) Compassion versus control: conceptual and practice pitfalls in the broadened definition of child abuse, *Journal of the American Medical Association,* **237**(19):2086–8.

Rowe, J., Davies, K., Baburaj, V. and Sinha, R. (1993) F.A.D.E. A.W.A.Y. – The financial affairs of dementing elders and who is the attorney?, *Journal of Elder Abuse and Neglect,* **5**(2):73–9.

Salend, E., Kane, R., Satz, M. and Pynoos, J. (1984) Elder abuse reporting: limitations of current statutes, *Gerontologist,* **24**(1):61–9.

Sanders, A.B. (1992) Care of the elderly in emergency departments: conclusions and recommendations, *Annals of Emergency Medicine,* **21**(7):79–83.

Saper, R. and Laing, W. (1995) Age of uncertainty, *Health Service Journal,* **105**(5476):22–6.

Saveman, B.-I. (1994) Formal Carers in Health Care and the Social Services Witnessing Abuse of the Elderly in Their Homes. Unpublished dissertation. Sweden, Umea University.

Saveman, B.-I. and Norberg, A. (1993) Cases of elder abuse: intervention and hopes for the future, as reported by home service personnel, *Scandinavian Journal of Caring Science,* (7):21–8.

Saveman, B.-I., Hallberg, I.R., Norberg, A. and Eriksson, S. (1993) Patterns of abuse of the elderly in their homes as reported by district nurses, *Scandinavian Journal of Primary Health Care,* (11):111–16.

Schaufeli, W.B. and Janczur, B. (1994) Burnout among nurses: a Polish–Dutch comparison, *Journal of Cross-Cultural Psychology,* **25**(1):95–113.

Scrutton, S. (1990) Ageism: the foundation of age discrimination, in McEwen, E. (ed.) *Age: The unrecognised discrimination.* London, Age Concern.

Scull, A.T. (1977) *Decarceration.* Englewood Cliffs, NJ, Prentice Hall.

Seedhouse, D. (1994) Editorial: Health care values or business values?, *Health Care Analysis,* **2**:181–4.

Shah, G., Veedan, R. and Vasi, S. (1995) Elder abuse in India, *Journal of Elder Abuse and Neglect,* **6**(3/4):101–18.

Slater, P. (1993) Elder abuse and legal reform, *Elders,* **2**(3):23–8.

Slater, P. (1994) Social work and old age abuse: laying down the law, in Eastman, M. (ed.) *Old Age Abuse: A new perspective.* London, Chapman & Hall.

Smith, G. (1986) Resistance to change in geriatric care, *International Journal of Nursing Studies*, **23**(1):61–70.

Smith, S., Baker, D., Buchan, A. and Bodiwala, G. (1992) Adult domestic violence, *Health Trends*, **24**(3):97–9.

Snyder, J.A. (1994) Emergency department protocols for domestic violence, *Journal of Emergency Nursing*, **20**(1):65–8.

Social Welfare Department (1991) White paper on social welfare into the 1990s and beyond. Hong Kong, Hong Kong Government Printer.

Sone, K. (1995) Whistle down the wind, *Community Care,* 6 Jul, 16–17.

Spinellis, C.D. and Pitsiou-Darrough, E.N. (1991) Elder abuse in Greece: a descriptive study, in Kaizer, G., Kurry, H. and Albrecht, H.-J. (eds) *Victims and Criminal Justice.* Freibury, Eigenverlad Max-Planck-Institute.

Sprey, J. and Matthews, S.H. (1989) The perils of drawing policy implications from research: the case of elder mistreatment, in Filinson, R. and Ingman, S.R. (eds) *Elder Abuse: Practice and policy.* New York, Human Sciences Press.

Staffordshire Social Services (1994) *Guidelines on the Protection of Vulnerable Adults.* Stafford, Social Services.

Starak, Y. (1988) Hong Kong: a model of 'social happiness' for the new China, *International Social Work*, **31**(3):211–17.

Starr, R.H. (1988) Physical abuse of children, in van Hasselt, V.B., Morrison, R.L., Bellack, A.S. and Hersen, M. (eds) *Handbook of Family Violence.* New York, Plenum Press.

Steele, R.F. (1980) Psychodynamic factors in child abuse, in Kempe, C.H. and Helfer, R.E. (eds) *The Battered Child*, 3rd edn. Chicago, University of Chicago Press.

Steinmetz, S.K. (1990) Elder abuse: myth and reality, in Brubaker, T.H. (ed.) *Family Relationships in Later Life*, 2nd edn. Newbury Park, CA, Sage.

Steinmetz, S.K. and Amsden, G. (1983) Dependent elders, family stress and abuse, in Brubaker, T.H. (ed.) *Family Relationships in Later Life.* Beverly Hills, Sage.

Steinmetz, S.K. and Straus. M.A. (1973) The family as a cradle of violence, *Society*, **10**(6):50–6.

Stevenson, O. (1989) *Age and Vulnerability*. London, Edward Arnold.

Stevenson, O. (1995a) Abuse of older people: principles of intervention, in DOH/SSI *Abuse of Older People in Domestic Settings: A report on two SSI seminars.* London, HMSO.

Stevenson, O. (1995b) Foreword, in Kingston, P. and Penhale, B. (eds) *Family Violence and the Caring Professions.* Basingstoke, Macmillan.

Stevenson, O. and Parsloe, P. (1978) *Social Services Teams: The practitioner's view.* London, HMSO.

Stevenson, O. and Parsloe, P. (1993) *Community Care and Empowerment.* York, Joseph Rowntree Foundation.

Straus, M.A. (1979) Measuring intrafamily conflict and violence: the conflict tactics (CT) scale, *Journal of Marriage and the Family*, **41**:75–88.

Straus, M.A. and Gelles, R.J. (1986) Societal change and change in family violence from 1975 to 1985 as revealed in two surveys, *Journal of Marriage and the Family*, **48**(Aug):465–79.

Straus, M.A., Gelles, R.J. and Steinmetz, S.K. (1980) *Behind Closed Doors: Violence in the American family*. New York, Anchor/Doubleday.

Sullivan-Marx, E.M. (1995) Psychological responses to physical restraint use in older adults, *Journal of Psychosocial Nursing*, **33**(6):20–5.

Szasz, T. (1961) *The Myth of Mental Illness*. New York, Hoeber-Harper.

Szasz, T. (1973) *The Manufacture of Madness*. London, Palladin.

Tatara, T. (1990) *Summaries of National Elder Abuse Data: An exploratory study of state statistics*. Washington, DC, National Resource Centre on Elder Abuse.

Tattam, A. (1989) Blowing the whistle, *Nursing Times*, **85**(23):20.

Tattum, D. and Herbert, G. (1993) *Countering Bullying: Initiatives by schools and local authorities*. Stoke-on-Trent, Trentham Books.

Taylor, S. (1989) How prevalent is it?, in Stainton Rodgers, W., Hevey, D. and Ash, E. (eds) *Child Abuse and Neglect: Facing the Challenge*. London, Batsford/Open University Press.

Thomasina, D.C. (1991) From Ageism to Autonomy, in Binstock, R. and Post, S. (eds) *Too Old for Health Care?* Baltimore, Johns Hopkins University Press.

Tomita, S.K. (1994) The consideration of cultural factors in the research of elder mistreatment with an in-depth look at the Japanese, *Journal of Cross-Cultural Gerontology*, **9**:39–52.

Tomlin, S. (1989) *Abuse of Elderly People: An unnecessary and preventable problem*. London, British Geriatrics Society.

Tornstam, L . (1989) Abuse of the elderly in Denmark and Sweden. Results from a population study, *Journal of Elder Abuse and Neglect*, **1**(1):35–44.

Townsend, P. (1962) *The Last Refuge*. London, Routledge & Kegan Paul.

Townsend, P. (1981) The structured dependency of the elderly: the creation of social policy in the twentieth century, *Ageing and Society*, **1**(1):5–28.

UKCC (United Kingdom Central Council for Nursing, Midwifery and Health Visiting) (1994) *Professional Conduct – Occasional Report on Standards of Nursing in Nursing Homes*. London, UKCC.

US Congress House Select Committee on Ageing (1980) *Elder Abuse: The hidden problem*. Washington, DC, United States Government Printing Office.

US Congress House Select Committee on Aging (1991) *Elder Abuse: What can be done?* Washington, DC, United States Government Printing Office.

van Hasselt, V., Morrison, R., Belack, A. and Hensen, M. (eds) (1988) *Handbook of Family Violence*. New York, Plenum Press.

van Weeghel, J. and Faber, E. (1995) Reporting Elderly Abuse. Paper presented at European Congress of Gerontology, Amsterdam.

Vernon, M. and Bennett, G. (1995) Commentary: Elder abuse: the case for greater involvement of geriatricians, *Age and Ageing*, **3**(24):177–9.

Vousden, M. (1987) Nye Bevan would turn in his grave, *Nursing Times*, **83**:18–19.

Walker, A. (1981) Towards a political economy of ageing, *Ageing and Society*, **1**(1):73–94.

Weiss, J.G. (1988) Family violence research methodology and design, in Ohlin, L. and Tonry, M. (eds) *Family Violence*. Chicago, University of Chicago Press.

Whittaker, T. (1995) Violence, gender and elder abuse: towards a feminist analysis and practice, *Journal of Gender Studies*, **4**(1):35–45.

WHO (World Health Organisation) (1995) How to prevent burnout, *International Nursing Review*, **42**(5):159.

Wiener, C.L. and Kayser-Jones, J. (1990) The uneasy fate of nursing home residents: an organisational–interaction perspective, *Sociology of Health and Illness*, **12**(1):84–104.

Wilkinson, T.J. and Sainsbury, R. (1995) Diagnosis-related groups-based funding and medical care of the elderly: a form of elder abuse, *New Zealand Medical Journal*, **108**(994):63–5.

Williams, C. (1995) *Invisible Victims: Crime and abuse against people with learning disabilities*. London, Jessica Kingsley.

Williams, J. (1995) Elder abuse: The legal framework, in Action on Elder Abuse Working Paper No. 2 (1995) *Elder Abuse and the Law: Papers from the 1st Annual Conference of Action on Elder Abuse, Lancaster University, March 1994*. London, Action on Elder Abuse.

Wilson, G. (1991) Elder abuse – a hidden horror, *Critical Public Health*, **2**:32–8.

Wilson, G. (1994) Abuse of elderly men and women among clients of a community psychogeriatric service, *British Journal of Social Work*, **24**(4):681–700.

WISE Senior Services (1993) *Fiduciary Abuse Specialist Team (FAST)*. Santa Monica, LA, WISE Senior Services.

Wolf, R.S. (1988) Elder abuse: ten years later, *Journal of the American Geriatric Society*, (36):758–62.

Wolf, R.S. (1992) Making an issue of elder abuse, *Gerontologist*, **32**(3):427–9.

Wolf, R.S. (1993) Responding to elder abuse in the USA, in Action on Elder Abuse Working Paper No 1, *A Report of the Proceedings of the 1st International Symposium on Elder Abuse*. London, Action on Elder Abuse.

Wolf, R.S. and Pillemer, K.A. (1989) *Helping Elderly Victims: The reality of elder abuse*. New York, Columbia University Press.

Wolf, R.S. and Pillemer, K.A. (1993) What's new in elder abuse programming? Four bright ideas, *Gerontologist,* **34**(1):126–9.

Wu, S.S. (1991) The problems of older persons caused by migration, *Social Welfare Quarterly,* **116**:22–6.

Yllö, K.A. (1993) Through a feminist lens: gender, power and violence, in Gelles, R.J. and Loseke, D.R. (eds) *Current Controversies in Family Violence.* Newbury Park, CA, Sage.

Zlotnick, A. (1993) Training strategies for elder abuse/inadequate care, *Journal of Elder Abuse and Neglect,* **5**(2):55–62.

Index